Radical Writing on Women, 1800–1850

Radical Writing on Women, 1800–1850

An Anthology

Kathryn Gleadle
British Academy Post-Doctoral Research Fellow
London Guildhall University

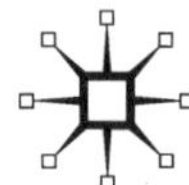

First published 2002 by
PALGRAVE MACMILLAN
Houndmills, Basingstoke, Hampshire RG21 6XS and
175 Fifth Avenue, New York, N.Y. 10010
Companies and representatives throughout the world

PALGRAVE MACMILLAN is the new global academic imprint of the Palgrave Macmillan division of St. Martin's Press, LLC and of Palgrave Macmillan Ltd. Macmillan® is a registered trademark in the United States, United Kingdom and other countries. Palgrave is a registered trademark in the European Union and other countries.

ISBN 0–333–72612–X hardback
ISBN 0–333–72613–8 paperback

This book is printed on paper suitable for recycling and made from fully managed and sustained forest sources.

A catalogue record for this book is available from the British Library.

Library of Congress Cataloging-in-Publication Data
Radical writing on women, 1800–1850: an anthology / [compiled by]
    Kathryn Gleadle. p. cm.
    Includes bibliographical references and index.
    ISBN 0–333–72612–X (cloth)
    1. Women—History—19th century. 2. Women—History—19th
    century—Sources. 3. Women—Social conditions—19th century.
    4. Feminism—History—19th century. 5. Sex role—History—
    19th century. I. Gleadle, Kathryn.

HQ1154 .R28 2002
305.4'09'034—dc21   2002019512

10   9   8   7   6   5   4   3   2   1
11   10   09   08   07   06   05   04   03   02

Printed and bound in Great Britain by
Antony Rowe Ltd, Chippenham and Eastbourne

Contents

Acknowledgements

The following libraries kindly permitted me to quote from material in their care: the British Library of Political and Economic Science; the Syndics of Cambridge University Library; The Mistress and Fellows, Girton College, Cambridge; Birmingham City Archives; the Friends House Library, London; and the Working-Class Movement Library, Salford. My thanks also to Helen Plant and Jane Rendall for allowing me to cite from their unpublished papers. In common with all others working in this field, I owe a tremendous debt to Jane Rendall for her inspiration and kind support. I wish to thank the British Academy for their financial support; and London Guildhall University for providing a welcoming academic home during the closing stages of this project. I am extremely grateful to Clare Midgley and Sarah Richardson for their encouragement and advice. Helen Rogers has been patient, kind and supportive and valiantly read an early and chaotic draft. Philippa Gray's friendship, wine-drinking and irreverence were particularly appreciated as the book reached completion. Finally, my family have nobly endured my continuing passion for early nineteenth-century feminism and its consequent incursion into our lives.

Notes on the Text

Original spellings and punctuation have been retained, although obvious errors have been silently corrected.

Bracketed numbers in the main body of the text refer to documents in the anthology.

Introduction

It has become a commonplace of feminist history that in the politically repressive climate of the post-revolutionary years, the voice of Mary Wollstonecraft was silenced. The fate of her reputation was apparently sealed in 1798 when William Godwin's revealing memoirs brought to light her suicidal tendencies and the nature of her relationship with Gilbert Imlay. According to the conventional narrative, this moment signalled a closure in the articulation of revolutionary feminism, as female authors were constrained to forget the lessons Wollstonecraft had taught them. They must bow their heads and succumb to a new, restrictive cultural order.[1]

However, it is now becoming increasingly apparent that such a picture requires considerable modification. As this collection seeks to demonstrate, feminism was alive and kicking in early nineteenth-century Britain. Indeed, to many it was a palpable threat. Witness Lord Shaftesbury during a debate on Jewish emancipation fearing that 'perhaps they would have a final struggle for a male Parliament';[2] or consider the hysterical tone of the *British and Foreign Quarterly Review* which portrayed Caroline Norton's campaign for greater maternal custody rights as a treacherous bid by female emancipationists to loosen all social ties.[3] Contemporary periodical publications could point to a continuing, rich vein of feminist discourse, citing such writers as Catherine Macaulay, Mary Wollstonecraft, William Thompson, Anna Jameson and Harriet Martineau.[4] Indeed, the prevalence of feminism was such that a women's rights position could be parodied, alluded to and satirized in contemporary literature. Both Charles Dickens's *Dombey and Son* and William Thackeray's *Vanity Fair*, for example, introduce cameo feminist characters.[5]

In tracing the history of early nineteenth-century feminism, two (overlapping) traditions – political radicalism and religious dissent – stand pre-eminent.[6] A growing body of work has now pointed to the existence of feminist discourses within a number of political movements: from the post-Napoleonic reform societies; the campaign for the freedom of the press; Carlile's Zetetic movement; Owenism, and the Chartist movement. In the case of the reform societies of the late 1810s, feminism was no more than a brief spark – a flash of possibilities brought about by the sudden conjunction of extensive female political activism and a particular set of political languages. In this context a small minority of political activists queried the masculinist language of Paineite rights and suggested the possible inclusion of women. In so doing they could defy the customary articulation of popular constitutionalism, to insist that women too, had enjoyed political rights as ancient Britons [**163–4**].

Within the context of Carlilean republicanism, feminism assumed more complex guises. Richard Carlile attracted a sizeable constituency of female support, particularly in towns such as Manchester, Blackburn, Ashton, Bolton and Bath where women established their own republican societies.[7] Although female political rights were an important component of feminist discussions in this milieu, activists were also drawn to heretical views of sexuality, marriage and birth control. Iain McCalman has painted a fascinating portrait of the feminism of this circle.[8] However, despite the fact that this network led to the first 'feminist' journal to be edited by a woman – Eliza Sharples's *Isis* – female autonomy was often compromised in other corners of the movement. A male-centred libertinism characterized much of the writing to emerge from these circles; and whilst feminist demands were frequently discussed, they were not automatically conceded [**14, 93, 129–31, 146, 166–7**].

In the Chartist movement, a tiny number of female associations pushed for the political rights of women to be considered; but across the movement at large, feminist discussions could be highly diffuse. Whilst many Chartist leaders, not least Feargus O'Connor, were highly critical of the concept of female enfranchisement, a number of high-profile Chartists did advocate the enfranchisement of (single) women. Such a position could coexist, as in the case of John Watkins and R. J. Richardson, with more patronizing attitudes as to women's intellectual abilities and domestic roles. At the same time, Chartists such as Goodwyn Barmby and W. J. Linton, who were also active in progressive Owenite and feminist circles, articulated less ambivalent feminist positions, as did a handful of individual female activists, such as Susanna Inge [**170–7**].[9]

The complex relationship between early socialism and feminism in Britain has been richly illustrated in Barbara Taylor's magisterial study.[10] The Owenite emphasis upon the centrality of the environment in the production of character was full of potential as a feminist model. It enabled radical thinkers to conceptualize the extent to which supposedly innate female characteristics were socially produced. This was not a simple project, however. Many Owenites remained fully persuaded that certain traits – such as morality and mothering – were an inherent facet of femininity [29–31]. Other shibboleths of Owenite thought could also be appropriated to a feminist agenda. The disparagement of private wealth could fit very neatly into feminist analyses which blamed the wider socio-economic system for the objectification of women [16–17]. Moreover, the Owenite critique of the contemporary marriage system served to open up debates on the marital relationship and the right to divorce [132–6, 152], whilst Owenite communitarian projects promised (in theory) to emancipate women from the drudgery of housework through the collectivization of house and child-care and the use of mechanical devices [36, 92, 94–5, 106]. Yet it is possible that it was the practice of Owenite politics that was at least as empowering for women as its theories. Whilst it is widely accepted that the seven Owenite communities were far from successful in implementing new gender relations, female participation in the cooperative societies and trades unions which the movement spawned could help to give women a sense of control over their lives [73–6]. Also, the movement afforded to certain gifted women – such as Margaret Chappellsmith, Frances Morrison and Emma Martin – opportunities to act as lecturers, missionaries and journalists for the cause (although the opprobrium they attracted may have deterred many women from wishing to follow their path).

Nevertheless, it would be mistaken to assume that Owenite feminism was a stable and unified phenomenon. As Taylor herself shows, male agendas (concerning sexual relations, for example) could be widely at variance with the needs and desires of female activists. Furthermore, the pages of Owenite journals reveal a fractured, amorphous and frequently derivative feminism. The *New Moral World* was heavily dependent upon the works on female emancipation that were emerging from the journals of rational dissent, from progressive novelists and poets, and from older authorities such as Mary Wollstonecraft or Shelley. But equally, conservative voices on such topics as female education and the marriage system were common, and works such as the preceptive *The Women of England* by Sarah Ellis were actually reviewed sympathetically.[11] Similarly, the 'Woman's Page' which appeared in the Owenite journal the *Pioneer*, was praised by Barbara Taylor as the most important platform for working-class feminism during this period.[12] Nonetheless, James Morrison's editorial comments reveal a more ambiguous feminism. He chastises women, for example, for kissing in public; holds mothers responsible for the high levels of infant mortality and talks of the 'particular spheres' of the sexes.[13]

Owenite feminism was further complicated by the impact of continental socialism, in particular Fourierism and Saint-Simonism. Charles Fourier advocated large-scale communities, or phalansteries, in which cooperative housecare would liberate women from domestic drudgery. (He also argued for a revolution in amatory practice – in which the sexual desires of all would be met and fulfilled. This aspect of the Fourierite agenda tended to be repressed within the British context, however) [36]. The Saint-Simonians preached societal renewal through reorganizing society along scientific lines, their ideas forming an early exposition of state socialism. They also looked to a female messiah to regenerate society through the values of love and harmony. Both these movements were made familiar to British socialist audiences from the early 1830s, when journals such as the *Crisis* and later, *The Shepherd* (both of which were associated with James Elishama Smith) translated and popularized many of their ideas. In the interpretation and dissemination of these movements within British progressive culture, activists tended to stress those aspects of the Fourierite and Saint-Simonian agenda which emphasized women's unique and moral purpose. Moreover, their ideas often became entwined with those of Southcottianism [31,48].[14] Some British radicals looked not only to France for inspiration, but to the United States of America. The flowering American transcendental movement formed many points of contact with those British progressives who sought not merely social or political change, but spiritual growth. The American feminist Margaret Fuller, for example, was courted by British Fourierites such as Hugh Doherty, and her work received a warm welcome across the radical press [154].[15]

Within popular politics there was, by the mid-century, a rich but conflictual history of feminist thought. This is true equally of the other major intellectual tradition which fostered feminism during this period – that of religious nonconformity. There is of course, no neat line of demarcation between political radicalism and religious dissent. This is evident if we consider such sects as Southcottianism, many leading figures of which, such as Zion Ward and James Elishama Smith, were also important activists in Owenite circles. Followers of Joanna Southcott, a working-class woman from Devon, believed her to be a prophetic messiah and her insistence upon women's unique spiritual mission amounted, it has been claimed, to a 'theological feminism' [**48, 136**].[16]

Attempts to reorientate biblical teachings to construct an empowering role for women are also in evidence in the republican movement. Eliza Sharples, in particular, made a significant contribution to feminist exegesis by portraying Eve as the bearer of knowledge. By taking the fruit of knowledge, Sharples accredited Eve as the creator of human society, and called upon women to rejoice in her actions.[17] Sharples also enunciated a desire to acknowledge women's spiritual status: 'I think we have souls, which no scripture has yet granted; that we are worthy of salvation, which no religion has yet promised us; that we are as men in mind and purpose.'[18]

Such a concern to confirm the importance of women's souls was central to the Quaker denomination. The Quakers sanctioned female preaching throughout this period (although by the mid-century this custom was on the wane). It is widely accepted that such practice did not necessarily entail any greater authority for women within the movement itself. Nevertheless, much research remains to be done upon the feminist consciousness of contemporary Quaker women (particularly given the fact that Quakers were strongly represented in the later women's rights movement).[19] It is significant that one of the period's most committed and active feminists, Anne Knight, was herself a Quaker [**192–4**].

There is much to be uncovered with regard to the formation of female identities within other religious denominations, such as the Baptists and the Congregationalists. The broader relationship between rational dissent and the emergence of modern feminism has, however, received greater attention. The close association which existed between Mary Wollstonecraft and such networks has, of course, long prompted such questions.[20] And, in recent years, historians have considered the continuing relationship between Unitarianism and feminism throughout the first half of the nineteenth century. Unitarians shared with Owenism a faith in the power of the environment to shape and mould the individual. Drawing closely upon the theories of John Locke and David Hartley, which posited a psychological theory of associationism, Unitarians placed an enormous emphasis upon the role of educational experience in the development of the individual – whether male or female. Their faith in the human ability to reason, and conviction that religious duty lay in developing one's powers of rationality to better serve God, meant that Unitarians were renowned for their educational progressivism, and in particular for the excellent education they frequently afforded to girls. Although in many socio-economic contexts this coexisted with a continuing belief in the essentially domestic and relative nature of women, many Unitarian families (particularly those close to political radicalism) developed highly progressive views on women's position.[21]

In London in particular, a network of radical reformers who were inspired by the political and intellectual basis of Unitarianism, but wary of its social conservatism, made a significant contribution to the development of feminist debate. These 'radical unitarians' were greatly influenced by the ministry of William Johnson Fox at South Place Chapel in Finsbury. Infusing the ideals of the cooperative movement with the teachings of Christ, they became involved in a number of practical initiatives to effect a change in women's position. These included lobbying for a reform to the laws governing prostitution, and also the establishment of a feminist-minded adult education and recreational institute, the Whittington Club [66].[22]

There are, however, additional ways in which the language of feminism and that of dissent might merge and overlap. The growing acceptance of biblical exegesis (particularly, but not exclusively, within the Unitarian tradition) encouraged the application of German scholarly methodologies so as to interrogate traditional interpretations of the Bible. This provided a useful tool for those who wished to question received theological wisdom as to the role of Eve (and the Genesis story more broadly),[23] or who sought to reconsider biblical pronouncements on such issues as divorce.[24]

Equally, the political, social and economic position of certain religious groups could prove particularly conducive to the questioning of established authority. Women, as well as men, could protest against the imposition of church rates or declaim against the withholding of civic liberties (prior to the repeal of the Test and Corporation Acts, in 1828). Nonconformist urban liberals, who championed a concept of active citizenship, flourished in such pressure-group movements as the anti-slavery cause and the repeal of the Corn Laws [**42, 188–92**]. Women, who could be equally implicated in the project of citizenship, were mobilized en masse in these campaigns. Occasionally, this activism could lead to the articulation of feminist viewpoints. In Birmingham, for example, little-known anti-slavery activists, such as

Mrs Toll and Margaret New pursued a feminist agenda. Indeed, participation in such campaigns had the opportunity to bring activists into contact with transatlantic feminist networks, such as the Garrisonian abolitionists, who championed women's rights.[25]

Liberal political ideologies (which were frequently but not necessarily associated with middle-class dissenters) also provided useful philosophical frameworks in which those sympathetic to women's rights could stake their claims. The issue of contractual government, for example, was central to the language of many such feminists. Many queried why women, as tax-payers, should remain disenfranchised; or asked why women should consent to a government which demanded their obedience and yet deprived them of civil rights [35, 167–8, 183–7].[26]

Utilitarianism performed a similar function. The Benthamite insistence on considering the 'greatest happiness of the greatest number' in the formulation of public policy immediately raised the question as to whether women should be included within this philosophical equation. Despite its eclectic intellectual roots,[27] by the 1820s utilitarianism had become identified with a cohesive coterie of metropolitan liberals, unitarians and 'philosophic radicals', such as John Stuart Mill and Thomas Perronet Thompson, many of whom were prepared to apply a feminist lens to their philosophical theories. The issue of female enfranchisement, in particular, aroused fierce debate within the utilitarian camp, prompting extensive discussions as to the nature and justice of female rights [180–3]. Utilitarianism also functioned as a crucial intellectual nexus for many pioneering socialists, notably William Thompson, Anna Wheeler and Frances Wright, all of whom enjoyed warm relationships with Jeremy Bentham.[28]

Discussion on women's rights was not confined to the select chambers of middle-class intellectuals, however. It is clear that within many liberal families, discussions on women's rights continued to form a lively part of family intercourse throughout the period. Isabel Petrie Mills for example, recalled discussing women's suffrage at the Bright family home, near Rochdale during the 1840s.[29] There are also many examples of juvenile feminism during these years. Women such as Lucy Aikin, Julia Smith and Margaretta Grey all recorded how, as children, they used to battle with boys over the rights of women.[30] An unpublished poem of 1814, in the Birmingham City Archives, elaborates upon heated discussions as to the relative rights and abilities of men and women which had evidently been exercising the sons and daughters of that family.[31] The young Elizabeth Barrett (Browning) even composed her own 'Essay on Women' in 1822.[32] Such consciousness may suggest the possible continuity of progressive parenting, which encouraged girls to develop self-respect and confidence in their opinions. Certainly work in progress on the social and intellectual life of rational dissenters (as well as others of liberal or latitudinarian religious views) in Edinburgh and York, indicates the rich, stimulating and empowering environment into which many contemporary women were born.[33]

It should not be assumed that feminism was always born of dissenting traditions. We have as yet little detailed knowledge of women's experience of, and response to, Anglicanism. Nevertheless, two important feminist works from this period, Anne Richelieu Lamb's *Can Woman Regenerate Society?* and *Domestic Tyranny*, by 'A Philanthropist', both emphasized the importance of the authors' Anglican faith.[34] Women's involvement in the pastoral and community activities of the Anglican church may (particularly given the influence and authority of the Church) have served to strengthen the confidence of middle-class women as public agents, particularly within the local context.[35]

All these examples point to the need for a sensitive appreciation of the ways in which people appropriated or adapted radical ideas in the workings of their own lives and relationships. We need to consider, that is, the conceptualization of feminism as a social practice (through family-based decisions such as child-rearing, education, the nature of spousal relationships and so on). Whilst histories of feminism have tended to concentrate upon public activities and proclamations perhaps there is also a need for a private history of feminism. There are frequently hints that some contemporaries exhibited a disjunction between the attitudes they practised in private and those they articulated in public. Anne Knight recorded that many publicly active men were privately in favour of female suffrage. In a list compiled for her own purposes, she included, amongst others, Joseph Sturge (the Quaker philanthropist), Henry Vincent (the Chartist lecturer), and George Thompson (MP and anti-slavery compaigner).[36] Certainly for many, feminism was a hidden or private agenda – a personally held belief that for reasons of cultural or political expediency was repressed. Caroline Norton, for example, expressed markedly different views in her published work than in her private letters [102].

Conversely, however, one senses that in the most advanced literary and radical circles, the endorsement of women's rights was a fashionable position which could be rather facilely adopted. Men such as Edward Trelawny and Edward Bulwer Lytton could be overbearing, contemptuous and violent towards their wives, and yet periodically profess sympathy with progressive formulations of women's position.[37]

Throughout this period, then, feminist discussion was varied and vibrant, and appeared in a remarkably diverse number of contexts. (This emerges starkly in the Biographical Notes at the end of this volume, which illustrate the breadth of ideological and personal motivations which could lead any one individual to formulate radical ideas on women.) Moreover, feminism extended far beyond the circles of metropolitan radicalism. The *Monthly Repository* observed in 1829 that a village discussion society in Blackwood village had taken two nights to consider 'Whether Men are endowed with Faculties superior to those of Women';[38] and the pages of progressive journals printed letters from readers across the country, who were engaged in feminist debate.[39] This evidence of the continued breadth and vigour of feminist debate in the 1800–50 period calls into question the extent to which Wollstonecraft's fire had ever been truly quenched. The widespread citations of Mary Wollstonecraft during these years confirm this impression. Whilst Wollstonecraft's friend and coadjutor, Mary Hays, may have chosen to omit Wollstonecraft from her *Female Biography* (1803) [1], a host of other writers showed little compunction in including Wollstonecraft in their female biographies. To include Wollstonecraft in such works could signal a feminist sympathy which was not otherwise made explicit in the text. For instance, both Mary Pilkington's *Memoirs of Celebrated Female Characters* (1804) and the anonymous *Eccentric Biography* (1803) defended Wollstonecraft's personal life, as well as drawing attention to the *Vindication of the Rights of Woman* and the laudable theories which they believed to lie behind it.[40] As many of the extracts in this anthology indicate, Wollstonecraft's life and ideas remained a source of inspiration and authority for progressive authors. She was discussed in the pages of Owenite and Chartist journals and the newsletters of adult improvement institutes. Her ideas were debated in monographs upon sexual reform, marriage and female employment.[41] Some sympathizers attempted to rid her name of its scandalous piquancy. As *Tait's Edinburgh Magazine* put it, 'Women dread something they know not what in her writings; whereas the fact is, that the philosophy of Mary Wollstonecraft, in her apology for her sex and the Rights of Women, is severe and even stoical.'[42] Contemporary women often discussed her amongst themselves. Listen to Elizabeth Gaskell, playfully suggesting to Anne Shaen that she set Wollstonecraft's words to music,[43] or Mary

Moulton-Barrett teasing her teenage daughter Elizabeth Barrett (Browning) in 1821 for her sympathy with Wollstonecraft's 'visionary' system of marriage.[44]

Nevertheless, to see Wollstonecraft's work as *the* catalyst, pushing forward the feminist agenda is stereotypical. Other feminist productions, of different trajectories, cut across the feminist intellectual chronology provided by the *Vindication of the Rights of Woman*. Indeed, Wollstonecraft's project of 'vindicating women's rights' was not itself original. Her work was preceded, for example, by the spirited *Female Rights Vindicated* (1758), a text which enjoyed currency across these years.[45] More importantly, a considerable amount of early nineteenth-century radical writing on women demonstrated its deep roots in Enlightenment feminism not by carrying Wollstonecraft's mantle per se, but rather by using the tools of Enlightenment scholars, such as comparative history and anthropology [2–3, 11–13, 120]. Equally, running in parallel with the discourse of explicit feminist polemic, ran other genres (including educational pamphlets, law manuals, medical treatises and political manifestos) in which feminist ideas could surface, founder and re-emerge, providing discrete chronologies for the articulation of feminist and proto-feminist agendas. Meanwhile within literary texts, those interested in progressive treatments of women's position, could find the imaginative space to develop alternative views of women's potential or to delineate more subversive aspects of female characters. By casing their narratives within traditional dénouements (such as marriage),[46] or giving minor characters the most telling lines, novelists could also ensure that their novels would still reach the shelves of Mudie's circulating libraries.[47]

If the genres used to express heterodox opinions on women were diverse, then so too were the political aspirations of such interventions. 'Women's rights' had no stable, unitary meaning, but could be inflected differently in various contexts.[48] Hence there was no automatic domino-effect which located women's rights on an intellectual matrix with support for the rights of slaves, or the rights of the people. Mary Ann Radcliffe prioritized the rights of women over those of black people [71];[49] whilst S. Hatfield noted with evident distaste that 'the lower orders of society' were 'over-leaping the bounds by which they ought to be limited'.[50] For the more conservative, such as Hatfield, the language of women's rights formed part of a discursive lexicon which was further associated with their 'privileges'.[51] This could lead to arguments that were strikingly at variance with Wollstonecraft's desire for women to act as rational, independent beings. The anonymous author of *Domestic Tyranny*, for example, insisted that men had misused the 'powers intrusted [*sic*] to them for the protection and benefit of the weaker sex'.[52]

If even the language of 'women's rights' was not a unifying concept, it is not surprising that other aspects of feminist discourse could be equally diverse. Feminism could be highly individualistic, and feminist debate was marked as much by divergence, as by consensus. Apparently 'obvious' aspects of the feminist agenda might fracture as they became assimilated to individual life-experiences, discrete political viewpoints and moral or religious preoccupations. Many of the documents represented here crackle with ambiguities and tensions. Lucy Aikin, for example, believed in female suffrage, but was opposed to divorce reform. She supported calls for tighter laws regarding the procurement of prostitutes, but believed that otherwise British women enjoyed a comparatively good legal position. Furthermore, she celebrated the fact that (elite) women now had access to 'explore most branches of knowledge', but professed to be 'totally opposed' to opening up professions and trades to women.[53]

As this suggests, it would be simplistic to imply that the plethora of feminist voices presented in this collection amount to a smooth and unbroken feminist tradition. There are clearly continuities between many of the ideas discussed (particularly in the 1840s) and later women's rights campaigns (and some overlap of personnel). Equally telling however, are the ruptures, the broken threads, and the discursive ellipses. Some elements on the early feminist agenda had but an intermittent history, or faded completely into obscurity. The relationship between vegetarianism and feminism [98] (and also sexual radicalism and feminism [Ch. 7, 141–7]), for example, went into something of an abeyance from the mid-century, to be revived again in the 1880s;[54] the link between evolutionary theories and women's rights [20, 109] became far more problematic and complex with the rise of social Darwinism;[55] whilst the possibilities of nudism for a feminist programme were rarely to be revived [158].

Indeed, this is perhaps one of the excitements of studying feminism during these years. We are witnessing a confluence of ideas in flux, before they became woven into a neater, more coherent whole. Indeed, there are many unexpected feminist moments in this period. One of the most striking is the accession of Queen Victoria in 1837. Whilst a number of progressive writers exploited her constitutional role as a rhetorical strategy with which to explode the myth of women's political ineptitude [167, 169], for others her sovereignty held more visionary potential. One writer insisted that Victoria's reign furnished 'an opportunity for turning the tide in the fortunes of women ... this is the appointed season for withdrawing from their necks the yoke of bondage which they have so long worn'.[56] Similarly, the young Elizabeth Blackwell dreamed of the Queen leading a great moral reformation of society with a 'priesthood of women, clubs, social unions, colonial operations, a true press, and radical action'.[57] Such rhapsodies are testament to the potent emotional needs of many contemporary women for greater freedom, autonomy and action. But they also indicate the ways in which some aspects of feminist thought, particularly the most contingent, could be ephemeral.

This proliferation of feminist discourse did not, of course, emerge within a cultural vacuum, but was an active response to both the range and scope of contemporary debates on women, as well as to particular perceptions of women's position. This was a complex process. Radical voices on women were not simple, unmediated reflections on the lives of contemporary females, and the majority of women rejected feminist analyses. This is perhaps not surprising in the case of working-class women. Most women already tended to play a significant role in structuring neighbourhood networks and values, and in defending community and family welfare. The chequered impact of growing industrialization meant that, for the majority of women, protecting the economic and social needs of their families and communities remained their first priority. This was reflected by the nature of their involvement in political movements such as Chartism, as well as their role in community protests, as in the Highland riots, for example. The centrality of these concerns probably explains the comparative rarity of working-class feminism outside the orbit of Owenism.[58]

The picture is rather different for middle-class women. Recent studies indicate that despite the undeniable and multi-faceted oppression women faced (particularly with regard to access to education, employment, financial status and patriarchal marital and sexual relationships), the early part of the nineteenth century actually witnessed some significant cultural shifts in women's status. Elite and middle-class women consolidated their involvement in cultural activities, such as book-clubs, lectures, sermons and the like; whilst the mushrooming philanthropic movement endowed women with the authority and confidence to act in the local and public sectors. Equally, the growing trend for female participation in pressure-group movements, as already noted, indicated the burgeoning civic and political consciousness of middle-class women.[59] Indeed, many of the feminists represented here, including Mary Gillies, Mary Hughes, Anne Knight, Harriet Martineau, Margaret Mylne, Barbara Leigh Smith and Harriet Taylor, came from precisely such environments. In other words, feminism was far more intricate a phenomenon than merely a reaction to women's oppression: it was also a response to change.

In order to fully understand this process, it is helpful to locate these progressive articulations on women within a broader discursive context. For example, Amanda Vickery has similarly suggested that the seemingly conservative language of 'separate spheres' may be interpreted as a reactive phenomenon.[60] That is, the proliferation of texts emphasizing women's domestic nature may be seen not as a reflection of women's actual status in the early nineteenth century, but rather as a conservative response to their increasing engagement and visibility in the public sphere. In other words, feminism was operating within a discursive landscape in which changes and developments in women's position were prompting the reconfiguration of contemporary sensibilities concerning appropriate female behaviour and roles. This alerts us to the importance of perceiving feminist discussions as part of a dialogic process, in which a range of views and opinions on the woman question prompted rich debates. (Contemporary journalists noted the almost exhaustive discussions on women's roles, attitudes and potential.[61])

Such a process was greatly stimulated by the growing hold of Evangelical sensibilities. By essentializing the supposedly female characteristics of loving, caring and morality, Evangelical literature not only provided a route whereby women could claim a duty to intervene in community and philanthropic endeavours, it also paradoxically, refocused attention upon women's domestic and maternal roles. This was a complex ideological configuration; but undoubtedly, the Evangelical insistence on recognizing women's worth and significance played an important part in shifting cultural attitudes towards positive roles for women. Indeed, Evangelicalism has earned a prominent place in social histories of feminism.[62] Whilst acknowledging Evangelicalism's importance to the longue durée of growing female confidence and consciousness, its relationship to the specific political demands for women's emancipation which comprise the present volume, is extremely problematic – not least because Evangelical vocabularies could directly conflict with feminist arguments for political rights and employment opportunities. Nevertheless, many who expressed radical views on women did not necessarily object to the greater discursive emphasis upon women's maternal and domestic roles, championed by the Evangelicals. A small number of those who articulated radical views on women's position even saw the pronouncements of women like Sarah Lewis (whose *Woman's Mission* noted approvingly the growing recognition of women's dignity and value, and acknowledged the potential of women's domestic influence[63]), as a welcome contribution to the debate.[64]

Such surprising and intricate conjunctures between diverse political positions are telling. Indeed, it is perhaps useful to consider this as a period in which opinions and attitudes towards women were far more contested, contradictory and interesting than they have often been portrayed. Furthermore, in addition to the calls to reinvest motherhood with greater meaning and significance, there were a myriad of other potentially empowering paradigms of womanhood within contemporary culture, but which had no necessary connection to feminism. Here we might think of the plucky heroines popular to melodrama; female preachers in plebeian Methodism as well as Quakerism; powerful aristocratic dowagers; authoritative philanthropists; female trade unionists; salonnières; petticoat reformers; temperance lecturers and so on. Feminism, that is to say, was operating within a context in which ideas on women were neither rigidly prescribed nor invariably restrictive.

To acknowledge the fluidity and contestation of voices on women in this period raises the important question of how 'feminism' is defined in this volume. The term 'feminism' was not coined until the end of the nineteenth century and its use prior to this period is certainly problematic. In selecting extracts, I have, on the whole, attempted to choose those which appear to have been self-consciously and deliberately attempting to alter the balance of power between the sexes; which have an awareness of the social and cultural oppression of women and which either explicitly positioned themselves (or were perceived by contemporaries) to champion emancipationist doctrines on women. My aim, however, has not been to reify and discipline progressive writing on women into a narrow feminist canon, but rather to prompt debate as to the nature of feminism during this period. Certainly it is not possible to chart a unified feminist polemic during these years – far from it. The voices here, as already indicated, are testament to the sheer mutability and variety of feminist discussion. For this reason, I have chosen the more amorphous term 'radical' in many instances – for this captures my intention of presenting documents which deliberately presented unorthodox views, or which knowingly went against the grain. Indeed, I have included a small number of extracts which do not conform to even a broad conventional understanding of the term 'feminism'. These include works such as *Kalogynomia* by Thomas Bell [**141**] (which articulated a powerful avowal of female sexual passion); and the prophecies of Joanna Southcott [**48**] (which amounted to a fierce onslaught upon the masculinist construction of religious authority). Neither of these authors, however, elaborated upon the wider social and political position of women. Equally, I have included a number of extracts which defy simple ideological characterization, comprising as they do varying and ambiguous demands for female emancipation as well as clear affirmations of male patriarchal or sexual privileges.[65] It is hoped that the incorporation of such documents will lend a more provocative edge to the collection, as well as illustrating the ebb and flow of unorthodox views on women amongst the varying radical subcultures of the day.

The radical writings on women which comprise this volume therefore represent the stimulating currents of (often conflicting) ideas on women. They indicate the great fecundity of progressive thought, and perhaps more fundamentally, affirm the multivocal nature of early nineteenth-century pronouncements on women.

Notes

1 See for example Harriet Jump, who maintains that 'Revolutionary feminism effectively ceased to exist'. Jump (1997), p. xiv. For details of Wollstonecraft's life see Tomalin (1985).

2 Cited in Nadia Valman, 'Women Writers and the Campaign for Jewish Civil Rights in Early Victorian England', in Gleadle and Richardson (2000), p. 93.

3 *British and Foreign Quarterly Review* (1838), vol. 7, no. 13, pp. 269–411.

4 See for example, 'A Blast against the Monstrous Regiments of Women', *Tait's Edinburgh Magazine* (November 1835), vol. 2, p. 702.

5 Miss Crawley had 'read Voltaire, and had Rousseau by heart; talked very lightly about divorce, and most energetically of the rights of women'. Thackeray (1848, 1968 edn), p. 130. In *Dombey and Son*, the feckless husband of sensible Susan Toots says of his wife that, 'Nobody but myself can tell what the capacity of that woman's mind is. If ever the Rights of women, and all that kind of thing, are properly attended to, it will be through her powerful intellect.' Dickens (1844–46, 1970 edn), p. 946. Publications such as the *Metropolitan Magazine* also provided satirical representations of contemporary feminist positions. See, for example, 'Man and His Missus, by one of the Henpecked', *Metropolitan Magazine* (1848), vol. 51, pp. 140–52.

6 The best introduction to feminism in this period is Rendall (1985).

 7 For illuminating discussions of the post-war reform societies and the republican movement see Epstein (1994), chs 3 and 4.
 8 McCalman (1980).
 9 Jones (1983); Schwarzkopf (1991); Thompson (1984), ch. 7.
10 Taylor (1983).
11 *New Moral World* (20 Feb 1841), vol. 9, no. 8, pp. 116–17.
12 Taylor (1983), pp. 96–8.
13 See the 'Woman's Page' in *The Pioneer* in the following issues: (10 May 1834), no. 36, p. 346; (24 May 1834), no. 38, p. 371; (31 May 1834), no. 39, p. 383.
14 K. Gleadle, '"Our Several Spheres": Middle-Class Women and the Feminisms of Early Victorian Radical Politics', in Gleadle and Richardson (2000), pp. 134–9.
15 Transcendental feminism in Britain awaits detailed investigation. However see Cooper (1872), p. 312; examples of reviews of Margaret Fuller include *The Reasoner* (10 June 1846), vol. 1, no. 2, pp. 29–30 (by Charles Lane) and *The Truth-Seeker* (February 1850), no. 1, pp. 13–19; *People's Review of Literature and Politics* (April 1850), no. 3, p. 122. J. F. C. Harrison provided an insight into British transcendentalists in (1961), part 3, ch. 2.
16 Clark (1995), pp. 108–11; Harrison (1979), p. 110; Taylor (1983), pp. 162–7.
17 Rogers (2000), ch. 2.
18 'First Discourse of the Lady at the Rotunda' (Eliza Sharples), *Isis* (11 February 1832), vol. 1, no. 1, p. 4.
19 Isichei (1970), p. 108.
20 Philp (1986); Tomalin (1974).
21 See, for example, the documents relating to Lucy Aikin, Julia Smith, Harriet Martineau and Mary Hughes.
22 For Unitarianism see Gleadle (1995); Watts (1998). As well as documents from individual members of this radical unitarian milieu (the central writers represented in this collection include Sarah Flower Adams, William Bridges Adams, William H. Ashurst, Eliza Meteyard, William Johnson Fox, Mary Leman Grimstone, Mary Gillies, Matilda Mary Hays, Mary Howitt, William James Linton, Harriet Martineau, Harriet Taylor; whilst the following authors were part of their broader network: Catherine Barmby, John Epps, Elizabeth Hennell, Anna Jameson, Geraldine Jewsbury, Eliza Lynn Linton, J. S. Mill, Bessie Rayner Parkes, Barbara Leigh Smith and Samuel Smiles) – see documents **77–80**, **137–40**.
23 The *Annual Review* (1803), vol. 2, pp. 449–50 praised S. Hatfield's *Letters on the Importance of the Female Sex* for its positive retelling of the story of Eve, and suggested that her interpretation should be brought to the attention of biblical scholars. Charlotte Brontë also considered the feminist implications of competing interpretations of Eve in *Shirley* (1849; 1985 edn), ch. 18. See also the ideas of Eliza Sharples, above p. 5.
24 See for example W. J. Fox, 'Politics of the Common Pleas', *Monthly Repository* (1836), vol. 10, p. 398.
25 For female agitation against the Test and Corporation Acts see K. Gleadle, 'British Women and Radical Politics in the Nonconformist Enlightenment', in Vickery (2001), pp. 128–9. For women and anti-slavery consult Midgley (1992 and 1993). Evidence regarding Birmingham feminists is located in

Taylor (1974), p. 178. See also Simon Morgan, 'Domestic Economy and Political Agitation: Women and the Anti-Corn Law League, 1839–1846', in Gleadle and Richardson (2000), pp. 115–33.

26 These arguments were not, of course, unique to middle-class liberals, but also surfaced in Chartist demands for women's rights [**173–4**].

27 Utilitarianism drew upon discussions concerning the nature of utilitarian morality developed by William Paley and David Hume; theories of psychological associationism, as propounded by David Hartley; radical political discussions concerning constitutional reform, and debates over political economy, such as those stimulated by David Ricardo and Adam Smith. The classic work on this area is Halévy (1952).

28 Dooley (1996), ch. 3, provides an extended discussion of the relationship between utilitarianism and feminism.

29 Crawford (1999), p. 80.

30 Le Breton (1864), p. 259; William Smith Papers, Cambridge, Add MS 7621; Butler (1869), pp. 14–15.

31 Hutton Beale Papers, 116 /2, Birmingham City Archives.

32 Kelley and Hudson (1984), vol.1, p. 133.

33 Unpublished papers of Plant (2000) and Rendall (2000)

34 Lamb (1844), p. 164; 'A Philanthropist' (1841), p. 52.

35 For an overview of women's philanthropic activities and their implications see Prochaska (1980).

36 Anne Knight papers, Friends' House, MS vol.s495, p. 214.

37 See the Biographical Notes at the end of this volume.

38 *Monthly Repository* (1829), vol. 3, p. 76.

39 Interestingly, there are clusters of contributions from the West Country. See for example *Educational Circular or Communist Apostle* (March 1842), pp. 37–8; *Howitt's Journal* (15 May 1847), vol. 1, no. 20, p. 40; *Lion* (19 December 1828), vol. 2, no. 25, pp. 776–80.

40 See also Betham (1804) for a more restrained but not uncritical account of Wollstonecraft's life. The strategy of employing collective biography to pursue a feminist agenda has an interesting pedigree. See Scott (1774) and Benger (1791).

41 From a plethora of examples, one might pick *National Association Gazette* (15 January 1842), no. 3, p. 23; *New Moral World* (3 August 1839), vol. 6, no. 41, p. 655; *The Pioneer* (7 June 1834), no. 40, p. 397; Walker (1839); Kitchener (1812), p. 103; Radcliffe (1810), p. 398. Jutta Schwarzkopf makes the interesting point that Chartist newspapers tended to confine their discussions to Wollstonecraft's views on female education: Schwarzkopf (1991), pp. 64–5.

42 'Review of Mrs. Hugo Reid's "Plea for Woman"', *Tait's Edinburgh Magazine* (July 1844), vol. 11, p. 423.

43 Elizabeth Gaskell to Anne Shaen (24 April 1848), in Chapple and Pollard (1966), p. 57.

44 Mary Moulton-Barrett to Elizabeth Barrett Browning [*c.* September 1821) in Kelley and Lewis (1984), vol. 1, p. 132.

45 It was reprinted in 1780 by E. Hayley, and then again by James Jollie of South Shields in 1833 (see documents **5, 26, 89**). It is also interesting to note that feminists Clementia and Peter A. Taylor possessed a copy of

another early feminist tract by 'Sophia' – *Woman Not Inferior to Man* (1739): Crawford (1999), p. 677.

46   See for example Chapter 4, n.15.

47   Charles Mudie, the owner of the circulating libraries, was a man of strict Evangelical and moral views, who would only stock material he felt to be inoffensive. Tuchman (1989), passim.

48   Extreme political radicals could have quite a different perspective as to what constituted women's rights. Thomas Spence, for example, who suggested that women would 'vindicate the rights of the species', believed that women's fundamental rights lay in providing 'from the elements the proper nourishments of their young'. Spence (1797), p. 5.

49   Joseph Banks, an admirer of Radcliffe's work, shared such sentiments. Gascoigne (1994), pp. 51–2.

50   Hatfield (1803), p. 90.

51   See also *Laws Respecting Women* (1777); Scott (1774), v; *The Rights, Privileges and Laws of Women* (1815).

52   A Philanthropist (1841), p. 13.

53   See Le Breton (1864), pp. 362–3, 368–70.

54   For vegetarianism and sexuality in the later period see, respectively, Leneman (1997) and Bland (1995).

55   For the later period see Jill Conway, 'Stereotypes of Femininity in a Theory of Sexual Evolution', in Vicinus (1972), pp. 140–54.

56   A Philanthropist (1841), pp. 23–4.

57   Ross (1950), p. 159.

58   A good introduction to these topics may be found in Thomis and Grimmett (1982).

59   See for example Colley (1992), ch. 6; Vickery (1998).

60   Vickery (1993).

61   See for example, *Eliza Cook's Journal* (14 December 1850), vol. 4, no. 85, p. 97, and Smith (1850), p. 77.

62   For an extended discussion see Rendall (1985), ch. 3.

63   See Lewis (1839), pp. 11–12, 44–5, 56–7, 51–2.

64   See for example, the views of Sophia Chichester: Gleadle (2000), p. 138. Anna Jameson referred to Lewis's and Marion Reid's books as 'two admirable little books': Jameson (1846), p. 215n; Marion Reid herself, however was very critical of Lewis: Reid (1843), ch. 3.

65   See for example documents **70**, **122**, the documents concerning sexual radicalism (especially **126–30**), or the unstable Chartist feminism of John Watkins and R. J. Richardson (**173–4**).

Part I
Defining the Problem

'Is there yet a slave-class? Alas! the ancient slavery subsists; one half of humankind is yet despoiled of its individuality, of its natural liberty and self-sovereignty.'[1]

Introduction

This first section of the anthology considers how radical thinkers and writers variously conceptualized the nature of woman, women's position within society, and the varying strategies proposed to raise women's social status. In formulating their ideas, contemporaries drew upon an enormous range of disciplines: history, anthropology, literature, religion, political theory and science all contributed to (and complicated) the rich debates that raged during these years.

Although consensus did emerge within discrete political contexts (as, for example, the agreement within socialist circles as to the relationship between women's ills and the capitalist system [16–17]), on the whole, arguments proliferated and diverged to produce a web of competing emphases and meanings. Certain tropes recurred repeatedly – by far the most frequently employed (as the documents illustrate throughout the anthology) was that of slavery. It is perhaps not surprising that a culture both steeped in biblical and classical learning and galvanized by the anti-slavery campaign should find the emotive image of the slave a particularly accessible resource. But to evoke the spectre of the slave triggered a plethora of meanings: the black African labourer, whipped and punished into toil and submission; the household slave deprived of all autonomy within the domestic setting of ancient households; and the Eastern slave consigned to sensual degradation in the harems which haunted the orientalist imagination.[2] The strength of the image was its sheer versatility. It also enabled feminist theorists to draw upon the extensive idioms of the anti-slavery movement, particularly with regard to the psychology of slavery. Men, it was suggested within feminist letters, were just as vitiated by the system of gender oppression as their subjected women, and enslaved women would be too inured to their oppression to seek emancipation. Such arguments should not, of course, be interpreted as an objective assessment of the realities of gender relations; rather they were conceived as a rhetorical strategy, a means of entry into the ideological registers of the writer's audience.[3]

To categorize women as slaves essentialized their role within patriarchal society. Certainly, a number of feminist writers believed that the lessons taught by history and anthropology confirmed the view that women were universally in subjection to men, thus leading to the articulation of theories of a universal male conspiracy [4, 5, 27, 73]. History, however, is a plastic tool. For writers were also keen to point out that women had actually played diverse and often inspiring historical roles. By the early nineteenth century, women's history was emerging as an empowering project, with polemicists focusing upon the intelligence, fortitude and courage displayed by women in diverse historical contexts. For many the cultivation of a female tradition of history, frequently relying upon a biographical methodology, was an obvious vehicle with which to display women's potential for greater social and political roles in contemporary society [1–7, 164–5]. Whilst the genre of historical biography proved a diffuse one, open also to conservative purposes,[4] its subversive potential was recognized by both feminist authors and their audience.

This approach to history rested a little uneasily with those analyses drawn from the Enlightenment tradition, which sought to provide a more critical account of women's changing position in relation to social development.[5] Here again, there seemed to be no obvious nexus of agreement. Did women's status provide a reliable indicator of the progress of Western civilization? Had Christianity functioned as the catalyst to improvement, as many commentators claimed [11, 13, 47]? Such questions exercised the minds and thoughts of numerous radicals. Yet what was often at stake in these discussions was contrasting intellectual models of change itself. Whilst some rested upon schematic formulas of societal progress which traced the evolution of different modes of social and economic organization (in which debate was further prompted by the insights gleaned from anthropology), others stressed rather the potential for varying degrees of intellectual attainment which were prompted by environmental conditions [18–19, 21–2, 161]. Those moving in the most advanced coteries of scientific pursuit might perceive change in cosmic, evolutionary perspectives – emphasizing the capacity for physiological change as a precursor to new gender roles [20, 109].

However, it was still convenient to dwell upon examples of positive female role models from the modern era. It was commonplace to treat one's reader to a roll call of recent female achievement, with success stories from the decorous field of literature proving a popular theme. If women had the potential to perform intellectual tasks with such ease, what was preventing them from making a more profound contribution to their own social and cultural worlds [41]? For many the answer was simple: an integral facet of male domination lay in men's iniquitous command of female socialization. The characters and intellects of young girls were compressed into narrow moulds so as best to fit them for male consumption as pleasing and passive companions [18–19]. But the extent to which such cultural pressures were responsible for the presentation of apparently 'typical' female traits of loving, self-sacrifice and grace was deeply and often bitterly contested. The Owenites, in common with many of their peers, had a tendency to blame social conditioning for those (supposedly) female characteristics they most deplored: such as the propensity to gossip, the display of shallow intellectual judgement or a devotion to the ephemeral. Nevertheless, they often identified women with the virtues of loving and sharing – qualities they placed on the political map as an antidote to the divisiveness and competition of capitalism.[6] For many thinkers, herein lay women's potential to assist in the reformation of modern society. Whilst other activists might despair of such a position as mere sentimental cant [29–30] many contemporary feminist writers expanded at length upon innate gender differences, arguing not that women were 'equal but different', but actually '*superior* and different' [26–8].

It was not merely women's personalities or intellects which became disputed in these competing arguments of 'nature versus nurture'. The female body itself was the site of considerable debate, as progressives considered (sometimes with the assistance of unorthodox medical theories) the extent to which female physical attributes were themselves socially produced [20–5].

If agitators analysed the cause of women's oppression so variously, it is not surprising that their formulas for change were equally diverse. As future chapters will indicate, improved education, enfranchisement, employment opportunities, reform of the laws and a revolution in sexual manners were all proposed as essential measures to emancipate women during this period. It is possible, however, to discern certain overarching strategies. For those allied to radical political movements, feminist solutions were usually presented through the prism of their wider agendas. Socialist feminists repeatedly insisted that women's liberation would have to be realized through a seismic cultural and economic shift that would prioritize the community rather than the individual. The redoubtable socialist and co-founder of the Communist Church, Catherine Barmby, presented a far-reaching programme of political, eccelesiastical and domestic reform to ensure women's liberation [34]. Many of her coadjutors in Owenite-influenced circles, reflected upon capitalism's tendency to atomize society – both through capitalist enterprise and the nuclear family. Consequently, they urged the need for women's collective action – a proposal which alarmed those Owenites who feared the privileging of gender over class needs [37, 73–6, 94].

However, it was not only feminist Owenites who argued for the need for women-only societies to effect reform. Such demands were frequent, often prompted by suggestions that women should follow the example of male radicals and organize themselves into campaigning for change [35, 38, 67–8]. Significantly, only a handful of societies did emerge.[7] Most contemporary feminists tended to use strategies which might enable them to work more comfortably within the confines of early Victorian mores. This is seen, for example, in the frequent recourse to literature as a vehicle to air progressive debates on women's position – a model which will recur during the course of the anthology. Moreover, many feminist-minded women, with their family schooling in laissez-faire liberalism, reacted with disdain to proposals for collaborative action. This emphasis upon the role of the individual in proving herself worthy of emancipation strayed into some more unlikely currents of proto-feminist expression. A number of women, as they sought possible models of female excellence, stressed the importance of remaining true to Christian ideals of self-sacrifice [39–46], or interrogated the Christian tradition to suggest even more profound means to reorientate women's role within society [47–8].

Notes

1 Lamennais (1840), p. 29.
2 See Chapter 6 for further elaboration of these tropes within the specific context of women's marital experiences. There were dissenting voices concerning the fate of women in the East. See Killham (1958), pp. 138–9 and document **110**.
3 For example Anne Knight's own, incessant attempts to rouse a women's rights campaign [**192–4**] was strikingly at odds with her arguments elsewhere that as an enslaved community, women were unable to fight for their liberation: 'Letter to editor from Anne Knight', *People's Press* (October

1847), vol. 1, no. 9, pp. 269–70.
4 For the conservative and Evangelical, such writings gave the opportunity to construct a canon of the pious and pure. See Timpson (1846).
5 For a useful overview see Rendall (1985), ch 1.
6 For further discussion of the Owenites' view of the female character see Taylor (1983), pp. 24–32.
7 For example, the Women's Elevation League (1853) with which Anne Knight was involved: Schwarzkopf (1991), p. 254; or the Ladies' Friendly Society within the Whittington Club: Gleadle (1995), pp. 167–8.

1
Analysing Woman's Position

'Does History speak?'

1. *Mary Hays's* Female Biography *was an impressive survey of the lives of famous and achieving women. As Lucy Aikin wrote to the dissenting radical Susannah Taylor in Norwich, 'There is a singular work lately published, of which I should much like to hear your opinion, Mary Hayes's [sic] "Female Biography". She is a great disciple of Mrs. Godwin,[1] you know, and a zealous stickler for the equal rights and equal talents of our sex with the other ... I am afraid the gentlemen will get a peep at her book and repeat with tenfold energy that women have no business with anything but nursing children and mending stockings.'[2]*

My pen has been taken up in the cause, and for the benefit, of my own sex. For their improvement, and to their entertainment, my labours have been devoted. Women, unsophisticated by the pedantry of the schools, read not for dry information, to load their memories with uninteresting facts, or to make a display of a vain erudition. A skeleton biography would afford to them but little gratification: they require pleasure to be mingled with instruction, lively images, the graces of sentiment, and the polish of language. Their understandings are principally accessible through their affections: they delight in minute delineation of character; nor must the truths which impress them be either cold or unadorned. I have at heart the happiness of my sex, and their advancement in the grand scale of rational and social existence. I perceive, with mingled concern and indignation, the follies and vices by which they suffer themselves to be degraded. If, through prudence or policy, the generous contention between the sexes for intellectual equality must be waived, be not, my amiable country-women, poorly content with the destination of the slaves of an Eastern haram [*sic*], with whom the season of youth forms the whole of life! ...

To excite a worthier emulation, the following memorial of those women, whose endowments, or whose conduct, have reflected lustre upon the sex, is presented more especially to the rising generation, who have not grown old in folly, whose hearts have not been seared by fashion, and whose minds prejudice has not yet warped.

Mary Hays, Female Biography (1803), vol. I, pp. iii–vi

2.   *In 1810 Lucy Aikin published an ambitious poem that attempted to trace the evolving position of women through various historical epochs. Twenty-two years later she admitted that the quality of the poetry was not high, but she defended the feminist principles that inspired the subject matter.*[3]

> Does History speak? drink in her loftiest tone,
> And be Cornelia's[4] virtues all your own.
> Thus self-endowed, thus armed for every state,
> Improve, excel, surmount, subdue, your fate!
> So shall at length enlightened Man efface
> That slavish stigma seared on half the race,
> His rude forefathers' shame; and pleased confess
> 'Tis yours to elevate, 'tis yours to bless;
> Your interest one with his; your hopes the same;
> Fair peace in life, in death undying fame,
> And bliss in worlds beyond, the species' general aim.
> 'Rise,' shall he cry, 'O Woman, rise! be free!
> My life's associate, now partake with me:
> Rouse thy keen energies, expand thy soul,
> And see, and feel, and comprehend the whole...'

Lucy Aikin, Epistles on Women (1810), p. 80

3.   *Ellen Weeton's essay, unpublished in her own lifetime, explicated a recurring theme concerning the comparative treatment of women in barbarous and civilized societies.*

Woman almost ever since the creation has been a humbled, degraded being indeed, when compared with man. With as just a sense of right and wrong, as strong a feeling of liberty and oppression, the same warmth of gratitude and resentment, she has been treated as if her capacity were little above the level of a brute ... I would not be understood to argue that woman is superior to man; I should blush to advance so weak an opinion. I would only affirm that they are *equal*, and ought to be treated as such in every respect ...

In proportion as the mind of man has been more cultivated, and become more refined, the intellect of woman has been more highly appreciated by him. He finds, *when he begins to use his understanding*, that he is not so much wiser, so much better, as he used to flatter himself he was; and as he still rises in knowledge, he more clearly perceives the equality of her whom he had been taught from infancy to look down upon.

In barbarous nations, strength of body is looked upon as the most admirable qualification – here, woman *must* sink in estimation; but in enlightened nations, where superiority of mind is most sought, and most highly admired when found, woman will inevitably rise up to the level of man in wisdom, virtue, and dignity. May it not then be justly inferred, that whoever censures woman as inferior to man, debases himself by it. If the censure is in a slight degree, he sinks a little more below the level of a truly enlightened mind; and in proportion as he is more severe, so much the nearer does he approach to the tyrant, the barbarian, and the savage.

Ellen Weeton, 'An Essay' (1810) in Bagley (1969), vol.I, pp. 312–13

4. Numberless circumstances have been recorded in ancient history, during intermediate ages, in which female abilities and talents have been displayed in various gradations and extremes, anterior to that grand epoch, in which a woman was so conspicuously chosen to assist in the great work of atonement, in producing the Redeemer.

No age has passed, in whose annals have not been recorded acts of female heroism and greatness – of deeds, in which have been displayed illustrious virtue and magnanimity: deeds which have reflected on that sex the brightest lustre, and strikingly discovered the natural richness of their minds, which, receiving very few advantages from a narrow system, long laid down and established, for their education, they must either have made efforts to free themselves from the mental shackles with which they were bound, and force themselves into acts worthy a human soul, or continue to drag little better than a torpid existence, in that state to which the meanness of their acquired knowledge seemed to condemn them ...

The untaught soul, that is suffered to lie in rudeness and error, although derived from the same source, has the evidences of its natural powers considerably lessened, compared with that enlightened mind which is enabled to seek into its own expectation. This is the cause whence many illiberal opinions of the opposite sex have suspected female faculties of inferiority: for men, taking the laws of order into their own hands, appeared to form a masculine plot, unfavorable to the advancement, by declaiming against the amiableness, of feminine knowledge, beyond the sphere of domestic life: but although these regulations were no proof of men's wisdom, they added to their importance by the exercise of greater power.

Miss S. Hatfield, *Letters on the Importance of the Female Sex* (1803), pp. 13–14, 25–6

5.   *This author considered the many achievements of women across history, drawing particular attention to those such as Joan of Arc, who had distinguished themselves in battle.*

If under the oppressive tyranny of the men, we have been able to give such striking instances of our fortitude, chastity, and abilities for learning; how much more conspicuous might we have expected to find the glorious actions of the sex, had we been in every thing upon a footing with them; – opportunities equally favourable to acquire; and occasions equally frequent to testify our knowledge and our skill! In all that is immediately dependant upon ourselves, how greatly superior do we appear, even under our disadvantages? The goodness of our heart, and our virtuous disposition, are ever transcendent. Let our opponents search all history, ancient and modern, and produce such instances of chastity in the men, as have here been promiscuously cited ... the conduct of men is so analogous in all ages, and in every part of the globe, that one would be inclined to imagine they have entered into an hereditary and universal combination against us. It is indeed the opinion of many, that they are prompted by instinct to oppress us.

A Lady, *Female Rights Vindicated* (1833; first published 1758), pp. xxxii–iii, 48

6.   *The following extract comes from the report of a lecture given by the Owenite Emma Martin, at the John Street Institute, Tottenham Court Road, London.*

... she went into a line of reasoning showing from the biographical history of various illustrious females, their general mental capacity to acquire, and readily communicate to their offspring, all the higher and more important knowledge of serene society, politics etc. being fully equal to man...

She then entered into a historical statement of woman in various ages and countries, and urged it as the duty of all Governments to take charge of, and regulate, such matters; and concluded by lamenting that women were generally found to hug the chains that held them in bondage, which was mostly attributable to single family arrangements: and contended for, and urged the necessity of women, in order to improve themselves, to make common cause with the men.

London Social Reformer (May 1840), vol. 1, no. 1, pp. 1–2

7.   Taxed with the want of benevolence and patriotism, set aside with the epithet of trifler; branded with the name of fool; all and every such degrading appellation, let woman, then, cast off, and point with pride to the page of history to refute the charge. In that page may be seen enrolled the names of female warriors, stateswomen, patriots, philanthropists, martyrs and the learned.

Anne Richelieu Lamb,[5] *Can Woman Regenerate Society?* (1844), pp. 166–7

'Touching on better days ...'

For some, an important part of their analysis was the assumption that women's situation was improving, or soon to improve.

8.   It is extremely gratifying to see women, not only advancing with the times, but using their utmost endeavours to aid and to quicken that advance. A time has now arrived when the sex may hope to attain its due rank in society; and, actuated by a laudable desire to be useful as well as agreeable, we hope to see women strenuously exert their long dormant power and assert their claim to be considered as rational and intellectual beings, and legally to be placed upon an equal footing with men.

'Study of Political Economy made Pleasant', *The Tatler* (24 January 1832), vol. 4, no. 435, p. 78

9.   I heartily rejoice that the baby is a girl; you will give her strength to endure and struggle with the evils which are the birthright of her sex. She will add to the number of well-educated women, who, I am afraid form but a very small portion of humanity. But I forget the difference in age. This little baby belongs almost to the third generation. She will be in her bloom, when we shall be old women, if not

dead. Great changes may take place before she attains womanhood.

Louisa Hill to Caroline Southwood Hill[6] (9 July 1840)
in Maurice (1913), p. 8

10. … I believe we are touching on better days, when women will have a genuine, normal life of their own to lead. There, perhaps, will not be so many marriages, and women will be taught not to feel their destiny *manque* if they remain single. They will be able to be friends and companions in a way they cannot be now. All the strength of their feelings and thoughts will not run into love; they will be able to associate with men, and make friends of them, without being reduced by their position to see them as lovers or husbands. Instead of having appearances to attend to, they will be allowed to have their virtues, in any measure which it may please God to send, without being diluted down to the tepid 'rectified spirit' of 'feminine grace' and 'womanly timidity' – in short, they will make themselves women, as men are allowed to make themselves men … I do not feel that either you or I are to be called failures. We are indications of a development of womanhood which as yet is not recognised. It has, so far, no ready-made channels to run in, but still we have looked, and tried, and found that the present rules for women will not hold us – that something better and stronger is needed … There are women to come after us, who will approach nearer the fulness of the measure of the stature of a woman's nature. I regard myself as a mere faint indication, a rudiment of the idea, of certain higher qualities and possibilities that lie in women, and all the eccentricities and mistakes and miseries and absurdities I have made are only the consequences of an imperfect formation, an immature growth … A 'Mrs. Ellis'[7] woman is developed to the extreme of her little possibility; but I can see there is a precious mine of a species of womanhood yet undreamed of by the professors and essayists on female education, and I believe also that we belong to it.

Geraldine Jewsbury to Jane Welsh Carlyle[8] (?1849) in Ireland
(1892), pp. 347–9

'Every variety of treatment'. Catechizing progress

Some writers, however, were extremely sceptical as to the degree to which social progress or Christianity had wrought any progress in women's position.

11.   In Christian Europe, woman has received every variety of treatment – having been esteemed an angel, and drudged like an ass.

[Maria Jewsbury[9]], 'A Brief Historical Notice of the Position of Women in Society', *Athenaeum* (28 January 1832), no. 222, p. 66

12.   Savage man kicks and beats woman, and makes her toil in the fields; semi-civilized man locks her up in a harem; and man three-quarters civilized, which is as far as we are got, educates her for pleasure and dependency, keeps her in a state of pupilage, closes against her most of the avenues of self-support, and cheats her by the false forms of an irrevocable contract into a life of subservience to his will.

[W. J. Fox], 'A Victim', *Monthly Repository* (1833), vol. 7, p. 177

13.   There is nothing more utterly fallacious than the prevailing notion of the improved position of woman in her connection with man and society. Short-sighted enthusiasts look back to more or less remote periods, and discover woman as a tent-bearer, a half beast of burden; and then, when they turn to the present, and find her as she is, they raise a loud cry of what Christianity and modern civilization have done for women. Now, I deny that it has done anything more than change the phasis of injustice under which she has so long been writhing. ... In that era of barbarity, men and women were *alike* roughly treated, by themselves, each other, and by Nature; and if the advancement of the state of womankind has been marvellous, let us not ascribe it to an improved estimation and treatment, but rather to a social advancement and civilization common to both. If anything, the treatment of woman is relatively worse ...

John Stores Smith, *Social Aspects* (1850), pp. 100–1

'What is this but aristocracy?'

For political radicals, exposing the iniquities of women's position was but part of a wider agenda which sought to lay bare the inequalities they believed to fracture contemporary society.

14.   The great mass of mankind have immense improvements to make in mental and political freedom and knowledge, before they will be able steadily to contemplate and perfectly understand, in all its bearings, that happy state of society to which all good minds look forward with hope, either for themselves or their descendants; and, if such be the case with Man, how much has Woman still to perform, who is so many degrees behind him in freedom and knowledge. That she is so, is no reproach to her intellectual capacity; to man alone it is entirely attributable: he has been enthralled, enslaved, deprived of his natural rights, by the odious inventions of kingly tyranny and priest-craft; and the natural consequence of his degradation of mind has been, that in all the relations of domestic life he has become as great a tyrant as the king or priest; recompensing himself for the loss of public freedom by being a private despot. Of course, in domestic as well as political government, it is necessary for the oppressed to be ignorant, and for this reason ignorance has been represented as perfectly meri-torious in woman, and the severest sarcasms, and the most clamorous invectives, have been by men heaped upon those, who have had the temerity to think for themselves and venture from the beaten track. Even now, when Women are certainly more instructed than formerly, it is only in arts perfectly useless both to themselves and others – mere inventions to kill time: and for a woman to interest herself in any question, either of government or religion, is considered as the very height of arrogance and presumption; even though she has, as it were, a double interest in the cause. Thus has Man, in debasing and degrad-ing the mind of Woman, by the natural re-action of the sentiments which he has inculcated, prepared the way for that state of abject slavery and superstition, in which almost all the nations of the earth are at present involved.

But you, my Countrywomen, possessed as I know you are, of minds capable of the very highest improvement, shake off that lethargy which has so long benumbed your faculties – exert your reasoning powers – read, reflect, and inquire – prove yourselves worthy of being, not only conducted, but *conductors* on the great march towards truth and freedom; and your exertions will animate Man with double zeal to proceed in his arduous and glorious enterprize. Prove yourselves, therefore, worthy of being wives and mothers to future citizens, of a future, enlightened, and happy republic.

> 'An Address to the Female Republicans', by a Female Materialist and Republican, *Newgate Monthly Magazine* (January 1825), vol. 1, pp. 236–7

15.   ... it is degrading to human nature to admit the superiority of one being over another, merely because the *gender* is different. What is this but aristocracy? If we admit the right of man to rule over woman, merely because he is *man*, then we may, upon the same principle,

admit the authority of one man to tyrannize over another, merely because he is of noble blood, *high born*. We are now making a bold stand against all these artificial aristocracies of birth, and are determined to acknowledge only moral and intellectual superiority. This will always attain its own place, if not kept down by artificial laws and tyrannical customs. Certainly, nothing can be more unjust than that law of public opinion and of political jurisprudence which gives a fool (merely because he is a man) a political and domestic authority over a woman, who may, in every other respect except the circumstance of sex, be his decided superior. We say, most decidedly, it is a tyrant's law.

[James Morrison], 'A Page for the Ladies', *The Pioneer* (29 March 1834), no. 30, p. 273

16.   Averse, as I have always been, to enter on the subject of private property, knowing that prejudice too frequently prevents its being rightly comprehended, and occasions the party who broaches it to be regarded as a romantic enthusiast, or as one ready to depart from the observance of any moral or social obligations; yet, so deeply connected is it with the destiny of woman, that I can no longer be silent. Were it possible to regard woman's happiness as a matter of minor importance, it might be foregone, but not otherwise. To see my sex appreciated, and understood by society as a whole, to behold her endowed with the bright qualifications enumerated by Mrs. Jameson;[10] the enjoyer and bestower of felicity, is, and has been for some time, my fervent desire. I know this consummation, so devoutly to be wished for, can never take place, while the existing arrangements of private property remain; and, in proportion as my wish is sincere, do I wish to see these barriers removed, and plenty, peace, and purity reign in happy unity.

Kate Barmby, 'Condition of Women', *New Moral World* (6 April 1839), vol. 5, no. 24, p. 372

17.   The new financial pontificate of protesting England. Holder of that now universal bond of union, which has usurped catholic supremacy over that of Rome. And which cements, albeit with poor protection, the multifarious governing interests of all the property-holding, trading, speculating, and money-fingering classes of the whole complex civilizational system. But which leaves the governed interests of the great proletariat mass, and those of the whole sex of woman, to shift for themselves. ... the universal interests of the female sex – the true parent sex of all humanity – being left without promise, or even thought, of rescue, to all the natural, and all the legally organised, rapacity of unchallenged unassailable male supremacy.

[Frances Wright], *England, the Civilizer* (1848), p. 396

'Unnatural traditions': the socialization of women

18.   Men and women are trained to their different moralities from infancy.

A little girl as soon as she becomes a conscious being, becomes a creature living, moving, and acting for *others*. She walks prettily, and has red shoes or blue ribbons to attract notice; the real, but concealed object being to promote her self-interest. This object being kept constantly out of view, is by some female, natures lost sight of. Habit teaches them to live, enjoy, act, think, hope, fear, only through others; never in and by themselves.

One of the fundamental principles of human nature, the selfish principle, is in women, forced down. They have no independent exercise of either the senses or the intellect. Hence they become lame, mutilated beings, unable to provide for their own happiness.

'D', 'Devotion and Self-Sacrifice', *Monthly Repository* (1836), vol. 10, pp. 426–7

19.   If all women were not brought up in such unnatural traditions of what is 'feminine' and 'maiden like', and 'sensitively delicate', they would not feel it a bounden obligation to tell lies, and deny an honest lawful affection for a lover. But they are crushed down under so many generations of arbitrary rules for the regulation of their manners and conversation; they are from their cradle embedded in such a composite of fictitiously-tinted virtues, and artificial qualities, that even the best and strongest amongst them are not conscious that the physiology of their minds is as warped by the traditions of feminine decorum, as that of their persons is by the stiff corsets which, until very recently, were *de rigueur* for preventing them 'growing out of shape'.

Geraldine Jewsbury, *The Half Sisters* (1848; 1998 edn), pp. 159–60

'Among the principles of creation': the uses of science

20.   *Here, Mary Leman Grimstone locates her comments concerning artificial gender differences within the context of evolutionary change.*[11] *The idea* *that plant and animal life would mutate and develop could be useful to a feminist agenda that claimed new forms of womanhood would emerge once environmental conditions had been altered.*

I perceive that the thing originated is not perfect, but instinct with the principle of perfectibility. This principle, decidedly perceptible in the human being, is latent in all, and through human agency developed in all. Fruits, flowers, vegetables, are by culture carried forward into varieties and excellencies unknown to the original stock. The same may be said of all the lower animals.

I regard man as the youngest animal on earth, or, to speak more distinctly, as a species newly on it. ...

That striking differences have existed, and do exist, between the sexes, I admit; that they are natural or necessary, I deny ... The general differences which attach to sex *en masse* are *artificial* differences – as artificial as those of class, having their origin in similar causes, and flowing into similar consequences.

M[ary] L[eman] G[rimstone], 'Self-Dependence', *Monthly Repository* (1835), vol. 9, pp. 597, 601

The phrenology movement argued that particular characteristics and abilities were located at specific points in the brain. Although the movement did not, in itself, promote a feminist agenda, individual practitioners often used its methods to draw feminist conclusions.[12]

21.   He [John Epps] was at this time [late 1820s] lecturing on Phrenology in Panton Sq, Haymarket, and in Buckingham St., Strand. His liberal views on the education of woman, then so uncommon, proved deeply interesting and attractive to many. He demonstrated that men and women have the same faculties, and that the different degrees of development of those faculties depend to a great extent on the education received. He made clear in what way nature had constituted woman on an equality with man, and *how* his rights were hers. He maintained that any branch of study she may please to pursue should be open to her.

Ellen Epps, *Diary of the Late J. Epps* (1875), p. 183

22.   *This extract comes from the report of a lecture given by the phrenologist, Mrs Hamilton, at a unitarian chapel in Greenock.*

... after folding up her handkerchief in the form of a brain, and setting it down before her on the desk, she began to describe how all the bad thoughts, words, and actions of mankind were produced from external impressions, made through the medium of the eyes, the ears, and other organs of the senses, and that all the errors and ignorance, faults and follies of women, were caused by their being exposed to the foul and contaminating moral influence of bad men; and that phrenologists had proved, and she herself would prove, that women's brains were capable of being improved to a degree which would make them equal and even excel the men in all the better accomplishments of our common nature, and give them power to break the chains of the tyrant and the oppressor, and set them completely free.

Crisis (3 May 1834), vol. 4, no. 4, p. 32

'Of the weakness of women'? Women and physical strength

Whilst many writers wrote of women's inferior bodily constitution (and hence their greater need for protection and consideration [27]), a number of radicals argued that physical characteristics were also socially constructed.

23.   *James Lawrence's idiosyncratic text was written (inconsistently) in his own phonetic system.*[13]

If the female can approach the male as near in corporeal as in mental powers, may indeed admit ov a doubt; but perhaps from the same cause that the labouring man is robuster than he hoom fortune never necessitated tu work; that the bargeman is stouter than the gentleman; and the swain in the hamlet more hardy than the Lord of the Manor; may not the male possess greater bodily strength than the other sex. In countries, whare the women are accustom'd tu toil in the fields, tu support immense burdens, tu undergo every fatigue, and tu face every change ov heat or cold, they are not distinguishable from the men by the weakness ov their frame, or the tenderness of their constitution. – During wun ov our late armaments, while the terror ov the press gang retained the colliers at home, the barges in sum ov the coal counties ware managed by females; and it is no uncommon object on the Thames tu see women ov all ages rowing and punt-pushing, even whare the stream is most rapid. What travelling Englishman is not surprised at the masculin appearance ov a poissarde[14] at Calais? and a fishwoman at Billingsgate would put to flight a hole troop ov Saint James's maccaronies.[15]

But can enny wun dout ov the equality ov the sexes, when thare are so menny examples ov female abilities to wun's consideration?
[James Henry Lawrence], *An Essay on the Nair System* (1800), pp. 4–5

24. Much of the weakness of women is owing to the want of work, – to the want of common exercise; inaction palsies their limbs, shrivels their muscles, tortures their nerves, - and thus renders them fair, it is said, to look upon.
Anne Richelieu Lamb, *Can Woman Regenerate Society?* (1844), p. 169.

25. The torture, the stake, the axe, or the gibbet, have not spared *her*; until a very few years the lash numbered *her* as its victim. In fact, no species of punishment has been introduced, at all supporting the proposition of woman's inferiority in strength of body or of mind.
Kate [Barmby], 'Woman and the Laws', *New Moral World* (29 June 1839), vol. 5, no. 36, p. 562

'By far *more* excellent than man'?

26. If there is any advantage with respect to corporeal distinction, it most certainly is on the side of women. The most curious and finest production in nature is indebted to them for its existence; and their peculiar grace and beauty make all men, for a time, own them their superiors.
A Lady, *Female Rights Vindicated* (1833; first published 1758), p. 136

27. *The following work included a forthright preface which made explicit the author's agenda: 'my task will hence be to prove, that man a vile barbarian, who, by his strength of* arm *or* head, *seeks rather by his overbalanc'd power to tyrannize o'er* Woman, *than justly to protect from every wrong the* feeble *structure of her sex. ... I should hope, to* strengthen *and* improve *the female's understanding; to* inspire *her with courage so as fearlessly to assert her rights'. [iii, iv–v]*

At all times, the calm and beauteous appearance of her countenance, irresistibly commands the veneration and respect of every *rational* observer; this, with her superior gentleness of manners, to which added a natural sympathizing disposition, (so peculiar to her sex), are of *themselves* calculated to soothe the savage breast, appease the tyrant's wrath, and, further, to render perpetually happy the life of that Man, who *unites* himself with her in the sacred bonds of love and friendship. SURELY then these considerations, divided from all others, must be sufficient to prompt mankind to venerate, I had almost said adore, the fair objects so wisely framed, to work such *wondrous* changes in our natures. Does this not prove to us, that she's by far the *most perfect* of the human species, by far *more* excellent than Man ...

... possessing, as Women do, such *admirable perfections* and *equal liberties* as those I just alluded to, they never were created or designed to be the SLAVES or DUPES of any earthly being; And, that being (in strength and constitution) the weakest of the human species, and formed, but to be *succoured by the hands of Men*, their claim to Male protection is both right and reasonable ...

The Rights, Privileges and Laws of Women (1815), pp. 2–3, 6

28. But see how I am talking with you, just as if you were, not only a man, but a man superior to most men in elevation of thought and range of research! Well, the greatest compliment a man can pay to a woman is to remember that her mind is in many respects equal, in some superior, to his own. And this because men fancy that women are not to be reasoned with. All folly! But then, men are such fools.

Edward Bulwer Lytton to Mrs Cunningham (25 February 1826) in Lytton (1883), vol. 2, p. 53.

In Owenite circles ideas concerning women's moral or intellectual superiority were frequently contested, as the following debate [29–30] indicates.

29. ... the immutable laws of Nature cannot be reversed, and *she* in her infinite wisdom, has stamped upon men and women a moral and intellectual difference, which no social arrangement can ever amalgamate. Woman, to be the loved and loving being for which she is so beautifully qualified, must preserve her own distinct moral peculiarities, and these, man can never understand...

'Concordia', 'To Robert Owen, Esq.', *The Crisis* (10 August 1833), vol. 2, no. 31, p. 254

30. This intensity of woman's love, which Concordia considers so distinguishing a mark of excellence in her sex, I believe to be the fatal result of her vicious and slavish training, and the profound ignorance in which she is kept as to the nature of those social laws which work her degradation and misery; under *such laws*, I hold that woman's love is the symbol of her deep degradation, moral and social; and I could as soon admire the prostrate worshippers of Juggernaut,[16] as I could, under present social arrangements, admire the *humiliating* idolatry of 'woman's love' for man, such as he has been, such as he must continue to be, till he discovers the error of his ways, and aspires to nobler views.

[Anna Wheeler], 'Vlasta', 'To the Editor of the Crisis', *Crisis* (31 August 1833), vol. 2, no. 35, pp. 279

'Different, aye! ... but, oh! never, never inferior'

31. *'Universalism', was a theory developed by the editor of* The Shepherd, *James Elishama Smith. A combination of religious millenarianism and social radicalism, it argued that there was an analogy between the physical and the metaphysical world. In particular, it expounded upon the concept of 'polarity': hence God and Satan could be understood as two elements of one entity. This doctrine of polarity was fully elaborated in the area of gender difference.*[17]

The characters, offices, and duties of the two sexes are eternally distinct, and never can be confounded. But they are equal. Woman in moral action and re-action is equal to man in physical and intellectual action and re-action. The denial of this equality is the feature of the old world, and constitutes the oppression of woman.

'Analytical Synopsis of Universalism', *The Shepherd* (17 March 1838), vol. 3, no. 38, p. 301

32. We grant that her intellect is of a different nature, but not that it is inferior.

'Woman', *Eliza Cook's Journal* (16 June 1849), p. 108

33. *In her novel,* Amymone, *Eliza Lynn (later Linton) admitted that she wished readers to draw direct parallels between her story of ancient Greece and modern society.*[18] *The eponymous heroine is the daughter of a slave and therefore has no civic rights. Yet she is full of pride, as well as an innate yearning that her considerable natural gifts might be put to a purpose:*

[Amymone] wore that fixed mask of cold haughty pride, of unbending will, which seemed to place her, like some pale colossal statue, above the weaknesses of her sex. Such can be the strength of the despised and contemned; such the justice with which women are placed as inferior to their lords! As different, aye! – completing that nature which without them is imperfect; but oh! never, never inferior! – through all their weakness, all their irresolution, perfect in their place, equal-mated with the stronger! ...

Amymone was not of those who dread their own thought until confirmed in it by some outward sign. She was rather one, whose active intellect and fierce passions required something definite, some action by which they might work; one who would for ever try the secrets of the future, not from timidity but from restlessness; from an energy which, if unsatisfied, would feed upon itself and consume its own life.

Eliza Lynn, Amymone (1848), vol. 1, pp. 116–17, 160

Notes

1   i.e. Mary Wollstonecraft.
2   Lucy Aikin to Susannah Taylor (27 January 1803) in Le Breton (1864), pp.125–6.
3   Lucy Aikin to Dr William Channing (7 April 1832) in ibid., p. 259.
4   Mother of the Gracchi (second century BC) and celebrated as an ideal Roman matron.
5   Little is yet known about Anne Richelieu Lamb. Jane Rendall wonders whether she might possibly have been the author of several articles in the *English Woman's Journal* under the initials, A.R.L: Rendall (1985), p. 317; although it is evident that she married to take the surname, Dryden, subsequent to her 1844 work.
6   Caroline Southwood Hill (1808–1902), radical educationist and daughter of the sanitary reformer, Thomas Southwood Smith. Her daughter, Octavia Hill was a famous housing reformer. Hill moved in radical unitarian and Owenite circles. Her husband, James Hill, the father of Louisa (from a previous marriage) was editor of the Owenite paper, the *Star of the East*. Maurice (1913).
7   Sarah Stickney Ellis, author of the prescriptive *Women of England: their social duties and domestic habits* (1839).
8   Jane Welsh Carlyle (1801–66), the wife of historian Thomas Carlyle. A formidable intellectual in her own right, Carlyle had an intense and often turbulent relationship with Geraldine Jewsbury. Clarke (1990), chs 4, 5, 7.
9   For Maria Jewsbury's authorship, see Clarke (1990), pp. 229–30n.
10   Anna Jameson. See Biographical Notes: also praised in document **41**.
11   For an interesting discussion of contemporary evolutionary theories see Killham (1958), ch. 11.
12   Much work still remains to be done on the gendered dynamics of this movement. Cooter (1984).
13   Spelling reform was also advocated by other radicals of the day, such as William Godwin. St. Clair (1989), p. 21.
14   Poissarde: a fishwife.
15   'Macaroni' was the term applied to the dandies of the day. St James's Park was the fashionable place for them to be seen.
16   An idol of Krishna, pulled through the streets of Orissa on an enormous chariot. Worshippers were said to have flung themselves beneath its wheels.
17   Harrison (1979), pp. 156–7; Taylor (1983), pp. 170–1.
18   Lynn (1848), vol. 1, p.v.

2
Agendas for Change

Blueprints for reform

*Documents **34** and **35** are indicative of the broad canvas of feminist thought in the early nineteenth century, encompassing demands for political, civic, domestic and spiritual freedom and sexual reform, as well as suggesting specific remedies such as petitioning and feminist organizations.*

34. *The following extract comes from Catherine Barmby's wide-ranging essay, and provides an elaboration of her three central demands.*[1]

1st.   We demand the political emancipation of woman, because it is her right, possessing as she does with man, a threefold being, sentimental, intellectual, and physical, because she is subject to like wants, expected to pay the same taxes, taxation without representation being tyranny, and because all other laws act as severely, many more severely upon her than upon man. We demand, therefore, that the mind of woman be acknowledged in the electoral and administrative departments of legislation, with which she is compelled to act in accordance, or to suffer the penalty.

2nd.   We demand the ecclesiastical emancipation of woman, because from her strong percipient power she has the ability to educate, and thus to benefit society; because the rights of the child demand the ecclesiastical freedom of woman, and because the heart of woman is destined to illumine and hallow the feelings of goodness when addressing itself to the assembly, as the mind or intellect of man is destined to strengthen the being, and to impart to it wisdom. We have the priest, we therefore demand the priestess, the woman-teacher of the word, the woman apostle of God's Law!

3rd.   We demand the domestic emancipation of woman, that is to say, we claim her freedom at the hearth and the board. We demand for her independence in the pursuit of those labors for which she is most particularly adapted, and which alone can be her security from the tyranny of her husband, and her preservation from the oppressions of society. In fine, we demand the emancipation of the hand of woman from mere household drudgery, so that her sentiment and intellect be protected, and with them her ministerings of good be insured. ... To effect the domestic emancipation of woman, the present organization of society is inefficient ... in a community of goods and labors properly organised, woman as well as man would have the liberty of working in those functions which Nature has assigned her; and possessing, in virtue of her common works, a share in the common property, she will become independent as man in all the relations of domestic life.

> Catherine Barmby, 'The Demand for the Emancipation of
> Woman, Politically and Socially', *New Tracts for the Times*
> vol. 1, no. 3 reprinted in Taylor (1983)

35.   Let them [women] endeavour to exchange an irresponsible and pernicious influence for the free and legitimate exercise of constitutional rights, and let them use every available means to accomplish that object – the first and most important step towards their complete social regeneration.

'But what are the means to be employed to bring about this change?' They are simple – for they are comprised in two words, education and agitation.

(1). To the momentous subject of education, the attention of all those is directed who are looking forward with hope to the emancipation of their countrywomen ...

(2). The second instrument to be employed to effect our social regeneration is agitation. It comprises active and passive resistance.

The active means of agitation we possess are chiefly derived from the press ... could the women of this country be excited to contend for their rights, the press would become, in their hands, an engine of enormous power ...

If we are individually weak, we are collectively strong. Union and association are therefore pre-eminently necessary for us. The very appearance of combination in a sex deemed incapable of moral energy would produce an extraordinary effect. Those who now laugh at the idea of female emancipation, would find their mirth suddenly checked, when they saw associations of enlightened and determined women springing up in every town and village, and numbering thousands and tens of thousands amongst their numbers. Even those most opposed to our views would be unable to close their eyes to the fact, that when women systematically begin to investigate their grievances, a great social revolution is at hand, and the tyranny of sex is nearly over ... The right to petition the legislature is, I believe, not denied us. Why do we not exercise that right to lay our complaints before Parliament? ...

I now come to speak of the passive resistance, which is a principal means of agitation. The principle has been laid down, that 'those who are not represented in the state are not bound to contribute to its burthens.' I think I have shown that women are not represented, and why should they not use the same means that have proved so successful in the case of the oppressed, both in England and in Ireland? What has passive resistance not done for the Catholics and the Dissenters? Would they have obtained the remission of even a fraction of their grievances, if their refusal to pay tithes, church-rates, and other equally obnoxious imposts, had not made our *just* and *wise* legislators fear for themselves?

In conclusion, then, let me call on my dear countrywomen no longer to remain voluntary slaves.

'An Outline of the Grievances of Women', *Metropolitan Magazine* (May 1838), vol. 22, no. 85, pp. 19, 26, 27[2]

36.   *For Fourierists (in common with many other early socialists) women's emancipation could only be secured through a wholesale reformation of social organization into cooperative communities.*

Civilization, or the system of separate households, offers no remedy for the ills of woman, offers no escape from sorrowful and painful subjection, to the daughters of the people. It is in vain that legislation, morals, and education combine to reform the manners, to stem the tide of corruption, to regenerate woman, to strengthen family relationships: all must fail, as society is now constituted. Remove corruption, then you efface misery; establish unitary education, then you will give free developement [*sic*] to the faculties; and assure independence by labour. The question is not whether it is desirable or not to give to woman political rights, and to put her upon an equality with man. In the present state, it would be but a new source of disorder. But perhaps it may be said, that in the present state, every industrious, artistic, and scientific path is opened to woman, and that a great number earn their own livelihood. It is true; but nevertheless, the difficulties of a profession for a woman are very great; first, by education, which seldom prepares them for it; secondly, by the obstructions which surround all social undertakings. Besides, how can women, absorbed in household details, the fatigues and the cares of maternity, occupy themselves with regular labour? It is in this sense that the independence of woman cannot be reconciled with separate households, and that even the right to labour cannot be granted her ... Even if the laws permitted divorce, is she in circumstances to profit by it – must she not endure all, suffer all, for the sake of her children? In the present social state, no remedy can be found for the ills and oppression of woman.

Fourier's system, insensibly introducing, without struggle, without injury to any interest, a society in society, resolves all the difficulties in the position of woman. Without changing the legislation, or proclaiming new rights, he stops at once all the sources of corruption, reforms education and manners by the effects that naturally flow from his system, in which *Unitary Education and the independence of woman are ensured by the rights of labour*; independence rendered possible by Associated Households, Attractive Industry, and continually increasing Wealth.[3]

Gatti de Gamond, *The Phalanstery* trans.
by S. C. Chichester (1841),[4] pp. 127–9

37. *Proposals for women-only organizations, such as those suggested in document [35], evoked considerable debate. Many, particularly within socialist circles, feared that gender-exclusive societies would damage the wider cause of social progress.[5] However, such plans were given forthright support in* The Pioneer:

Divided as men are – and we vow it grieves us much to see their scattered situation – women are infinitely more so. Men have their public meetings, their social meetings, their newspapers, their magazines, their male speakers, and their male editors, and men with men correspond in all quarters of the world, upon the most extensive scale; but woman knows nothing of woman, except through the medium of man – a dense medium, which distorts her native character, and bedaubs it with the false colouring of the sex, whose feelings, on a thousand delicate subjects, must be the very reverse of her own. How can woman redeem herself from such shackles of ignorance and mental slavery? By application to man? Fool she must be, if she apply to man to get a knowledge of herself, and the interests of her own sex. By taking counsel in part with man? This nominal reputation of man for practical skill and experience will ruin her cause, if she let him have any thing to do with it; for if ever a man is introduced amongst the other sex, they will stick to him like feathers on a tarred seaman, and he will carry the whole union on his back. Men having nothing to do with women; they are two distinct animals altogether; they have each a sphere of their own, with which the other cannot, without creating mischief, interfere. Therefore, we say, let woman look to herself, consult with woman on her own affairs; allow no male to enter her meetings, until she has obtained sufficient skill and experience to act in public, and then let her assembly rooms be thrown open.

And what are women to consult about? say some. Why, their own affairs, to be sure; their own rights and privileges. Let them make rules and regulations for managing domestic matters, morals, &c., or any other matters which peculiarly interest them, as women; and let these be submitted to the General Union of both sexes; and, if approved, let them be acknowledged as obligatory, both at home and abroad; and let him that will not submit be degraded, as unworthy the name of man. By this means the women may, in a few months, do an immensity of good; they may reform drunken husbands, procure clean and comfortable homes, get good clothes and education for their children, &c. &c. Who are afraid of female legislation but profligates? Woman will only interfere where woman finds herself aggrieved; and has she not a right to interfere? He who denies the right of woman, declares himself a rebel.

[James Morrison], 'A Page for the Ladies', The Pioneer
(8 March 1834), no. 27, p. 238

38.   The abstract right of women to equality has been argued successfully, and (I think) sufficiently. Let them act upon it, and prove their fitness for exercising their rights; above all, let them show some desire to possess them; at present the cause has fewer advocates among women than among men. The most practical plan appears to me to be for some of the most talented women of the country to form a 'Women's Club', to act politically, with a view to influencing the public and the legislature on important political questions; especially those which particularly affect women. They should, I think, recognise the doctrine of equality of rights, but not bring it out very prominently, as they would make more way by showing their power to enter fully into the detail and statistics of political questions. After the club had lasted two or three years, men might be permitted to become associates (but not members), and in time the two sexes might really meet on equal terms to discuss their mutual interest. This club, however, should be directed by the *elite* of the women in England, so that it might never *deserve* ridicule. I should be proud of the honour of being an associate of such a club, but it is of no use for men to take the initiative. To all women who ask for their rights, we can only say as Leonidas said to Xerxes when he asked for his arms – 'Come and take them'.[6]

People's Review of Literature and Politics (February 1850), no. 1, p. 48

'Her own will and determination'

Many progressive women believed that their true position in society could not be achieved but by individual assertions of women's capabilities and worth.

39.   I am sorry that I cannot accede to your request – that I would send some communication to be read to your assembled friends on the 25th. I do not approve of the tone used by some of the public advocates of Woman's Rights; & I do not think that any good object will be attained by the formation of such a society as you tell me of. I therefore do not wish my name to be connected with its proceedings by any act of my own.

Harriet Martineau to 'Madam' (20 March [1849]) in
Sanders (1990), pp. 115–16[7]

40.   *Elizabeth Pickett explained a similar position to her friend Anne Knight, who had been urging her to join a woman's suffrage campaign:*

Think not my honoured Friend that I less regard the vital subject of our sex's influence – because I venture in some respect to differ from yourself as to the present mode of proceeding for the attainment of the rights you seek. The first difficulty you have to overcome is to convince Men aye & women too that our sex possess Mental & Moral power & energy to enable them to enter into & compass the bearings of legislative subjects – and this is not so much to be accomplished by the open assertion of womans rights – however truthfully & eloquently they may be enforced – as by the practical exhibition of that power in furtherance of the great & universal cause of truth &

justice – within the sphere – narrow & restricted tho' it be which under present circumstances is open to Womans usefulness.

> Elizabeth Pickett to Anne Knight (April 1850) Friends House Library, Temp MSS 725/5/38

41.   *Famous, successful women were of course, particularly useful in the cause. In this extract from the leading Owenite newspaper of the day, the author noted the significance of the works of such writers as Anna Jameson and Christian Johnstone.*[8]

We rejoice to find that many highly respectable and esteemed public writers of the day, are using their endeavours to correct the present absurd and cruel notions of female virtue, and to point out the tyranny and grossly immoral tendency of our present marriage laws; and, more than all, do we rejoice that this important, yet, in some respects, thankless task, has been undertaken by woman herself; satisfied, as we are, that if she is ever to occupy her proper station, as an independent being in society, it will be mainly owing to her own will and determination so to do.

> 'Social Condition of Woman', *New Moral World* (30 March 1839), vol. 5, no. 33, p. 360.

42.   ... the strenuous and persevering efforts which have been made by a large portion of British females, in favor of Negro emancipation – efforts which have been happily crowned with signal success ... I trust may be considered as a pledge and forerunner of their own emancipation from the state of civil bondage, which now fetters their condition both of body and mind.

> A Philanthropist, *Domestic Tyranny* (1841), p. 55

'High principle and self-sacrifice'

43.   The wider the field of action, the wider also is the field for self-renunciation.

> Marion Reid, *A Plea for Woman* (1843), p. 12

44.   We hear for ever of the self-devotion of our sex. In nine cases out of ten such a feeling would be more aptly named by the designation of self-abasement or self-annihilation ...

> Anne Richelieu Lamb, *Can Woman Regenerate Society?* (1844), pp. 94–5

45.   She [Emma Shaen] is a decided Chartist and 'Rights of Woman' personage, but has her aristocratic education to thank for a very strong dislike to all improprieties and oddnesses. She quite recognizes the wickedness of making self-development the object of life – to my surprise, for she joins in so many things with the party who do this; yet even goes further in condemning it than I should dare to do.

> Emily Winkworth to Catherine Winkworth[9] (3 May 1848)
> in Shaen (1908), pp. 30–1

46.   How many instances one sees almost daily of the marvellous energy and high principle and self-sacrifice of woman! I am always thankful to see it, for it is in this way that women will emancipate themselves.

> Mary Howitt to her sister (2 September 1850) in Mary Howitt, *An Autobiography* (1889), vol. 2, p. 62

'The doctrines of our Redeemer'

For many, religion formed a powerful means of furthering women's role within society.

47.   The writings of women are full of eloquent complaints of the unhappy destiny of their sex, but they do not ascend to its cause and suggest a remedy. It is most unfortunate that a mistaken piety has often turned their endowments against themselves; and the most gifted and virtuous, who might have done so much to elevate the character of women and help them to advance in worth and in happiness, have only confirmed the system under which they suffer, and even represented their grievances as the unquestionable will of Him whom we believe to be a God of justice and love. Those who plead so earnestly for their own degradation, and appeal to Scripture to maintain it, do not seem to consider that the injunctions respecting married people in the Epistles prove clearly how entirely those early Christians, who learned the doctrines of our blessed Redeemer from his own lips, understood those doctrines as a law of Liberty.

> [Henry Brougham[10]], Lydia Tomkins, *Thoughts on the Ladies of the Aristocracy* (1835), p. 50

Joanna Southcott's voluminous prophecies are not readily reduced to indicative extracts. The following can only give a flavour of the passion of her voice, and her repeated insistence upon the central role of women in effecting spiritual redemption.

48a.   ... I shall now answer for myself, *to such poor deluded men*, who judge of things they know nothing about ... And this is the darkness of men's understanding: seeing the day-light of the gospel thrown open before them *by a woman*, bright as the fervent sun; truths of the prophecies clear as the moon; which is as much too strong for their weak judgment as the fervent sunshine is for their eye-sight – for they can no more look into the divine brightness and beauty of the one than the other.

Joanna Southcott, The Second Part of the Continuation of Joanna Southcott's Prophecies (1813), p. 96

48b.   ... for know, when the Woman is freed from the transgression, and her Redemption takes place, then comes the REDEMPTION of MAN; but how vain and how simple is every man to believe that his redemption can take place, that is born of a woman, as long as the woman stands under the transgression of the Fall! For I tell you all, being saved from the transgression, is to be freed from the transgression; or let men answer ME, if they place it another way, to a temporal sense, how are these Women to be saved that had never any Children? So let men mark in what manner the Scriptures are penned; and let men mark, from the Apostle, how much more he recommends the virtues of a *single Woman*, as living to the LORD, than the married Woman that lives to please her husband.[11]

Joanna Southcott, The Kingdom of Christ is at Hand (1805),
pp. 23–4.

Notes

1   Barmby also suggested the establishment of a female-only magazine, as did Harriet Martineau: Le Breton (1864), p. 363; Eliza Meteyard celebrated *Eliza Cook's Journal* for being a progressive, woman's journal – see *Eliza Cook's Journal* (7 July 1849), vol. 1, no. 10, p. 155. For another broad schema for women's emancipation by another in Barmby's network see the interesting essay: 'Independence of Woman', by 'Pause' in Bath, *Educational Circular or Communist Apostle* (March 1842), pp. 37–8.

2   The article was widely believed to have been written by Caroline Norton. See Killham (1958), pp. 148 ff. A more likely author is, perhaps, Mary Leman Grimstone, whose style and idioms bear striking resemblance to this essay. It is worth noting that the opening lines of the article echo the text of a little-known Grimstone essay – 'Drawing Room', *Tatler* (1 September 1832), no. 54, p. 394. See also document **187**.

3   For a further exposition of the value of 'associated households', see document **96**. 'Attractive industry' was a central tenet of Fourier's ideas. He believed that in the harmonic state, labour could be organized so as to be wholly satisfying and appealing to each individual: Beecher (1986), ch. 14.

4   Zoë Gatti de Gamond was a Belgian writer and acolyte of Fourier. Sophia C. Chichester (1795–1847) was a wealthy patron of progressive causes. She was particularly associated with James Elishama Smith, James Pierrepont Greaves and the Ham Common Concordium. Gleadle, '"Our Separate Spheres": Middle-class Women and the Feminisms of Early Victorian Radical Politics', in Gleadle and Richardson (2000), pp. 136–9. For full biographical details see Latham (1999), chs 5–8.

5   See the debates in *The Crisis* (17 August 1833), vol. 2, no. 33, p. 263; (24 August 1833), vol. 2, no. 34, p. 268; (7 September 1833), vol. 3, no. 1, p. 5.

6   Leonidas, King of Sparta, was killed in battle in 480 BC, when fighting the Persians, led by King Xerxes.

7   See also Harriet Martineau to [?] G.H. Lewes (15 December 1850) in Smith (2000), vol. 2, p. 534.

8   Christian Isobel Johnstone (Mrs) (1781–1857), a Scottish writer and joint editor of *Tait's Edinburgh Magazine* from 1843–46.

9   Emily Winkworth (1822–87) and her sister, Catherine Winkworth (1827–78) came from an intellectual family in Manchester, and were friends of Elizabeth Gaskell. Emily married the radical, feminist William Shaen (brother of Emma Shaen) in 1851. Catherine achieved high repute as a German translator. Shaen (1908).

10   The pamphlet is attributed to Henry Brougham in the British Library catalogue.

11   Although Southcott repeatedly insists that women are to be redeemed through childbirth, she makes it clear that this might be a metaphorical process i.e. through bringing the spiritual seed to mankind.

Part II

Female Roles

We should think that there could not be two opinions as to the propriety of her moving in the sphere which God and nature intended her
to fill; the only difficulty is in deciding what that true and natural
sphere is. As long as opinions are so various on that point, it is not very
philosophical to use the phrase as if its meaning were quite undis-
puted.[1]

Introduction

What was the purpose of women's lives? Were they to develop their minds and souls so as to best fit them for the rearing of a new generation of temperate, cultivated citizens; was their role to soothe and support their husbands; should they nurture their intellects and skills so that they themselves might contribute to social welfare and progress; or, was their duty purely and simply to themselves? Although adherents to the concept of female emancipation were least likely to advance the argument that women's duty lay in ministering to their husband's welfare, they might espouse any or all of these positions – their emphases often shifting with the sands of their audience. Their responses were further complicated by the matrix of ideological pressures bearing upon feminist votaries. For many, feminism was construed from, as much as it was in opposition to, religious sensibilities (of duty and sacrifice); political theories (of class oppression, for example) and prevailing notions of the paramount importance of maternal influence.

Radical discussions on female education tended to focus upon the ends to which female cultivation should be put. As such they are a useful gauge for assessing the climate of progressive opinion on such topics as the relative merits assigned to female employment or domesticity. Nevertheless, such writing was entwined with other, more conservative, discourses upon female education. From the 1790s an influential model of female educational improvement, fuelled by Evangelical preoccupations, had called for a revolution in educational practice. Hannah More's insistence that women's education should aspire to strengthen and develop their moral and mental capacities, and her fundamental faith that the intellect and virtues of the nation were inextricably linked to the quality of mothering received by its citizens, became widely disseminated.[2] Few feminists were prepared to reject altogether the critical relationship between female education, motherhood and the welfare of the nation (and indeed, the race [65]). Indeed, such utilitarian views of female education – that women should be educated for the good of society – provided a convenient chassis on which to build arguments for improved educational access. Consequently, the egregious consequences of failing to educate women, and, in particular, the social imperative of ensuring well-educated mothers so as to best raise their children, proved a recurring theme [54, 56–7].

To emphasize the importance of the mother could also provide an ideological nexus for discrete aspects of the reforming agenda: large numbers of political radicals were associated with moves to reform infant education – a project which they hoped would realize their vision of a people fit for political power. In so doing they popularized the theories of educationists such as Johann Pestalozzi (1746–1827), who dwelt at length upon the vital influence of the maternal role in the educational development of the young [100].[3] As this indicates, it is important to remember that debates over female education occurred in a variety of differing forums and were not always instigated primarily within the context of the 'woman question' itself. Debates for improved female education also arose, for example, within the context of other educational discussions including demands for national education [54]; the merits of coeducation [61, 63]; legislative proposals for educational reform [60] and the establishment of adult education institutes [65–6]. Whilst many writers fumed at the lack of public funding allocated to female education, others focused upon the need to expand women's opportunities for self-education [56, 67–8].[4]

Despite this, the question of female education also functioned as a useful vehicle with which to air broader debates concerning women's position. The issue of female nature and abilities, discussed in Chapter 1, frequently surfaced, as did the role of an inadequate education in the harmful socialization of women [50–1]. Although most radical commentators on women argued that it was unjust and immoral to educate women solely with reference to others, many still subscribed to an image of cosy domesticity and harmonious marriages which they suggested improved female education might augur [52–4]. The prevalence of such broad topics tended to give a peculiarly abstract air to many of the progressive debates on middle-class female education. (Interestingly, landmarks such as the establishment of Bedford College and Queen's College in London designed to improve the employment potential of young governesses, are rarely mentioned explicitly.[5]) Nevertheless, the instrumentality of education in its potential to widen women's employment prospects was recognized. [**66, 72, 83–4**]. In a culture that was setting an increasingly high premium upon the moral and social values of work and self-advancement, the persistent attention paid by feminist-minded thinkers to the importance of female employment is not surprising. As Eliza Meteyard explained in the preface to her novel *Struggles for Fame*, 'if a moral [to the novel] be asked for, it appears to me, clearly self-suggestive; that "Work *is* Worship," and the bread of labour, even of woman's labour, the sweetest gathered from the harvests of the earth'.[6]

Nonetheless, feminist motivations for promoting female employment were surprisingly diverse. Some concentrated upon (middle-class) women's limited access to the employment market, with writers pointing in particular to the desperate situation faced by widows, or the genteel poor [**71, 83**]. Although many women found employment in family businesses, teaching or needlework, there was a discernible narrowing of economic opportunities for women of this sector from the late eighteenth century. Many customarily female occupations were increasingly practised by men (including millinery, bookbinding and brewing).[7] This was a concern that exercised a wide constituency of contemporary liberal opinion – as the attempts to improve training and professional arrangements for governesses testify.[8] A second set of arguments (which frequently overlapped with the first) focused upon the wider personal and social benefits which female employment might secure. This included the pride and dignity women's financial independence could occasion, as well as a consideration of the improved marriages which might ensue were women no longer forced into marriages purely for financial gain [**72, 78, 80, 118**]. Opinions as to the kind of employment women might seek, nonetheless varied widely [**77–9, 81–4**].

By the mid-1840s some writers, particularly those who hailed from more exclusively literary (rather than radical political) circles, tended to view female employment as a channel for women's intellectual and practical energies. In other words, they articulated a perception of work that emphasized its potential for self-fulfilment [**84–7**]. This dovetailed into a proto-feminist literary tradition that was fostered by such writers as Germaine de Staël, whose novel, *Corinne* had been a central influence for many. Geraldine Jewsbury, for example, followed *Corinne* in exploring the complex psychology of female aspirations, and the moral imperative of developing the self [**85**]. It is worth noting that this strand of early feminist ideology appears to comprise a cross-current to that stream of thought which focused rather upon the desirability of self-denial and self-sacrifice [43, 45–6].

Discussions on women's employment within the socialist press were often infused with similarly lofty tones. This may well be due to the fact that journalists writing such material were often from middle-class circumstances themselves. Nevertheless, such forums also provided the space for more biting comment, focusing upon gender tensions within the employment market or women's right to fair remuneration. As Barbara Taylor and Anna Clarke have both demonstrated, the under-cutting of male employment by cheap female labour was a source of profound discontent and unease in many working-class communities during this period. During 1833–4, as the labour movement entered a new phase of militancy, arguments raged over the location of female employment within the labour market and the comparative merits of gender-segregated, or mixed-sex trades unions [73–6].[9]

For some writers the debate on female employment functioned merely as a rhetorical frame on which to expound upon women's abilities. Indeed, as many writers made clear, to argue that women had as much potential as men to fulfil professional tasks did not necessarily mean that they believed women *should* take up such work [72, 88]. The majority clearly envisaged that women would devote themselves primarily to domestic concerns once they were married. The construction of domestic roles within radical debates on women was, nonetheless, multifaceted. Such diversity was symptomatic of the varied perceptions of motherhood and family life prevalent in contemporary discourse. Specific cultural moments, such as the Queen Caroline affair, crystallized the sentiments of many, that women had a right to protection in their capacity as wives and mothers.[10] But such an assumption was to be bitterly contested in the heated debates surrounding the Infant Custody Act (1839) [102–4], which revealed starkly the deep seam of Victorian patriarchy. Meanwhile, Evangelical formulations of the domestic, serene mother, clashed with the vision of political radicals like the Chartists, whose 'militant motherhood' was fuelled by an insistence that mothers had a right and a duty to protect the family welfare by engaging in public, high-profile activism.[11] Therefore, the feminist-minded were operating within a landscape in which the maternal role was already highly contested and riven with conflicting meanings.

Whilst many radicals constructed motherhood as the epitome of female grace and nobility, wider ideological objectives could complicate attitudes towards maternity. As Elizabeth Hamilton had bitterly commented in 1803, 'some ill-advised advocates for the *rights* of our sex', had represented the management of the family as 'mean and degrading'.[12] Hamilton would certainly have despaired of those in the cooperative tradition, who believed that existing social arrangements, centred upon the nuclear family, made motherhood and family management a frustrating, isolating and exhausting prospect. Calls for cooperative housing, the professionalization of child care, and infant education were mostly designed to reconfigure the role of the mother, and to shift some of the pressures of domestic life onto the community and the state [34, 36, 94–6][13] (although they could also be used to reaffirm male desires for comfortable and peaceful domesticity [94]). James Lawrence even argued that mothers should receive an income from the state, dependent upon the number of children they had [129]. To some vegetarian activists, women's domestic drudgery could be vastly reduced by the adoption of a meatfree diet [98]. Other women may not have concurred with such radical political solutions, and yet still protested against the onerous and stultifying burdens of a life centred around domestic concerns [97].

Perhaps one of the greatest insights to be developed in such discussions, however, was a recurring rejection of the hierarchical relationship which had evolved between those who performed paid employment (men) and those who performed unpaid domestic labour (women). Feminists repeatedly insisted that were was no rational reason why women's greater involvement in domestic management should lead to a gendered hierarchy within the family [90].[14] This included strategic efforts to deconstruct socially gendered roles concerning domesticity and parenting [93, 105–8] (one Fourierist even questioning the biological basis for female breast-feeding [109]), as well as attempts to redefine the economic and social worth of domestic labour [70, 88, 91].

If, for some, motherhood and domestic responsibility encapsulated all that was unique and most dignified in women's social function, for others it was a problematic role which necessitated social and cultural innovation so as to enable women to find their true sphere as individuals and citizens in their own right.

Notes

1   Reid (1843), p. 23.
2   Myers (1982).

3   For Pestalozzi's ideas and influence see Stewart (1972), especially pp. 75–7.
4   Self-culture and self-education were a common feature of many middle-class women's lives. For glimpses into these processes see Watts (1998), passim, but especially pp. 153–6.
5   For further details, and contextualization, see Rendall (1985), pp. 131–2.
6   Meteyard (1845), vol. 1, p. vii.
7   See Hall (1992) ch. 8, for an excellent discussion. For a more optimistic assessment see document **36**.
8   Hughes (1993).
9   Taylor (1983), pp. 83–117; Clark (1995), ch. 7.
10 Clark (1995), pp. 164–74.
11 Clark (1992).
12 Hamilton (1803), vol. 1, pp. 370–1.
13 See also the philosophy of the First Concordists at Ham Common, whose educational establishment encouraged a dilution of the link between parent and child. Wright and Wright (1840), pp. 6–7.
14 Such ideas had been developed during the 1790s: Mary Robinson, for example, insisted that men recognize that domestic management did not reflect the 'constrained obsequiousness of inferior organization'. Robinson (1799), p. 66. See also 'On the Rights of Woman', *Cabinet* (1795), vol. 2, pp. 47–8.

3
Education

'The magnitude of the error'

49. *Sydney Smith's trenchant essay provides further insights into radical perceptions as to women's potential and abilities, outlined in Chapter 1. His cutting and satirical attack upon the objections raised to granting women intellectual development was to make it a widely cited essay in the years to come.*[1]

A great deal has been said of the original difference of capacity between men and women; as if women were more quick, and men more judicious – as if women were more remarkable for delicacy of association, and men for stronger powers of attention. All this, we confess, appears to us very fanciful ... As long as boys and girls run about in the dirt, and trundle hoops together, they are both precisely alike. If you catch up one half of these creatures, and train them to a particular set of actions and opinions, and the other half to a perfectly opposite set, of course their understandings will differ, as one or the other sort of occupations has called this or that talent into action: there is surely no occasion to go into any deeper or more abstruse reasoning, in order to explain so very simple a phenomenon. ...

It is said, that the effect of knowledge is to make women pedantic and affected; and that nothing can be more offensive, than to see a woman stepping out of the natural modesty of her sex, to make an ostentatious display of her literary attainments. ... When learning ceases to be uncommon among women, learned women will cease to be affected. ...

Now, there is a very general notion, that the moment you put the education of women upon a better footing than it is at present, at that moment there will be an end of all domestic economy; and that, if you once suffer women to eat of the tree of knowledge, the rest of the family will very soon be reduced to the same kind of aerial and unsatisfactory diet. ... Can any thing, for example, be more perfectly absurd than to suppose, that the care and perpetual solicitude which a mother feels for her children, depends upon her ignorance of Greek and Mathematics; and that she would desert an infant for a quadratic equation? ...

As it is impossible that every man should have industry or activity sufficient to avail himself of the advantages of education, it is natural that men who are ignorant themselves, should view, with some degree of jealousy and alarm, any proposal for improving the education of women. But such men may depend upon it, however the system of female education may be exalted, that there will never be wanting a due proportion of failures; and that after parents, guardians and preceptors have done all in their power to make every body wise, there will still be a plentiful supply of women who have taken special care to remain otherwise; and they may rest assured, if the utter extinction of ignorance and folly is the evil they dread, that their interests will always be effectually protected, in spite of every exertion to the contrary. ... There is in either sex a strong and permanent disposition to appear agreeable to the other: and this is the fair answer to those who are fond of supposing, that an higher degree of knowledge would make women rather the rivals than the companions of men ... We are quite astonished, in hearing men converse on such subjects, to find them attributing such beautiful effects to ignorance. It would appear, from the tenor of such objections, that ignorance had been the great civilizer of the world. Women are delicate and refined, only because they are ignorant; – they manage their household, only because they are ignorant; – they attend to their children, only because they know no better. Now, we must really confess, we have all our lives been so ignorant as not to know the value of ignorance. ...

Nothing, certainly, is so ornamental and delightful in women as the benevolent virtues; but time cannot be filled up, and life employed, with high and impassioned virtues. ... Compassion, and every other virtue, are the great objects we all ought to have in view; but no man (and no woman) can fill up the twenty-four hours by acts of virtue. ...

They have nothing serious to do; – is that a reason why they should be brought up to do nothing but what is trifling? They are exposed to greater dangers; – is that a reason why their faculties are to be purposely and industriously weakened? They are to form the characters of future men; – is that a cause why their own characters are to be broken and frittered down as they now are? In short, there is not a single trait in that diversity of circumstances, in which the two sexes are placed, that does not decidedly prove the magnitude of the error we commit in neglecting (as we do neglect) the education of women.

[Sydney Smith], 'Female Education', *Edinburgh Review* (January 1810), vol. 15, pp. 299, 301–2, 304–6, 307–8[2]

'Mis-education'

As Chapter 1 indicated, radical writers often dwelt upon the egregious conse-quences of female socialization. Many authors dwelt upon the role of education in warping women's minds and bodies.

50.   We deprive the nightingale of sight, in order that it may sing us sweeter songs; we render the captive weak, and demand him to be strong as the free; we stimulate his feelings to madness, and expect from him the exercise of reason; we spread our treasures before him, and mock if he ask to share them; we deprive him of liberty and bid him rejoice in his prison. This may be a metaphorical way of putting the case, but is it very far from the truth? Is the painted, gilded, varnished thing which we call education, and which some call over-education, worth presenting to the minds and hearts of a race of beings as influen-tial as women? – and, remembering the conventional morality in which, for the most part, a female is reared – the veil that is kept between herself and the knowledge of her true position in society – the little truth that she hears whilst hearing it might avail her – the enervat-ing treatment she habitually receives even from the nursery, till at least half way towards the grave, – remembering this, and much more, are we justified in attributing her faults and follies primarily to herself?

[Maria Jewsbury],[3] 'On Modern Female Cultivation', *Athenaeum* (11 February 1832), no. 224, p. 95

51.   ... the women of the higher classes are so mis-educated as to become, in character, vain, proud, and most unwomanly weak, and helpless, sacrificing the beauty of health and cheerfulness to the desire of appearing feebly and *femininely* delicate. To please the false tastes and diseased imaginations of their expected lords and masters, they are taught to pride themselves in infirmity, under the name of refine-ment, and the affectation of superior manners and graces; and instead of learning the important duties of wives and mothers, and rational

companions and helpers of man, they are taught to spend much of their time in decking their persons, endeavouring to improve their natural beauty and grace, and conceal their defects; and, unfortunately, such is the force of example, they are assiduously imitated in these time-wasting, frivolous customs and employments, by the females of the other classes, so far as they can obtain the means; every class, down to what is called the lowest, strives to imitate the appearance and fashions of the class above it.

'W.W.P.', 'Woman As She Is and As She Ought To Be',
New Moral World (12 January 1839), vol. 5, no. 12, p. 178

'The great end of education'

Most radicals asserted women's right to be educated for their own needs and development. However, many also wished to emphasize a broader agenda of reforming society.

52.   Our inquiring is not so much of how much they should learn, or how little they do learn – but of the prior question to what is it proposed they sd [*sic*] learn at all? Is the end desired to make us better ministrants to the pleasures of men and if so to what description of pleasure are they to produce or increase[.] On the answer to these questions will depend the solution of the next – is the object of educating them the production of the greatest amount of happiness themselves of which they are capable. By what strange process is it that the end talked of is always happiness or pleasure to men – true that is one of the ends proposed – but only by implication in the theory that the greatest happiness of each being accords well with the greatest happiness of all. We hear nought in disquisition on mens education of what sort of instruction will produce the greatest happiness [for] women. We hear of no profession of the act of making women happy ...

Harriet Taylor, 'Education of Women', [*c*.1832] in Jacobs
and Payne (1998), p. 7

53.   *The* Westminster Review, *in this review of Sarah Lewis's* Woman's Mission (1839), *protested at her assumption that women should be educated for the influence they had over others.*

... we consider it unworthy of a rational, moral, accountable being, to lay down the doctrine that virtue and intelligence are to be cultivated in one-half of the human race only, for the effect they are to have on the other. To tell a girl that her virtue is given her to improve her husband's children, and her intelligence to show her *how* to do it, is to place her at once in an inferior grade, to prevent her from attaining to any high degree of virtue or intelligence.

'Review of "Woman's Mission"', *Westminster Review* (1840),
vol. 34, p. 257

54. An essay on female education is ever a sort of writ of *ad quod damnum* to ascertain how much a woman may be allowed to know, without trespassing on the mental preserves of man, and how little, consistently with securing for him every possible advantage. Her education is never considered otherwise than with reference to him; though his education is never considered with reference to her.

The aim of female education has been to make woman a kind of *acephala*, that is, an animal without a distinct head. It is now about being felt, that this system does not work so well as it was hoped it would: that *indistinct heads* descend, by hereditary right, on to the shoulders of sons as well as daughters, and that by aid of a few sympathetic unions, we run a chance of having some with *no heads at all*. ...

... in what plan of education, public, private, or national, is *female* education even glanced at as a national or universal interest? Oh, no; feed the boys, and the girls will grow fat, is the principle upon which *mental* nourishment is purveyed. ...

The great end of education is to fit woman, as an individual, to create happiness for herself by means as purely self-dependent as the nature of things will admit; and to fit her, as a relative creature, to be a zealous and liberal labourer in the midst of the whole human family for the advancement of the whole human race. ...

There is an humble pair, in my own neighbourhood, whom I am silently observing with peculiar interest. He does not rise to the dignity of *making* boots, he only *mends* them. Their little place, which a large window leaves open to the street, is in good order, and while he sits at the lapstone, she sits at her needle. How delighted should I be to see her reading to him a philosophical treatise or a fine poem, and then, when the book was laid aside and the needle resumed, hear them digest in happy converse the mental aliment they had thus participated.

M[ary] L[eman] G[rimstone], 'Acephala', *Monthly Repository* (1834),
vol. 8, pp. 771, 772, 773, 777

55. *The Owenite* New Moral World *often published surprisingly cautious* *writing on this subject.*[4] *This letter to the editor was one of the more progressive treatments of the subject.*

Surely we cannot look at the evils in society, arising from the ignorance of woman, without seeing the absolute necessity of her mental and moral powers being cultivated. Has not society already suffered by that system of education which teaches accomplishments, to the exclusion of all that is useful? How can a woman train the youthful mind to a knowledge of its own character, or to a knowledge of nature's works, unless she has herself been properly instructed? Accomplishments, without a previous mental and moral training, are an evil. But when the two are united, it must produce an agreeable and useful being.

The present unnatural state of society is not only 'unjust to woman,' but unjust to all.

'Anna', 'Letter to the Editor', New Moral World (22 June 1839),
vol. 5, no. 35, p. 549

56.   The incalculable greatness of the evil influence which ignorance in its women must bring to bear on any community, and the evident tendency of a race of truly enlightened women to produce, in their turn, a more enlightened race of men, are certainly very good public reasons for the discontinuance of this system towards women. But far from being the only reasons – as is often assumed – neither of these is the best or truest argument for doing away with a system so partial and injurious. The intrinsic value of a human soul, and its infinite capability of improvement, are the true reasons for the culture of any human being, woman no less than man. The grand plea for woman sharing with man all the advantages of education is, that every rational being is worthy of cultivation, for his or her own individual sake. The first object in the education of every mind ought to be its own development. Doubtless, the improvement of the influence exerted upon others will be a necessary consequence; but it ought never to be spoken of as the first inducement to it. It is too much the custom, even of the most liberal in these matters, to urge the education and enlightenment of women, rather as a means of improving *man*, than as, in itself, an end of intrinsic excellence, which certainly seems to us the first and greatest consideration.

If woman be naturally more feeble of intellect than man, surely she has, on that very account, the greater need of all the advantages which education can bestow. What appearance is there, then, of great care having been taken to improve the soft and feeble character of her mind? Has a strengthening and envigorating [*sic*] system of education been provided for her? The defects of her mental powers having been so obvious, doubtless there are plenty of schools and colleges endowed for her benefit, that as far as possible these deficiencies might be remedied? No, indeed! this is very far from being the case. Should this being, said to be so feeble of intellect, feel any desire after knowledge, any impulse to advance farther than the mere alphabet of learning, difficulties multiply around her at every step. As might be expected, in the usual course of class legislation, almost all the public money given in aid of education is employed in removing obstacles from the path of that sex which possesses the power of granting the money; and the individual members of which, if they be so much stronger of intellect as they pretend to be, are more able to remove obstacles for themselves, or to advance in spite of them. ...

In general, when a girl returns from school, the only way in which she can continue her education is by private study – we might almost say stolen study – in the midst of continual distractions and interruptions. Those only who are very earnest will continue their studies long. Many very soon leave them off, and many more never think of them at all, but sink contented, at seventeen, into that elegant nothing – a finished young lady. If woman's mind is so feeble, why is she left to struggle with all those difficulties which are so sedulously removed from the path of man? Why are there not great public institutions for young women to attend, that they may have every assistance in carrying on the work of self-culture, when they arrive at the proper age for it, instead of being forced, as they now are, to struggle on alone and unaided; or if they have not energy enough for that, having recourse to novels, embroidery, working in worsted, or some such kill-time occupation?

Marion Reid, *A Plea for Woman* (1843), pp. 174–7, 196

57. Women have strong claims upon the consideration of society; first, because they constitute one-half of the human race; and, secondly, because the moral well-being of the other half mainly depends upon them.

[Samuel Smiles], 'Industrial Schools for Young Women', *Eliza Cook's Journal* (9 June 1849), vol. 1, no. 6, p. 81

'A useless life'

58. Why was not I fellow of a College with free access to the Bodleian? I might then have been *approfondie* in something; now I skim the surface of everything, and can get no further for want of assistance.

Caroline Cornwallis to Mrs Mossop (12 March 1820),
in Cornwallis (1864), p. 26

59. I have been pondering upon your observations as regards a young lady's life, and I do not agree with you. I allow that most girls *do* lead a useless life, but I cannot admit that such is a necessary consequence of our state. I think it is a fault of education ...

Bessie Rayner Parkes to Kate Jeavons (15 Mary 1846), BRP VI 49,
Parkes Papers, Girton College.

'Educate them in harmony with each other'

Many radicals perceived that to reform female education was not sufficient – the education of boys would also have to be recast if a real reformation in the relationship between the sexes was to be secured.[5] This involved the radical-minded tackling diverse issues pertaining to educational policy.

60. *Henry Brougham's education bill (1820) aimed to give England and Wales a parochial school system, similar to that which operated in Scotland. The bill foundered due to the opposition of dissenters, who resented the control which the act would have given to the Anglican church over religious education.[6] Mary Hughes, herself a rational dissenter, fumed at the devastating consequences she believed the act would have upon the provision of girls' education.*

I have read in various periodical publications, many serious and well-founded objections to Mr. Brougham's Education Bill, most ably pointed out, – but what appears to me beyond all comparison the most forcible of all, has scarcely been even adverted to by any – namely, the manifest tendency which it will *necessarily* have to *degrade* and *demoralize* a large part of the population of this country. Under a weak and most fallacious pretence of extending the means of instruction amongst the males, all females of the lower classes are by this Bill, and at no very distant period, to be plunged into the ignorance which involved their progenitors in the dark ages! The 'glad tidings' of the gospel are to be disclosed to *English women* only through the medium of the desk and pulpit, or by the *pure* and *correct* information which they may be likely to gain by inquiring of their husbands, brothers, &c. at home! for our liberal and enlightened legislators are about to *seal up* the *Bible* from their view! An act is about to be passed in the 19th century to reduce a vast majority of the females of this country, as nearly as may now be done, to a level with those of Hindostan!

It will perhaps be said by the promoters of the Bill, and with a smile of contempt, that no law of such a description has ever entered into their thoughts! But, is not completely withdrawing the means of instruction from the children of the present day, the most effectual, nay, the only method of securing the ignorance of the rising generation? If it is urged that no bar is placed by the Act before the doors of schools for girls, which are, or may be, opened in every town and village throughout the kingdom – let it be well considered, that the proposed Bill rests upon such a degree of additional parish *taxation*, as, it is pretty generally agreed, will come on 'like an *armed man*,' and speedily *batter down* all those institutions for the instruction of the poor which depend upon voluntary contribution. This, indeed, appears to be one main design of the measure, and it must be allowed to be *fitly framed* for effecting its worthy purpose.

Mary Hughes, 'Letter to the editor', *Monthly Repository* (1821), vol. 16, pp. 276–7

61.   *Here, writing in his own system of phonology, James Lawrence draws upon Wollstonecraft's proposal for a coeducational public education system.*

The authoress ov 'the Rights of Women' proposes the foundation ov public schools, whare the youth ov boath sexes might be educated tugether. During the existence ov the present institution ov marriage, this project wood be impossible but ware the recommended system introduced, nothing cood be productiv ov such good consequences. A yunion ov tue strangers wood not hav the same prospects ov stability, as wun between a pair hoo had had every previus opportunity of becoming acquainted with each other.

[James Lawrence], *An Essay on the Nair System* (*c.*1800), pp. 31–2

62.   From the earliest period of life, the boy is taught to be self-reliant, self-dependent, in a word (for this is the truth) selfish; while the girl, on the contrary, is taught to be self-sacrificing, dependent, and reliant on others, rather than herself, for her main sources of happiness. He is early encouraged to trust to himself for getting on in the world, while she is encouraged to trust mainly to others. The boy's intellect is cultivated to the disregard of his affections; whereas, her affections are cultivated to the disregard of her intellect. While woman is educated almost exclusively in reference to man, he, on the other hand, is never educated in reference to her, but only to himself. ...

While therefore it is requisite that the mental strength of woman should be increased, it is equally important that the sympathetic and moral character of man should be improved. It is impossible to have a pure womanhood pervading society while young men's notions of women are low and selfish, and while their daily practices are at variance with all purity and virtue.

> [Samuel Smiles], 'Men and Women. – Education of the Sexes', *Eliza Cook's Journal* (14 December 1850), vol. 4, no. 85, pp. 97–9

63.   Now is the time for renewing the subject, now to insist that girls and boys have the *same education* ...

> Anne Knight, Friends House Library, MS, vol. s495, p. 6

'The truest virtue'

The moral education of women was frequently envisaged to have empowering potential (in giving women the autonomy to make personal and moral decisions for themselves).

64.   She saw that actual female education was based on the notion that ignorance is innocence – a most woeful and mischievous mistake. The truest virtue is most consistent with the truest knowledge; and in proportion as knowledge is false, will virtue be frail. She saw with disgust and anger the stumbling-blocks thrown in her own way, while facilities were afforded to her brother ...

> Mary Leman Grimstone, *Cleone* (1834) vol. 1, pp. 108–9

'All the rights of membership': women and adult education

65.   *William Thompson was one of the first to call for women's admission to mechanics' institutes. By the 1840s a variety of self-improvement establishments, such as literary societies, adult education classes, mechanics' institutes and the like had extended their membership to women.*[7]

Let your libraries, your models, and your lectures, and all your means of improvement be equally open to both sexes. Equal justice demands it. Have not women an equal right to that happiness which arises from an equal cultivation of all their faculties that men have? ... Long have the rich excluded the poorer classes from knowledge: will the poorer classes now exercise the same odious power to gratify the same anti-social propensity – the love of domination over the physically weaker half of their race? By such conduct the best fruits of their own knowledge would be lost; they would have no endearing friends to whom they could communicate, with whom they could compare and improve their knowledge. The ignorance of their associates would thwart and render abortive all their efforts to render their knowledge available in the promotion of health, comfort, or social pleasures. By ignorant women their improvements could not be appreciated, but would be counteracted. ... If the minds of women be not equally improved with those of men, *home* will be rendered either unattractive to intelligent men, or will become more and more the nursery of the caprices and arbitrary commands of men, rooting out of their minds the very basis of morality. Till women are equally educated with men, men must remain eternally immoral and unintellectual, though acquainted with all the physical sciences; no partial improvement of half the race will make men better than the lordly owners of West India or Virginia slaves. Instead of confidence and sympathy, merited suspicion, cunning and overreaching, and all the blunders and vices of the stupidity of ignorant women will torment men's lives, and retaliate on them the misery produced by the degradation they uphold. Soon are the passions of the brute gratified; what then becomes of the slaves who have no intellectual qualities to command respect? If women remain ignorant, particularly under our present vicious system of isolated domestic training, the minds and dispositions of all the race must remain perverted, in spite of after education. ...

Have not women less physical strength than men? Are they not therefore peculiarly fitted for intellectual and social pursuits, which do not peculiarly require strength? Is not the presumption just, that as men excel in muscular, so would women, were their faculties fully developed, excel in intellectual power?

Mechanics! you have long been the slaves of ignorance. Women have been, in all ages, and are now, the slaves of the ignorance and imbecility imposed upon them by all men. In improving yourselves, improve equally the other half of your race also. Thus only, by making women your equals, will you accomplish the last great step towards becoming yourselves rational, beneficent, and happy.

W[illiam] T[hompson], 'To the Members and Managers of Mechanics' Institutes in Britain and Ireland', *Cooperative Magazine and Monthly Herald* (February 1826), vol. 1, no. 2, pp. 46–7

66.   *The Whittington Club, a venue for education and recreation established by metropolitan radicals in 1846, was promoted by its founders as an important vehicle for feminist reform.*[8]

We think, with others, that the admission of ladies as members of the association is an admirable step in co-operative advance; nay, we go further, and think that in a great measure the character and fixity of the institution will mainly depend on the spirit in which it meets the views of the age, on one of its most important questions; the limit must not, therefore, be fixed to mere amusement, but by full participation in the benefits to be offered. We are for womanly advance. We cannot sever the unity of her progress from our own, however modified it may be by sexual difference. In the better unity of her characteristics with that of man, seems to lie the real secret of the question as to woman as a moral and social agent: there is divisibility and yet unity; divisibility as far as moral action is concerned, unity as completing a reciprocating law that can only rightly influence through unity of its characteristics. Whatever may be the limits of 'woman's rights', we are quite contented to leave their development to the agency of time, perfectly convinced that her advance will be co-equal with our own, and as grandly developed; and that the concession of all those 'rights' which advanced knowledge in mental and organic phenomena may show, will not need to be enforced, by any other process than that of the beautiful agency of mind reciprocating mind. Institutions, therefore, that bring into action this mental co-operation, meet a great necessity; and will do more to raise the moral characteristics of man and the mental powers of woman than a whole statute book of laws, by divesting social intercourse of its present appetitive stigma, so unjust to women, so demoralizing to ourselves. Necessity now enforces woman to earn her bread (and we think happily) by what were once considered the masculine prerogatives of the pen, the pencil, or the voice; and brings her into competition with ourselves, without our allowance of one privilege in the unequal warfare. To equalize these privileges as regards reading-rooms, libraries, and ordinaries, would confer a large benefit: more especially in this metropolis

where is congregated so much necessary and influencing intellect. ...
As regards active agency, we think the literary ladies should be induced
to deliver in to the committee of management, written lectures on the
chief topics that relate to advance; which, after selection, might be
occasionally read at the soirees and scientific meetings. Glorious
minds might thus be brought to bear upon the spirit of the age in all
their high example of womanly grace combined with intellectual
strength.

[Eliza Meteyard], Silverpen, 'The Whittington Club and the Ladies'
Douglas Jerrold's Weekly Newspaper (24 October 1846), no. 15, p. 343

Educational societies

*In addition to calling for women's access to public and adult education on
the same terms as men, some radicals, drawing no doubt upon the rich tradition of female self-education,*[9] *suggested that women form their own
educational societies.*

67.   Why should they not join and form societies for the promotion
of morals, of religion, of education, and of the more popular branches
of science and literature? How many new lights, how many momentous truths might be elicited and disseminated by such co-operation.

Dr Alexander, 'On the Duties and Rights of Woman', *Star in the
East* (19 October 1839), vol. 3, no. 162, p. 46

68.   *This extract comes from an extraordinary feminist 'postscript' which
Mary Leman Grimstone attached to her novel,* Woman's Love.

If home be a woman's province, and in England, this axiom will find
as many female as male supporters, might she not, by looking beyond
and around it, become more efficient, and more happy in the office
she holds in it? Is there any reason why women should not join, and
form, societies? Who more fit to form *educational* societies, than those
engaged in the duties of maternity? Might they not advantageously
interchange ideas from the result of actual experiment and experience? Associations have been instituted for the advancement of
astronomy, geography, agriculture. ... But is there any comparison
between the advantages of discovering a star in the celestial, and the
moral, hemisphere?

Mary Leman Grimstone, 'Postscript' *Woman's Love*
(1832), pp. 365–6

'A college of my own': Tennyson and *The Princess*

Tennyson's The Princess *was widely regarded as a dignified plea for women's rights. The* Eclectic Review, *for example, wrote, 'here we have one of our most delightful poets, though commencing half in badinage, warming as he dwells upon her [Mary Wollstonecraft's] cherished subject, "the rights of women," and pleading those rights with a force and an eloquence which the world has scarcely witnessed before.'*[10]

69a.   *The narrator of the poem is staying at the home of Sir Walter Vivian. He tells his assembled friends of a story he has read of a 'feudal warrior lady-clad', and asks, 'lives there such a woman now?' One of the young ladies present replies animatedly:*

> Quick answer'd Lilia 'There are thousands now
> Such women, but convention beats them down:
> It is but bringing up; no more than that:
> You men have done it: how I hate you all!
> O were I some great Princess, I would build
> Far off from men a college of my own,
> And I would teach them all things: you should see.

Alfred Tennyson, *The Princess* (1847), p. 7

In reply, the narrator tells an extraordinary story of Ida, who establishes an all-female university with her two associates, Lady Psyche and Lady Blanche, both firm believers in the cause of female equality.

The Reasoner, *which praised the poem for pleading 'the cause of Woman's Rights with all the lore of a scholar, all the grace of an artist, and all the inspiration of a poet',*[11] *chose to illustrate the poem to its readers with the following extract – Lady Psyche's lecture to the new pupils in the Woman's College:*[12]

69b.   Deep, indeed,
> Their debt of thanks to her who first had dared
> To leap the rotten pales of prejudice,
> Disyoke their necks from custom, and assert
> None lordlier than themselves but that which made
> Woman and man. She had founded; they must build:
> How might they learn whatever men were taught:
> Let them not fear: some said their heads were less:
> Some men's were small; not they the least of men,

For often fineness compensated size:
Besides the brain was like the hand, and grew
With using; thence the man's, if more was more;
He took advantage of his strength to be
First in the field: some ages had been lost;
But woman ripen'd earlier, and her life
Was longer; and albeit their glorious names
Were fewer, scatter'd stars, ...
         even so
... in arts of government
Elizabeth and others; arts of war
The peasant Joan and others; arts of grace
Sappho and others vied with any man ... [13]

At last
She rose upon a wind of prophecy
Dilating on the future; 'everywhere,
Two heads in council, two beside the hearth,
Two in the tangled business of the world,
Two in the liberal offices of life,
Two plummets dropt for one to sound the abyss
Of science, and the secrets of the mind:
Musician, painter, sculptor, critic, more:
And everywhere the broad and bounteous Earth
Should bear a double growth of those rare souls,
Poets, whose thoughts enrich the blood of the world.'

Alfred Tennyson, *The Princess* (1847), pp. 30–2

Notes

1 See for example *Tait's Edinburgh Magazine* (July 1844), vol. 11, p. 423;
Clarke (1863), pp. 394–5.
2 The essay was ostensibly a review of Thomas Broadhurst, *Advice to Young
Ladies on the Improvement of the Mind* (London 1808).
3 See Chapter 1, n. 9.
4 See for example Eliza Murray, 'Comparison of the Sexes', *New Moral World*
(8 June 1839), vol. 5, no. 33, p. 516.
5 Some radicals attempted to put such ideals into practice, as in the Wisbech
infant school, run by Caroline Southwood Hill and James Hill, where boys
and girls were given equal intellectual and physical education. Taylor
(1983), p. 341, n. 50.
6 Stewart (1985), p. 127.
7 See Purvis (1989), chs 5 and 6.

 8 Gleadle (1995), ch. 5.
 9 For self-education see Peterson (1989), pp. 41ff.; Vickery (1998), pp. 257–60.
10 *Eclectic Review* (1848), p. 423.
11 Panthea (Sophia Dobson Collet), 'Tennyson's Princess', *The Reasoner* (1848), vol. 4, no. 91, p. 175. For the influence of this poem upon later campaigners for female higher education see Caine (1992), pp. 28–30.
12 The intrusion of a group of young men posing as female students leads to a bitter conflict. But finally Ida, the epitome of true womanhood, capitulates and gives herself up to the love of one of the intruders, although not without considerable inner turmoil: 'She still were loth to yield herself to one/That wholly scorn'd to help their equal rights/Against the sons of men, and barbarous laws …' (Tennyson, (1847), p. 154.)
13 In referring to great women of the past, such as Elizabeth I, Joan of Arc, and the ancient Greek poet Sappho, the approach here is similar to that pursued by other contemporary feminists. See Chapter 1.

4
Employment

'An incalculable addition to general happiness'

This chapter opens with two important contributions from the early years of the century, both of which are full of intriguing ambiguities.

70. *This essay was one of a number of interesting articles on women's position to be published in the lively* British Lady's Magazine.[1]

Is it too bold an attempt to persuade your readers that it would prove an incalculable addition to general happiness, and the domestic comfort of both sexes, if needle-work were never practised but for a remuneration in money? As nearly, however, as this desirable thing can be effected, so much more nearly will women be upon an equality with men, as far as respects the mere enjoyment of life. As far as that goes, I believe it is every woman's opinion that the condition of men is far superior to her own.

'They can do what they like,' we say. Do not these words generally mean, they have time to seek out whatever amusements suit their tastes? We dare not tell them we have no time to do this; for, if they should ask in what manner we dispose of our time, we should blush to enter upon a detail of the minutiae which compose the sum of a woman's daily employment. Nay, many a lady who allows not herself one quarter of an hour's positive leisure during her waking hours, considers her own husband as the most industrious of men, if he steadily pursue his occupation till the hour of dinner, and will be perpetually lamenting her own idleness.

Real business and *real leisure* make up the portions of men's time – two sources of happiness which we certainly partake of in a very inferior degree. To the execution of employment, in which the faculties of the body or mind are called into busy action, there must be a consoling importance attached, which feminine duties (that generic term for all our business) cannot aspire to.

In the most meritorious discharges of those duties, the highest praise we can aim at is to be accounted the helpmates of *man*; who, in return for all he does for us, expects, and justly expects, us to do all in our power to soften and sweeten life.

In how many ways is a good woman employed, in thought or action, through the day, in order that her *good man* may be enabled to feel his leisure hours *real substantial holyday*, and perfect respite from the cares of business! Not the least part to be done to accomplish this end is to fit herself to become a conversational companion; that is to say, she has to study and understand the subjects on which he loves to talk. This part of our duty, if strictly performed, will be found by far our hardest part. The disadvantages we labour under from an education differing from a manly one make the hours in which we *sit and do nothing* in men's company too often any thing but a relaxation; although, as to pleasure and instruction, time so passed may be esteemed more or less delightful.

To make a man's home so desirable a place as to preclude his having a wish to pass his leisure hours at any fireside in preference to his own, I should humbly take to be the sum and substance of woman's domestic ambition. I would appeal to our *British ladies,* who are generally allowed to be the most zealous and successful of all women in the pursuit of this object, – I would appeal to them who have been most successful in the performance of this laudable service, in behalf of father, son, husband, or brother, whether an anxious desire to perform this duty well is not attended with enough of *mental* exertion, at least, to incline them to the opinion that women may be more properly ranked among the contributors to, than the partakers of, the undisturbed relaxation of man. ...

Much has been said and written on the subject of men engrossing to themselves every occupation and calling. After many years of observation and reflection, I am obliged to acquiesce in the notion that it cannot well be ordered otherwise.

If at the birth of girls it were possible to foresee in what cases it would be their fortune to pass a single life, we should soon find trades wrested from their present occupiers, and transferred to the exclusive possession of our sex. The whole mechanical business of copying writings in the law department, for instance, might very soon be transferred with advantage to the poorer sort of women, who with very little teaching would soon beat their rivals of the other sex in facility and neatness. The parents of female children, who were known to be destined from their birth to maintain themselves through the whole course of their lives with like certainty as their sons are, would feel it a duty incumbent on themselves to strengthen the minds, and even the bodily constitutions, of their girls, so circumstanced, by an education which, without affronting the preconceived habits of society, might enable them to follow some occupation now considered above the capacity or too robust for the constitution of our sex. Plenty of resources would then lie open for single women to obtain an independent livelihood, when every parent would be upon the alert to encroach upon some employment, now engrossed by men, for such of their daughters as would then be exactly in the same predicament as their sons now are. Who, for instance, would lay by money to set up his sons in trade; give premiums, and in part maintain them through a long apprenticeship; or, which, men of moderate incomes frequently do, strain every nerve in order to bring them up to a learned profession; if it were in a very high degree probable that, by the time they were twenty years of age, they would be taken from this trade or profession, and maintained during the remainder of their lives by the *person whom they should marry.* Yet this is precisely the situation in which every parent, whose income does not very much exceed the moderate, is placed with respect to his daughters.

Even where boys have gone through a laborious education, superinducing habits of steady attention, accompanied with the entire conviction that the business which they learn is to be the source of their future distinction, may it not be affirmed that the persevering industry required to accomplish this desirable end causes many a hard struggle in the minds of young men, even of the most hopeful disposition? What then must be the disadvantages under which a very young woman is placed who is required to learn a trade, from which she can never expect to reap any profit, but at the expense of losing that place in society, to the possession of which she may reasonably look forward, inasmuch as it is by far the most *common lot,* namely, the condition of a *happy* English wife?

As I desire to offer nothing to the consideration of your readers but what, at least as far as my own observation goes, I consider as truths confirmed by experience, I will only say that, were I to follow the bent of my own speculative opinion, I should be inclined to persuade every female over whom I hoped to have any influence to contribute all the assistance in her power to those of her own sex who may need it, in the employments they at present occupy, rather than to force them into situations now filled wholly by men. With the mere exception of the profits which they have a right to derive from their needle, I would take nothing from the industry of man which he already possesses...

It would be an excellent plan, attended with very little trouble, to calculate every evening how much money has been saved by needle-work *done in the family*, and compare the result with the daily portion of the yearly income. Nor would it be amiss to make a memorandum of the time passed in this way, adding also a guess as to what share it has taken up in the thoughts and conversation. This would be an easy mode of forming a true notion, and getting at the exact worth of this species of *home* industry, and perhaps might place it in a different light from any in which it has hitherto been the fashion to consider it.

[Mary Lamb], 'Sempronia', 'Essay on Needlework',
British·Lady's Magazine (1815), pp. 257–60

71.   *In 1799, Mary Ann Radcliffe published her outspoken disquisition on female employment,* The Female Advocate; or, An Attempt to Recover the Rights of Women from Male Usurpation. *Eleven years later she brought out her memoirs, in which she included a reprint of the original essay. She was pleased to find that notable public figures, such as Joseph Banks, supported her ideas concerning the encroachment of men upon traditional female employments. Banks suggested to Radcliffe the possibility of a female petition to parliament, or a female society to campaign more effectively.*[2]

What can be said of men-milliners, men-mantuamakers, and men stay-makers? besides all the numerous train of other professions, such as hairdressers, &c. &c.; all of which occupations are much more calculated for women than men. ... 'Look,' says an observer, 'to the shops of perfumers, toymen, and others of a similar situation; and, above all, look to the haberdashery magazines, where from ten to twenty fellows, six feet high, may be counted in each, to the utter exclusion of poor females, who could sell a tooth-pick, or a few ribbons, just as well.'

A tax upon these fellows would be very salutary; *so say I*; yet, for a poor female individual to attack so numerous a body of men, however insignificant by custom, is a bold stroke. ...

... it was never intended that women should be left destitute in the world, without the common necessaries of life, which they so frequently experience, even without any lawful or reputable means of acquiring them, through the vile practice of men filling such situations as seem calculated, not only to give bread to poor females, but thereby to enable them to tread the paths of virtue, and render them useful members, in some lawful employment, as well as ornaments to their professions and sex. This lovely appearance, alas! is but too often thrown aside, and, frequently, *not* from vicious inclinations, but the absolute necessity of bartering their virtue for bread. Then is it not highly worthy the attention of men, men who profess moral virtue and the strictest sense of *honour*, to consider in what mode to redress these grievances! for women were ultimately designed for something better, though they have long fared otherwise. ...

... notwithstanding so many unfortunate females have been obliged to seek bread in the paths of vice, and so many young men have fallen victims to their folly and wickedness, still the same devouring jaws of destruction are open for its future prey; nor can they ever possibly close, until the grievous precedent of men usurping females' occupations is entirely done away, *or some proper substitute provided*, so as to enable women to share the common necessaries along with their fellow-creatures: till then, we need not wonder at the vast number of pickpockets and housebreakers, which, at all times, infest the streets, to the disturbance of all civil society ...

Are not women, by nature, of a more gentle and delicate composition than men, and less able to bear the hardships which so frequently are forced upon them? Has it not, in all ages, been the task, or rather the avowed choice, of the male part of the creation, to protect and defend the weaker sex? and is not the male part of the creation better able to bear cold, hunger, fatigue, and hardships than women are? Poor helpless women! who no sooner meet the heavy fate of indigence, than, from their appearance, they are bound to support a load of infamous censure along with it.

Witness the poor slaves; what exertions have not been used by the humane friends of liberty in their behalf? Yet less, much less, are their sufferings to be lamented than the poor females I speak of, who have been bred up and educated in the school of Christianity, and fostered by the tender hand of Care.

The slave is little acquainted with the severe pangs a virtuous mind labours under, when driven to the extreme necessity of forfeiting their virtue for bread. The slave cannot feel pain at the loss of reputation, a term of which he never heard, and much less knows the meaning. What are the untutored, wild imaginations of a slave, when put in the balance with the distressing sensations of a British female, who has received a refined, if not a classical, education, and is capable of the finest feelings the human heart is susceptible of? A slave, through want of education, has little more refinement than cattle in the field; nor can they know the want of what they never enjoyed, or were taught to expect; but a poor female, who has received the best instruction, and is endowed with a good understanding, what must not she feel in mind, independent of her corporeal wants, after the adversity of fate has set her up as a mark, for the ridicule, the censure, and contempt of the world? Her feelings cannot be described, nor her sufferings sufficiently lamented.

Mary Ann Radcliffe, 'The Female Advocate' in Radcliffe (1810),
pp. 405–6, 409, 419–20, 463, 469

'The mere removal of partial sexual restraints'

72. *William Thompson and his collaborator, Anna Wheeler, argued as J. S. Mill was to do in his* Subjection of Women (1869), *for the removal of all restraints that impeded women's access to the labour market. Thompson and Wheeler were sensitive, however, to the cultural barriers that would still remain, whilst recognizing the psychological benefits of offering women the possibility to work if they so chose.*

They [women] require no more of enjoyment than what their faculties, whatever they may turn out to be, equally cultivated with those of men, may be able to procure for them under *equal* competition; competition free to all, and equal as to women with men. They expect no removal of natural bars to their success. All they ask is, that to these natural bars in the way of their pursuit of equal happiness with men, no additional bars, no *factitious restraints*, shall be superadded. . . .

They ask the same means that men possess of acquiring every species of knowledge, of unfolding every one of their faculties of mind and body that can be made tributary to their happiness. They ask every facility of access to every art, occupation, profession, from the highest to the lowest, without one exception, to which their inclination and talents may direct and may fit them to occupy. They ask the removal of *all* restraints and exclusions not applicable to men of equal capacities . . .

Though, from the indirect operation of numerous causes, few women might avail themselves of the removal of all existing exclusions and restraints; though the habits of men, in the possession of all arts, trades, professions, and employments, might long render them unwilling to elect women, though of superior merit, to places which men had been accustomed to occupy; yet would the very eligibility be an incentive to knowledge and exertion amongst women: it would raise them in their own opinion: the barrier of sexual superiority and domination would be broken down: women would see a possibility, by means of improvement, of becoming the equals, not only in domestic but in civil life, with men. As they respected themselves and became respectable, the respect of men would follow on their own. Instead of being looked upon as the ignorant slaves of man's animal propensities, they would be the cultivated and equal sharers of the most exquisite mingled pleasures of sense and intellect of which human nature is susceptible.

William Thompson [and Anna Wheeler],[3] *Appeal* (1825),
pp. 157–8, 159, 164

'Woman for herself'

Thousands of female workers joined trade organizations and cooperatives in the upsurge of Owenite activity in the early 1830s. However, increasingly unions were becoming gender-exclusive organizations, not least because of the fears of male craft workers that cheap female labour was undercutting their wages. Such tensions became particularly acute in the tailoring trade because of the mass reorganization of the trade through piecework and subcontracting, which undermined the craft traditions of male tailors. The resultant strike activity against the employment of women aroused fierce discussion.[4]

73. Sisters, bondswomen, arise! and let us unite to gain our rights. Let us unite and teach the oppressors, our employers, their duty.

In manufacturing towns, look at the value that is set on woman's labour, whether it be skilful, whether it be laborious, so that woman can do it. The contemptible expression is, it is made by woman, and therefore cheap! Why, I ask, should woman's labour be thus undervalued? Why should the time and the ingenuity of the sex, that could be so usefully employed otherwise, be monopolized by cruel and greedy oppressors, being in the likeness of man, and calling themselves masters? Sisters, let us submit to it no longer; let us once get to the knowledge of our wrongs; and our cause is won. ... Woman's rights, like man's, have been withheld from motives purely political, by deep concerted plans of early oppressors. The sage priests of olden time well knew, if woman's penetrative and inquisitive mind was allowed its liberty, their well-laid schemes of bigotry and superstition would soon have come to light. But, to return to our immediate interest: let our class generally unite; let us make a beginning in Birmingham; there are great numbers of females employed in this town. If our first efforts are feeble, let us fear not; a change must come, and that speedily. The women of Derby have entered the bonds of union; let us, in compliment to these noble but oppressed women, plant the standard of female union in Birmingham. Women of Birmingham, your children's, your own, your country's interest demand it. Be slaves no longer, but unite and assert your just rights! With the anxious hope that we may soon establish a union that will be a shield from oppression of every kind.

[Frances Morrison], 'A Bondswoman', 'To the Females of the
Working Class', The Pioneer (8 February 1834), no. 23, p. 191

74.   Has woman a right to reduce the wages of man, by working for less than man? Certainly not, were woman considered equal to man, and did she enjoy the same rights and priviliges [*sic*]; but since man has doomed her to inferiority, and stamped an inferior value upon all the productions of her industry, the low wages of woman are not so much the voluntary price she sets upon her labour, as the price which is fixed by the tyrannical influence of male supremacy; therefore any attempt to deprive her of labour, because she works at a reduced price, is merely punishing woman for the cruel and pernicious effects of male supremacy. To make the two sexes equal, and to reward them equally, would settle the matter amicably; but any attempt to settle it otherwise will prove an act of gross tyranny.

[James Morrison], 'A Page for the Ladies', The Pioneer
(5 April 1834), no. 31, p. 286

The following two passages refer to a plan, mooted in the Owenite paper The Crisis, *regarding the establishment of a female employment association.*[5]

75.   The ladies, we understand, are at last resolved to behave themselves like men, and no longer to live a single life. Many of them have undergone the ceremony already, and commenced a lodge of their own. Some of the Unionists profess a little alarm at this. What are they alarmed at? and what right have they to interfere? Are not the women one half of humanity? Are they not fellow-labourers with the men? Are they not more oppressed, and more unequitably paid, than their robust partners? Who is a greater drudge than the common house-servant? and how few women, now, comparatively speaking, have any support or dependence but their own exertions! Marriage is becoming less and less frequent, for a living is becoming more and more precarious. These arguments ought to prevail with the rudest and the most illiberal mind: and it is only a rude and an illiberal mind that can require an argument to justify women in claiming, and men in giving, to woman rights equal to man himself.

Crisis (1 March 1834), vol. 3, no. 27, p. 221

76. I was sorry to read in your last number, as also to hear from some of my own acquaintances, that there is a jealousy in the men against Female Unions. What can be the cause of this, but the tyrannical spirit of the male? Is man not yet willing to relinquish the rod of authority … If they deny our right to unite, and claim equal privileges with men, then, Sir, I say, we deny their right to unite and claim equal privileges with their masters. But it is clear enough, from this whispering spirit of jealousy that is going about with its venomous tittle-tattle, that the men are as bad as their masters; that, in fact, they want to be masters themselves; and that life would not be worth having if the slave trade were completely abolished, and woman emancipated. But, I hope, Sir, that my fellow-countrywomen will despise these insinuations, these fears, and jealousies of the men, and consult their own interests, for it seems to be a law of nature that every species and every sex take care of itself, for there is a tendency in every other to make a slave of it. If we depend upon men, they will become our masters; therefore, I begin, now, to rejoice that there is an opposition to our Union, for it may stimulate us to self-exertion, which is the only way of effecting our deliverance. Then let our motto be, 'Woman for herself and man for himself'.

A Woman, 'To the Editor of the Crisis', *The Crisis* (8 March 1834), vol. 3, no. 28, p. 230

Female employment and the William Johnson Fox circle

The group of radical unitarians who clustered around the ministry of William Johnson Fox in the early 1830s debated the issue of female employment extensively. Their many-hued arguments were indicative of the kaleidoscopic nature of many radical voices on women, even within comparatively heterogeneous intellectual communities.

77. Many branches of trade and commerce should also be thrown open to women in a manner that should render them respectable.

Several of the bazaars have set an excellent example, by employing only females: in the shops of milliners, haberdashers, retail linen-drapers, &c. it is disgusting to see men officiate. The married woman who has been thus taught and trained in the middling class of life, would be able to assist in providing for her family and house, she would not be a useless burthen on the industry of her husband, and would thus ensure his respect with his love. The unmarried would, by the professions or trades which they exercised, keep a rank in society, and maintain the respect due to that rank: they would no longer feel the humiliation of having no social consequence but through the men, and their characters would acquire dignity and strength.

'On Female Education and Occupations', *Monthly Repository* (1833), vol. 7, pp. 497–8.

78.   The great occupation of woman should be to *beautify* life: to cultivate, for her own sake and that of those who surround her, all her faculties of mind, soul, and body; all her powers of enjoyment, and powers of giving enjoyment; and to diffuse beauty, elegance, and grace, everywhere. If in addition to this the activity of her nature demands more energetic and definite employment, there is never any lack of it in the world: If she loves, her natural impulse will be to associate her existence with him she loves, and to share *his* occupations; in which, if he loves her (with that affection of *equality* which alone deserves to be called love) she will naturally take as strong an interest, and be as thoroughly conversant, as the most perfect confidence on his side can make her.

Such will naturally be the occupations of a woman who has fulfilled what seems to be considered as the end of her existence and attained what is really its happiest state, by uniting herself to a man whom she loves. But whether so united or not, women will never be what they should be, nor their social position what it should be, until women, as universally as men, have the power of gaining their own livelihood: until, therefore, every girl's parents have either provided her with independent means of subsistence, or given her an education qualifying her to provide those means for herself. The only difference between the employments of women and those of men will be, that those which partake most of the beautiful, or which require delicacy and taste rather than muscular exertion, will naturally fall to the share of women: all branches of the fine arts in particular.

J. S. Mill, 'Essay' [1832] in Rossi (1970), pp. 76–7

79.   *Mary Leman Grimstone was one of the few radical writers to draw attention to the issues facing older women.*[6]

As regards the guardianship of the poor, and the regulation of public morals, the least reflection is sufficient to show that the united agency of the sexes must be more efficient than the agency of either alone. In every parish there are women, elderly and old, who yet in the vigour of their health and intellect, might bestow on general interests those powers which their grown-up families no longer tax. How much more might, and would, a female overseer of the poor do in acting for the poor, than any of that kind of superintendents have ever yet done. If *she* were applied to in the case of a lying-in woman, *she* would not order *dry bread*, as was done on a recent occasion. She who had been herself a mother, and given a mother's nourishment to a child, could appreciate the necessities and the sufferings of the creature who, in such a case, appealed to her. Was there a female police, acting in conjunction, and under wise regulation, with male officers, the young victim of folly might find a friend and an adviser, where she now only finds a further betrayer.

Mrs. Leman Grimstone, 'Quaker Women', Monthly Repository
(1835), vol. 9, pp. 34–5

80.   *J. S. Mill's* Principles of Political Economy *contained a chapter entitled, 'On the Probable Futurity of the Labouring Classes' which was largely written by Harriet Taylor. The* Westminster Review *praised this portion of the work for giving serious attention to the issue of female employment.*[7] *This passage elaborated upon the author's claim that industrial occupation should be freely open to both sexes. The argument was related to a broader purpose – that women's employment would help to keep the population down, by channelling female energies away from domesticity.*[8]

The same reasons which make it no longer necessary that the poor should depend on the rich, make it equally unnecessary that women should depend on men, and the least which justice requires is that law and custom should not enforce dependence (when the correlative protection has become superfluous) by ordaining that a woman, who does not happen to have a provision by inheritance, shall have scarcely any means open to her of gaining a livelihood, except as a wife and mother. Let women who prefer that occupation, adopt it; but that there should be no option, no other *carrière* possible for the great majority of women, except in the humbler departments of life, is one of those social injustices which call loudest for remedy.

J. S. Mill [and Harriet Taylor],[9] *Principles of Political Economy* (1848),
vol. 2, p. 321

'An innovation on all our English ideas'

As the preceding extracts have indicated, there was little agreement, even among advanced radical thinkers, as to what kind of employment would best suit women. Interestingly, there was evidently some hostility towards contemporary plans to facilitate young ladies' entry into the profession of governess.[10] Instead, many turned to France, where, they claimed, women were performing a wide range of jobs.[11]

81.   In all the relations between the sexes, she is the refiner and the comforter of man. It is hers to keep alive all those purer, gentler, and more genial sympathies ... without which man, exposed to the rougher influences of everyday life, and in the struggle with this selfish world, might degenerate (*do* degenerate – for the case is not hypothetical) into mere brutes. Such is the beautiful theory of the woman's existence, preached to her by moralists, sung to her by poets, till it has become the world's creed – and her own faith, even in the teeth of fact and experience! Let man, the bread-winner, go abroad – let woman stay at *home*. Let her not be seen in the haunts of rude labour any more than in those of vicious pleasure: for is she not *the mother?* – highest, holiest, dearest title to the respect and the tenderness of her 'protector *Man!*' All this sounds so very trite, one is ashamed of the repetition. Who has ever questioned the least of these truths, or rather truisms? No one; – the only wonder is, that while they are accepted, promulgated, taught as indisputable, the real state of things is utterly at variance with them; and they are but lying common-places at best. ...

She might be a clerk, – or a cashier, – or an assistant in a mercantile house. Such a thing is common in France, but here in England who would employ her? Who would countenance such an innovation on all our English ideas of feminine propriety?

Anna Jameson, 'Women's Mission and Woman's Position' in
Memoirs and Essays (1846), pp. 217–18, 236

82. I never *would* be a governess and give up independence, but I would if cast on my own exertions set hard to learn the higher branches of bookkeeping if one may so term it and see if like so many French women, I could not get some employment in managing a warehouse or some such thing. Such people have much better payment I think than a governess (considering), and all the unemployed hours to themselves. I should not mind losing caste at all, first all the worthless friends would be horrified and leave and the true remain. What a *sieve* such a step would be.

Bessie Rayner Parkes to Barbara Leigh Smith (13 February 1847),
BRP V 6², Parkes Papers, Girton College

83. Society has closed, against females of a certain station, every avenue to useful and honourable employment except the one of tuition. And to this profession, difficult as it is, and unfitted as many are from mind and temper for the exercise of it, do crowds of helpless females flock, whose necessities compel them to depend upon their own exertions for their support, and whose fears of sinking in society deter them from encountering its ban by entering upon employment more congenial to their talents, feelings, and dispositions. The prejudice against ladies being employed in various other occupations seems to be inveterate; so much so, that the liberal-minded and benevolent cannot escape the influence of it, even while attempting to render assistance. The present observations arise from a knowledge that, at this time, it is in the contemplation of some most excellent and religious persons to subscribe a sum of money for the purpose of founding an institution for the benefit of the daughters of their ministers, upon the plan of bringing them all up, whatever be their tastes, tempers, and dispositions, for governesses. The probability is, that if their benevolent design be carried into effect, it will place the greater part of their protegées in circumstances where they will feel more acute mental suffering than it would be possible for them to experience in any other situation.

Indeed, the proposal for establishing an institution for educating a number of persons of various bents and dispositions for the purpose of following one employment as the means of subsistence, appears so erroneous as to extinguish all hope of advantage to the majority of the objects of it. ...

There are other pursuits of a noble and elevating character which the female mind is capable of comprehending, if the means are afforded of so doing. The limited view of female power and usefulness which we have just alluded to, operates very prejudicially with regard to the happiness of young females who have a certain position in society; and who are, nevertheless, compelled by narrow circumstances to have recourse to daily exertion for support. It is not to be expected that more than a few should possess that peculiar species of talent which is required for governesses; though all can be fitted for usefulness in some sphere, indicated by their own peculiar talents and dispositions. Would it not, then, be desirable to cultivate the peculiar ability each may possess, and so train them for such situations as their inclinations and talents may make most available for their future usefulness and ultimate happiness? ...

But once let the ban be removed, which forbids to females of a certain class any other employment than that of tuition, and we should soon find an abundantly extensive field for the lucrative exertion of female talent. Practical chemistry; various mechanical arts, such as engraving, painting, carving, gilding, watchmaking; the useful trades, such as bookselling, &c. &c. would, according to the various tastes, afford the young females a means of subsistence, in a way agreeable to themselves and beneficial to society. The example of an institution for this purpose would have a valuable influence.

Mildred Ellis,[12] 'The Education of Young Ladies' (1838),
pp. 193, 194–5

'My heart beats to be with them'

The final section in this chapter focuses upon women's articulation of their psychological needs for useful employment.

84.   I often feel as if I were not in my proper sphere, as if I possessed talents that only want awakening – that are ready to bud, did they find the least encouragement, and – that will wither for want of it. I could, Tom, I think I could have been something greater, something better than I am, had not my natural genius been repressed, and – like the blighting winds to the rosebud – been shrivelled almost to nothing. Thou wilt smile at this as an effusion of vanity – I cannot help it – thou knowest not the ardour, the enthusiasm that often glows within me, almost beyond my power to conceal it. I cannot say to what my disposition would particularly lead me – to what science I mean; for to science it very strongly inclines. For want of a proper guide, I first turn to one and then to another. I cannot go regularly on in any, for want of a proper assortment of books. Why are not females permitted to study physic, divinity, astronomy, etc, etc, with their attendants, chemistry, botany, logic, mathematics, etc. To be sure the mere study is not prohibited, but the practise is in a great measure. Who would employ a female physician? who would listen to a female divine, except to ridicule? I could myself almost laugh at the idea. The more active employments on the great stage often interest me strongly. When I read of battles by sea or land, how my heart beats to be with them! and a partaker of the danger.

Ellen Weeton to her brother, Thomas Weeton, (15 November 1809)
in Bagley (1969), vol. 1, pp. 196–7

85.   *Geraldine Jewsbury's novel,* The Half-Sisters, *contrasts the lives of two women: Alice Bryant, a repressed and dissatisfied middle-class wife and Bianca Pazzi, her half-sister, a beautiful actress.* Douglas Jerrold's Shilling Magazine *raved over the result: 'Miss Jewsbury is a genius … She particularly demands the enlargement of the sphere of woman's activities; and her story is framed to elucidate the happier effects produced, both socially and individually, by the full development of the mental powers and affections of women.'* [13]

Here, the charismatic, but chaste, Bianca airs her views to her future husband, Lord Melton.

'Women, in general, have no settled occupation,' said Bianca, looking up. 'Those who have families, have, indeed, a legitimate employment, enough to employ all their energies. Those women, too, who have to gain their own living, have their hands pretty full. But, with these exceptions, women lead a life of nonentity, so far as the *real value* of their occupation goes. All they do is to pass away the time, and it is of little real consequence whether it be done or let alone. Look, for instance, at the great body of unmarried women, in the middle classes – they spend their days in the same kind of trifling that slaves in the East amuse themselves with, till some one comes to put them into a harem. They want an object, they want a strong purpose, they want an adequate employment, – in exchange for a precious life. Days, months, years of perfect leisure run by, and leave nothing but a sediment of *ennui*: and at length they have all vitality choked out of them. This is the true evil of the condition of women. The need of some sort of a stimulant becomes, at last, an imperative necessity – it is the cry of their expiring souls, an impulse of self-preservation: they possess unsatisfied, unemployed powers of mind – a strong vitality of nature, that must consume them, unless an adequate, legitimate employment be provided for them. They must find something that is *worth* being done; voluntary employment will not stave off the evil. The very possession of existence inspires a desire for activity, and it is melancholy to see the blind vague efforts women make to be useful; they do their various things, not as an imperative duty, but because they have "plenty of time", and play at being Lady Bountifuls and lady patronesses to poor people, to get rid of their own weariness. I do not set myself up as an example of what women in general should be, but this one blessing I have had to counter-balance the many questionable items in my position, I have had a definite employment all my life: when I rose in the morning my work lay before me, and I had a clear, definite channel in which all my energies might flow.'

Geraldine Jewsbury, *The Half Sisters* (1848; 1998 edn), pp. 248–9

In Shirley, *the book's eponymous heroine, Shirley Keeldar, a young heiress, is an effective and competent businesswoman. Her best friend, Caroline Helstone, as she hints in this passage, bitterly regrets her own lack of opportunities.*

86a.   'Caroline', demanded Miss Keeldar, abruptly, 'don't you wish you had a profession – a trade?'

'I wish it fifty times a-day. As it is, I often wonder what I came into the world for. I long to have something absorbing and compulsory to fill my head and hands, and to occupy my thoughts.'

'Can labour alone make a human being happy?'

'No; but it can give varieties of pain, and prevents us from breaking our hearts with a single tyrant master-torture. Besides, successful labour has its recompense; a vacant, weary, lonely, hopeless life has none.'

'But hard labour and learned professions, they say, make women masculine, coarse, unwomanly.'

'And what does it signify, whether unmarried and never-to-be married women are unattractive and inelegant, or not? – provided only they are decent, decorous, and neat, it is enough.'

Charlotte Brontë, *Shirley* (1849; 1985 edn), p. 235[14]

86b.   *This letter from Mary Taylor to her close friend, Charlotte Brontë, appears to have been prompted by reading the passage cited above, before she had seen the more radical passages on female employment which appear later in the novel.*[15] *Taylor herself had recently emigrated to Wellington, seeking greater opportunities than custom permitted to middle-class women in Britain.*[16]

I have seen some extracts from Shirley in which you talk of women working. And this first duty, this great necessity you seem to think that *some* women may indulge in – if they give up marriage & don't make themselves too disagreeable to the other sex. You are a coward and a traitor. A woman who works is by that alone better than one who does not & a woman who does not happen to be rich & who *still* earns no money and does not wish to do so, is guilty of a great fault – almost a crime – A dereliction of duty which leads rapidly & almost certainly to all manner of degradation. It is very wrong of you to *plead* for toleration for workers on the ground of their being in peculiar circumstances & few in number or singular in disposition. Work or degradation is the lot of all except the very small number born to wealth.

Mary Taylor to Charlotte Brontë (c. 29 April 1850)
in Smith (2000), vol. 2, p. 392

86c. *In this second extract from Shirley, Rose Yorke (who was modelled on Mary Taylor) provides further arguments for women's right (or indeed, duty) to put their talents to greater use. Although Rose attempts to assure her mother of her acquiescence in traditional female duties, the powerful language of the passage speaks for itself.*

'if my Master has given me ten talents, my duty is to trade with them, and make them ten talents more. Not in the dust of household drawers shall the coin be interred. I will *not* deposit it in a broken-spouted teapot, and shut it up in a china-closet among tea-things. I will *not* commit it to your work-table to be smothered in piles of woollen hose. I will *not* prison it in the linen-press to find shrouds among the sheets: and least of all, mother – (she got up from the floor) – least of all will I hide it in a tureen of cold potatoes, to be ranged with bread, butter, pastry, and ham on the shelves of the larder.'

Charlotte Brontë, Shirley (1849; 1985 edn), p. 385

87. *The Professor, Charlotte Brontë's first novel, was written in 1846, but not published until after her death, in 1857. The novel traces the fortunes of a young Englishman, William Crimsworth as he follows a teaching career in Belgium. Despite their comfortable financial circumstances, his wife insists on running her own business even after the birth of their son.*[17]
   In this extract the betrothed teachers, Frances Henri and William Crimsworth (the narrator), plan their wedded future:

'... we shall have both the same profession. I like that; and my efforts to get on will be as unrestrained as yours – will they not, monsieur?'
   'You are laying plans to be independent of me,' said I.
   'Yes, monsieur; I must be no incumbrance to you – no burden in any way.'

'But, Frances, I have not yet told you what my prospects are. I have left M. Pelet's; and after nearly a month's seeking, I have got another place, with a salary of three thousand francs a year, which I can easily double by a little additional exertion. Thus you see it would be useless for you to fag yourself by going out to give lessons; on six thousand francs you and I can live, and live well.' ...

'How rich you are, monsieur!' and then she stirred uneasily in my arms. 'Three thousand francs!' she murmured, 'while I get only twelve hundred!' She went on faster. 'However, it must be so for the present; and, monsieur, were you not saying something about my giving up my place? Oh, no! I shall hold it fast'; and her little fingers emphatically tightened on mine.

'Think of my marrying you to be kept by you, monsieur! I could not do it; and how dull my days would be! You would be away teaching in close, noisy schoolrooms, from morning till evening, and I should be lingering at home, unemployed and solitary; I should get depressed and sullen, and you would soon tire of me.'

'Frances, you could read and study – two things you like so well.'

'Monsieur, I could not; I like a contemplative life, but *I* like an active life better; I must act in some way, and act with you. I have taken notice, monsieur, that people who are only in each other's company for amusement, never really like each other so well, or esteem each other so highly, as those who work together, and perhaps suffer together.'

'You speak God's truth,' said I at last, 'and you shall have your own way, for it is the best way.'

Charlotte Brontë, The Professor (1857; 1989 edn), pp. 250–1

Notes

1 See, for example, 'On the Condition of Women', *British Lady's Magazine* (1815), vol. 1, pp. 181–2.
2 Radcliffe (1810), pp. 473–5.
3 For details of the collaboration see Dooley (1995), pp. 26–35.
4 Taylor (1983), ch. 4.
5 *The Crisis* (20 April 1833), vol. 2, no. 15, p. 119.
6 Although see Lamb (1844), p. 9, which was also addressed to older women.
7 *Westminster Review* (1848), vol. 49, p. 305.
8 See also document **139**.
9 For Harriet Taylor's co-authorship of this chapter see Jacobs and Payne (1998), p. 291.
10 For full details of these initiatives see Hughes (1993).
11 See also R.D.O., 'Situation of Women', *The Crisis* (22 December 1832), vol. 1, no. 42, p. 171.

12 Mildred Ellis, appears to have been married to Sir William Ellis, a manager of the Middlesex Lunatic Asylum.
13 *Douglas Jerrold's Shilling Magazine* (1848), vol. 7, p. 370.
14 See also *Shirley*, pp. 376–9.
15 Smith (2000) explains that Taylor would have been able to read this extract which was reprinted in the *Manchester Examiner*, p. 394n.
16 The promotion of female emigration was more typically a conservative project – perceived as a means of providing 'marriage fodder' and domestic services to the expanding expatriate community: Hammerton (1979). However, see also the interesting discussion of emigration in [Samuel Smiles], 'Employment of Young Women', *Eliza Cook's Journal* (5 January 1850), vol. 2, no. 36, pp. 145–7.
17 It is interesting to note that Brontë attempts to reassure her reader that an independent, working wife may still assume a meek, subordinate character in her domestic relationships: *The Professor*, p. 277.

5
Domesticity and Motherhood

In defence of domesticity

As the previous chapter indicated, many radical writers on women envisaged that even with expanded employment opportunities, most women would still wish to devote themselves to the home environment. Contesting opinions proliferated even within this framework, however.

88. Nature has generously done her part; and the powers of the female mind are equal to the highest attainments, as far as those of human[s] are permitted to go, whether they relate to the boundless ranges of science, or in exploring the depths of nature and of art, in the most abstruse and difficult researches.

Neither are their bosoms less capable of exercising the firmer and nobler dispositions of courage and resolution – had their country's cause commanded their aid in the council and in the field, the ardor of patriotism and heroic valor would have directed and sustained them there: or, had Religion or Justice called them to the pulpit and the bar – truth, persuasion, and zeal would not less have accompanied, and crowned their efforts.

But the ordinances of superlative Wisdom appointed a sphere for female action, more important and engaging. Society looked to that sex for happiness, for prosperity; duties, the most amiable, indispensable, and arduous – relations the most endearing – cares distinct and separate from those of the opposite sex, beautifully and reciprocally constituting appropriate convenience and variety. The regulations and management of private domestic life communicate their influence to the sphere of public action; and while its good order secures the comforts and happiness of one, it cannot fail to assist and promote the welfare and prosperity of the other.

Miss S. Hatfield, *Letters on the Importance of the Female Sex* (1803), pp. 28–30

89.   The regulation of domestic concerns is the department of the women, because the men's pride makes them fancy it beneath them, otherwise we should not be indulged in this small share of government.

A Lady, *Female Rights Vindicated* (1833; first published 1758), pp. 71–2

90.   I am fully aware ... that each sex has its own peculiar sphere of duties and employments, which should not be intruded upon by the other; otherwise the whole business and all the concerns of domestic life in particular would be disorganized and subject to confusion. But it is not necessary that this separation of duties should cause a separation of interests or throw the balance of power into one channel, which becomes thereby a source of tyranny and injustice, rendering the domestic circle a scene of perpetual dispute and disorder ...

A Philanthropist, *Domestic Tyranny* (1841), p. 36

91.   To be very successful in any of the professions may require more firmness of nerve and more steady concentration of intellect than to manage a family with propriety; but certainly the proper management of a family infers the presence and constant exercise of those mental faculties, a greater concentration of which than usual is occasionally required in the learned professions. Neither are there any rules or tables which can materially assist woman in the performance of duties the features of which are so various and shifting: each woman must use her own judgment in her own case, and continually adapt her conduct to its changing phases ... the domestic duties of the mass of women are more onerous, and require even greater mental exertion, than the duties connected with business of the mass of men.

Marion Reid, *A Plea for Woman* (1843), pp. 42–3

'Confined, like other domestic animals'

Although domesticity may have loomed large in the feminist imagination, for many, particularly for those in the socialist tradition, women's domestic roles were perceived as symptomatic of the oppressive and limited lives they believed women to lead.[1]

92.   Confined, like other domestic animals, to the house and its little details, their 'sober wishes' are never permitted 'to stray' into the enlarged plains of general speculation and action. The dull routine of domestic incidents is the world to them, except when an occasional vista opens upon the actors in real life, through the long aisles of superstition, or the unsubstantial glitter of meretricious public amusements.

Home, except on a few occasions, chiefly for the drillings of superstition to render her obedience more submissive, is the eternal prison-house of the wife: the husband paints it as the abode of calm bliss, but takes care to find, out-side of doors, for his own use, a species of bliss not quite so calm, but of a more varied and stimulating description. These are facts of such daily occurrence and notoriety, that to the multitudinous, unreflecting, creatures, their victims, they pass by as the established order of nature.

William Thompson [and Anna Wheeler], *Appeal* (1825), pp. 39, 79

93.   I do not like the doctrine of women keeping at home, and minding the house and the family. It is as much the proper business of the man as the woman; and the woman, who is so confined, is not the proper companion of the public useful man.

Richard Carlile, 'To the Lady of the Rotunda', *Isis* (3 March 1832),

vol. 1, no. 4, p. 56

94.   *This extract is indicative of the comprehensive potential assigned to unionism within Owenism, [see also 73–6]. Here, the principle of union is promoted as a panacea for women's domestic problems, including a blueprint for community playgroups.*

He may drink tea if he pleases; go to a coffee-house every night, and read the papers, and bring in fifteen shillings a-week to keep home and pay the rent withal. *He has a right to do this*, for he makes the money. But what is the woman doing? She is working from morning till night at house-keeping; she is bearing children, and suffering all the pangs of labour, and all the exhaustion of suckling; she is cooking, and washing, and cleaning; soothing one child, cleaning another, and feeding a third. And all this is nothing; for she gets no wages. Her wages come from her husband; they are optional; he can give her either twenty shillings to keep house with, or he can give her only ten … And it is high treason in women to resist such authority, and claim the privilege of a fair reward of their labour! Good Good! if we thought that the sex *woman* could patiently endure such a yoke of bondage, we should hate her most heartily! But how is she to prevent it? Why, by the very same means by which the men will prevent the tyranny of the master. Women will save themselves abundance of labour by association. We shall give an idea of what might be done by union. ...

Supposing, merely, ten matrons were in friendly union, might not one take charge of ten families of children for a day, and relieve all the other nine, who would each take the office in her turn, and thus be released for nine days out of ten, of the greatest proportion of her labour? Might not infant schools be instituted, *not* for teaching children to read; for amusing infants, and affording a comfortable opportunity for mothers, not only for improving their minds, but adding to the comforts of their husbands, and making home a place of attraction, instead of an object of aversion, as it is at present. What an agreeable change would this be both for parents and children! How gladly would the little creatures walk off to school in a morning, with their clean hands and faces, and laughing countenances, if, instead of drilling them there, like a parcel of mutes, forcing them to sit all day on a bench, with a little book in their hands, and two big tears rolling on their cheeks, they were amused and entertained by a variety of innocent plays: drawing their little horses, rolling their little wheelbarrows, whipping their wooden donkeys, jumping, and dancing, and singing; their little hearts distended with joy, and as happy to return on a morning to their amusement, as now they are loath! All this might be done by women, if they would merely commune with each other on the subject; and who better qualified than women for such legislation as this? Might not washing establishments be instituted, where each, in her turn, might assist in person, or by proxy, as she pleased, and thus divest the workman's fire-side, or his kitchen, of many of the disagreeable inconveniences which so often drive him to the public-house ... we are certain that homes will never be comfortable till this union be accomplished, and such projects as these, and many others, to which we shall allude, shall be carried into effect. It is for the happiness of man and woman that we write.

[James Morrison], 'A Page for the Ladies', *The Pioneer* (22 March 1834), no. 29, pp. 262–3

95. *The* Working Bee *was the journal of the Owenite community, Manea Fen. Despite the optimistic claims of socialists as to the possibility of female emancipation within their communitarian experiments, conventional patterns of gender behaviour continued to be replicated even within these progressive environments.*[2]

The change of circumstances to those who have just left the old world is great – much more than many could have anticipated. The little domestic cares, the management of a house, leave the female who enters a Community. The sound of the kettle, singing on the fire, (so dear to many a woman) the command of a servant – must be given up. Common meals, and parties who are appointed to the various departments, supersede these domestic habits and associations. All are placed upon an equality …

'To those Desirous of entering Community especially the females', *Working Bee* (4 July 1840), vol. 1, no. 5, (new series), p. 37

96.   Howitt's Journal *was a popular publication which provided a forum for many of the radical journalists within metropolitan feminist circles.*

It is desired, then, earnestly to recommend to the middle classes a combination to form Associated Homes; each home being separate and complete in itself, but contained within one building, or associated in a range of buildings, having a common kitchen and other offices, a common store of all kinds of provisions, and other articles essential to housekeeping, and an establishment of the needful number of domestic servants; the whole under the control of a certain appointed body, or of a capitalist who may choose to embark in [*sic*] such an undertaking; and every department under efficient superintendence. …

It is difficult to estimate the importance of this diminution of expense, with increase of comfort and refinement, and decrease of domestic drudgery. The time thus set free might produce effects so great and beneficial that we cannot see where they would end. The great duties of mothers, the great duties of wives, the true mission of women in the world, would then all have a chance to develop themselves. When the time comes, may women see and take advantage of their golden opportunity. May they have a due sense of their great responsibilities, and shun the temptation which may assail them to waste that great boon of peaceful leisure in frivolity or indolence. The women of the middle class have not, like those of the aristocracy, formed habits of luxury, ease, and the necessity of seeking excitement in society. They have been trained to industry, and to much self-command, self-denial, and patience. No conventional morality comes in to shield them and permit them any license. They have much to learn, but in many respects little to subdue; and may therefore be said to have a clear field before them, if the evils of their circumstances could be removed.

Opportunities for education, from the age of infancy upwards, would open in such establishments such as we cannot command now. This would be one of their great advantages. The numbers collected would form classes sufficient to pay the best teachers.

> Mary Gillies, 'Associated Homes for the Middle Classes',
> *Howitt's Journal* (15 May 1847), vol. 1, no. 20, pp. 271–3

97.   There is no *depth* in our domestic life, nothing beyond the *surface* of everyday concerns, and sometimes when I pump I find too little water in my well of hope or Faith: I say this to you alone, don't let any one else think I feel a deficiency.

> Bessie Rayner Parkes to Barbara Leigh Smith [1847], BRP V^2 , Parkes
> Papers, Girton Papers

98.   *The contemporary vegetarian movement tended to prioritize women's domestic role in effecting reform, but it contained within it a minority constituency of feminist voices.*[3] *Here Charles Lane considers the implications of meat-eating for women's domestic labours.*

The extra toil is not only great, but filthy. The woman's mind is absorbed in anxiously buying the right variety, and in cooking in the required way, to the exact minute. She has no chance for her own improvement; and that so frequently she does not desire it, is the saddest part of the story. ...

Seeing to what an extent the present and coming ages are dependent on female development, every sincere and religious man will adopt every practicable means for the elevation of the more susceptible half of the human race. The chains which slavery forges for itself are the last to be removed. Every man who desires that woman should be his COMPANION, and not his TOY or his domestic SLAVE, will henceforth refuse the dainty flesh, even though her daintier hands shall have prepared it.

> C[harles] L[ane], 'Religious and Moral Objections to Flesh Eating',
> *Truth-Tester* (1848), vol. 2, p. 130

'As if she were an angel'

Despite the palpable unease many felt at women's domestic role, eulogies on motherhood were common among progressive thinkers.

99.   It was the first time in my life I had seen a complete realization of my idea of a mother's love. She seemed, at times, as if she were an angel guarding an immortal soul.

'S.Y.' [Sarah Flower Adams], 'The Three Visits', *Monthly Repository* (1834), vol. 8, p. 730

100.   'It is my impression,' said Felix, 'that parents make the best teachers; – especially do I think, with Pestalozzi,[4] that a mother, even the most uncultivated, if she follow the dictates of maternal love, can educate her very young children better than any other can educate them. Who can sympathize with the child as she does? Who can have the patience with it that she has? Who have the vital interest in it that she feels? Oh! let mothers keep in view that the happiness, not merely of the young creatures committed to their care, but of the whole world, depends principally upon *them*, and they will rise to the work with all their best energies!' ...

'Oh, what a work! how full of beauty! Instead of shunning, who would not seek it? As sympathy strengthens between the child and mother, she will soon discover how infinite a power she may exercise by means of that sympathy. A saddened look – a sorrowful tone – will prove a correction, which the young thing that loves the light of kind looks, and the gladness of gay tones, will feel instantly, and answer to implicitly. Once establish this reciprocal feeling, – support it by perfect truth and tenderness on one side, and by inviting perfect confidence and affection on the other – and what is there to impede the progress of education?'

Mary Leman Grimstone, *Cleone* (1834), vol. 1, pp. 209–10; 216–17

101.   *Grimstone's close associate, William James Linton, developed the rhetoric of motherhood to reconfigure national identities and women's contribution to the state:*

If you would be honored as mothers, first teach yourselves how to render due honour to our common mother – our Mother-land! Recollect that this our English life is one half woman; and that woman has her duty there, her part to perform in the organisation and working of the whole. Her business, as much as man's, to understand the life, the purpose and mission of her country; her business and bounden duty to assist the man in his duty towards *their* country, whether by patriotic impulse, by counsel, or by more active compan-ionship; in all things feeling that Humanity is composed of two parts, equal though differing, two equal intelligences, to be harmonised

together for mutual aid, and in the common work of human progress.
W. J. Linton, 'Noble Women', *The Reasoner* (1848),
vol. 4, no. 88, p. 137

Infant Custody

The Infant Custody Act of 1839 permitted married women (providing they were not guilty of adultery) to apply to the courts for custody of children under seven years old, and for access to older children.[5] The Act was passed largely thanks to the efforts of Caroline Norton, whose estranged husband, George, refused to allow her custody of their sons following the breakdown of their marriage. The degree to which the Act may be seen as the result of a feminist viewpoint is open to debate. It appears, however, that some reformers, such as Edward Trelawny, did view the measure in this light.[6] Norton herself denied that her actions were prompted by feminist ideology, claiming that she believed, 'The natural position of woman is inferiority to man.'[7] In private, however, she expressed more heretical views on women's position.

102.   To-night Talfourd[8] (blessed be his name for that same, and a crown of glory to him! as the Irish say) has given notice of a motion in the House of Commons to alter this law. I thought you would be glad to know this, both for the sake of the sex (whom you have not the clever woman's affectation of thinking inferior to men) and for me, whose first glad feeling for many months of struggling has been the public notice of an effort, at least, to be made in behalf of mothers.
Caroline Norton to Mary Shelley (1 February 1837), in Perkins
(1909), pp. 137–8[9]

103.   *Debates over the Infant Custody Bill became highly intricate. Henry Brougham, who bore a bitter personal animosity to Norton, opposed the bill, but he used the opportunity of the parliamentary debates to discourse on the many legal and social injustices faced by women.[10] Norton therefore had to construct a case that women were particularly oppressed by the law regarding infant custody.*

I must deny either that the particular acts of oppression aimed at by the Infant's Custody Bill, *are* the *necessary* results of an inferior position; or that women *do* suffer equally in any other instance from want of legal protection ...

She is *not* left to the exercise of despotic power on the part of her husband as regards property, for the law compels him to provide for her; she is *not* left to his despotic power in the matter of personal violence and cruelty, for she *can* obtain a divorce, though it be only a divorce *a mensa et thoro* [legal separation]. It is in the single point of *her children* that she is *entirely* without remedy: it is in the single point of her children that her innocence or her ill-usage avail nothing.

[Caroline Norton], Pearce Stevenson, *A Plain Letter to the Lord Chancellor* (1839), pp. 5, 11

104.   … the great obligation conferred on our sex by that estimable character, Serjeant Talfourd; who in the great senate of the nation, and in spite of great opposition by persons of power and influence, has succeeded in obliterating from the statute book one of its most obnoxious enactments against the Rights of Women …

A Philanthropist, *Domestic Tyranny* (1841), pp. 34–5

Deconstructing motherhood

Other writers pondered more fundamentally on the cultural and social construction of motherhood.

105.   *J. S. Mill's scepticism concerning the educative responsibilities of motherhood were at variance with those in his network who celebrated pedagogical theories that promoted the maternal role [100].*

… as to the education of children: if by that term be meant, instructing them in particular arts or particular branches of knowledge, it is absurd to impose that upon mothers: absurd in two ways: absurd to set one-half of the adult human race to perform each on a small scale, what a much smaller number of teachers would accomplish for all, by devoting themselves exclusively to it; and absurd to set all mothers doing that for which some persons must be fitter than others, and for which average mothers cannot possibly be *so* fit as persons trained to the profession. Here again, when the means do not exist for hiring teachers, the mother is the natural teacher: but no special provision needs to be made for that case.

J. S. Mill, 'Essay' [1832], in Rossi (1970), pp. 75–6

106.   *For the Owenite George Petrie, the effects of a socialist reformation would be so profound that even the pains of child-birth would be assuaged.*

Listen to me, then, enslaved sisters, and I will lead you out of the 'land of Egypt, and out of the house of bondage' ... The only foundation on which the temple of human happiness can be erected, is a rational commonwealth, divided into communities of property; wherein no artificial distinctions will be known; where the irrational sounds of husband and wife, and master and mistress, will not be heard ... In such a state of society, the travail of the female will be divested of its pains; every attention will be paid to keep her mind in a state of equanimity, in order that she may grace the earth with an organization of the first order of human nature; in her parturition, she will be comforted and caressed by the whole community, whereby the natural suffering would be modified and softened, as well by superior science as by numerous acts of kindness performed by both sexes; the child, which would undoubtedly be the property of the community, would be nursed, trained, and reared to maturity ...

> [George Petrie], 'Agrarius', 'Moral Marriage and Priestly Marriage',
> *The Man* (September 1833), vol. 1, no. 13, p. 98

107.   We shall arrive at the conviction, that there is even a maternal nature in that portion of mankind which is of the male sex.

> C[harles] L[ane], 'National Female Education', *The Shepherd*
> (16 September 1837), vol. 3, no. 12, p. 92

108.   *In this essay, Catherine Barmby dwelt upon the differing class constructions of motherhood. The Poor Law Amendment Act (1834) to which she refers, placed the burden of supporting illegitimate children upon their mothers. This clause was repealed in 1844.*[11]

The mother, in the highest circles of life, when separated from her husband, in accordance with the law of divorce, may have all intercourse with her children denied to her, however free from suspicion her conduct may have been; while, in consonance with the New Poor Laws, the wretched creature, deficient, perhaps, in her morals, destitute of food and shelter, and, with these, of every thing that can render the society of her child aught but a torture, *is commanded to fulfil her maternal duties.*

> Kate [Barmby], 'Woman and the Laws', *New Moral World*
> (29 June 1839), vol. 5, no. 36, p. 562

109.   *This striking passage alludes, if ambivalently, to a belief in the possibility of male breast-feeding. It is clear that within progressive networks there was some interest in new theories concerning the mutability of the species, and even occasional hints of eugenic theories.*[12]

The efforts that are now made by the literary friends of the fair sex to raise the character of Woman, are amongst the pleasing signs of the times. These efforts give rise to multiplied speculations regarding her nature and destiny, manifesting, like every class of speculations in which the human mind engages, opinions wide as the poles asunder. Some there are who in the spirit of paradox boldly assert that there is nothing more than a formal distinction between the two sexes, and that even this is partly artificial, that woman suckles a child merely because man refuses to do it, and that the desire in man to contribute this infantine nourishment would not only cause its secretion, but actually produce a nipple to administer it. Those who make such sweeping assertions as this, may be supposed to make a multitude of others, less extravagant perhaps, but not more agreeable to the order of nature. That men have suckled is probably true. The evidence is strong, and the fact is quite possible, but it is an exception. …

'Review of "The English Maiden"', *London Phalanx*
(30 October 1841), no. 31, p. 493

Notes

1 By contrast, Fourierists argued that domesticity would be redefined in the ideal 'harmonic' state and be conceptualized as no more than an 'exchange of services'. Gamond (1841), p. 78.

2 Taylor (1983), ch. 8.

3 Gleadle (2002).

4 For Pestalozzi see p. 56 above.

5 See document **120** for a bleaker view of women's maternal rights even after the Act.

6 Erskine (1915), p. 165.

7 Quoted in Perkins (1909), p. 149.

8 Thomas Noon Talfourd (1795–1854) – a writer and lawyer who moved in liberal, literary circles. An MP for Reading, he was the chief parliamentary champion of the Infant Custody Act.

9 Mary Shelley declined to help Trelawny when he requested assistance in the campaign; yet she materially assisted Caroline Norton in the writing of her pamphlets. St. Clair (1977), p. 158–9; Perkins (1909), p. 133.

10 Chedzoy (1992), p. 177; for Brougham's complicated arguments see *Parliamentary Debates* (30 July 1838), 3rd series, vol. 44, pp. 779–88.

11 For further details see Thane (1978), pp. 31–2.

12 See document **20** and note; 'Politics', *The Shepherd* (31 March 1837), vol. 2, no. 8, p. 57 alludes to the possibility of improving the species through selective breeding. For Fourierite ideas concerning the potential for human evolution see Beecher (1986), pp. 338–41.

Part III

Marriage, Sexuality and the Female Body

'Morality is a science, and as such must be studied.'[1]

Introduction

Feminist letters throughout this period insisted upon exploring the most intimate recesses of women's lives. What was the nature of contemporary relationships? How prevalent was the problem of domestic violence? To what extent were women able to express their own sexuality? Should women be empowered to exert control over their own fertility? Such questions variously acknowledged the insidious imbrication of patriarchal privilege within both the public and private worlds. Indeed, the incessant tropes of liberty, freedom and independence within progressive discourses on marriage, and the reiterated images of confinement, harems and slavery [110–14] formed a compelling fugue to those evocations of domesticity simultaneously emanating from even radical quarters [88–91].

For many, the iniquitous marriage laws epitomized the ability of men to negotiate their dominance between the public and private domains [119–21]. Although women could have their property protected for their own use under the system of equity (a practice which was common among the upper classes and certain sectors of the middle class),[2] early feminists concentrated almost exclusively upon the ills of the common law. This entailed the loss of women's legal identities upon marriage: they were unable to make contracts, and were obliged to give up ownership of any personal property and freehold land to their husbands.[3] The ensuing demands for reforms to married women's legal position emerged not only from explicitly feminist quarters. A more attenuated tradition of legal discourse used Enlightenment paradigms of history and anthropology to consider women's legal rights in a broader, comparative framework.[4] Radical writers could utilize anthropological and historical observations as a vehicle with which to expose what they felt to be the egregious position of contemporary British women [**116, 120, 126**]. Certainly there was widespread cognizance of the fact that dominant attitudes towards marriage, divorce and sex were not divinely ordained, but were rather, socially produced. As Charles Southwell put it, 'it is clear that men's notions upon this subject, are determined by localities and contingencies'.[5]

Yet, at the same time, many radicals conceptualized sexual behaviour as being driven by natural laws. To prohibit the free expression of sexual desires through inflexible marital arrangements was, it was argued, to contravene nature itself. As the documents in this section illustrate, the views of William Godwin and Mary Wollstonecraft, concerning the inadequacy of marriage as a social institution were not extinguished in the conservative reaction that followed the French Revolution.[6] Rather they were rehabilitated by a new generation of radicals who moved within literary bohemian circles. In particular, the networks of the radical poet Percy Bysshe Shelley widely debated, and frequently practised, heterodox sexual relations. Shelley explicitly positioned Godwin as his intellectual mentor, not least with reference to his ideas on marriage; and there was considerable cultural inter-change between Godwin and the circle of intellectuals who clustered around the young Shelley (including Leigh Hunt, Edward Trelawny [**110**] and Thomas Jefferson Hogg [**156**]).[7] Central to the philosophy of these networks was the insistence that individual feelings should predominate over the dictates of social institutions; and correspond-ingly, that people should feel free to break the bonds of marriage when personal inclination so prompted [**128**]. As Claire Clairmont (Shelley's sister-in-law) observed in her diary in 1820, 'The words for piety, decorum, behaviour, respect for the opinions of the world are nothing but the coverings people put upon their souls when like Adam & Eve they are ashamed of its deformity.'[8]

Shelley's ideas and his revolutionary poetry were to be widely discussed in radical political circles throughout this period – from Carlile's zetetic movement of the 1820s, through to the Owenites in the 1830s and 1840s. Shelley was, declared the Owenite paper, the *New Moral World*, 'one of the prophets and poets of the future'.[9] Indeed, Shelley functioned as a central conduit between the Godwinian tradi-tion and the emergence of Owenite sexual radicalism.[10] It would be misleading, however, to consider political radicals such as these as operating in a simple dialectical relationship with conventional sexual mores. They were part of a much broader, richer cultural environment. For a start, many plebeian communities still sanctioned common-law marriages as well as informal 'remarriage' once a relationship had broken down.[11] Alternative sexual lifestyles were also practised by certain religious sects. However, the desire for a more liberated sexual culture might merge and overlap with authoritarian and patriarchal attitudes towards women. The Swedenborgians, for example, failed to categorically deny their detractors' taunts that they condoned polygamy and adultery, and their suggestion for the state regulation of prostitution was constructed upon a model of male sexuality as a rampant and irreducible force.[12] Such a formulation boded ill for female needs, desires, or even protection.

Sexual libertinism could be defended in the name of women's rights – as in the case of James Henry Lawrence – whose views on female sexuality and the possibility of dispensing with all stable partnerships were hotly debated in radical literary and political circles [**126–9**]. The relationship between libertine and feminist traditions remained knotty and ambiguous, however. In the Owenite movement, there are clear indications that numbers of female followers feared that a relaxation of sexual behaviour might merely intensify their own social and personal vulnerability.[13] Barbara Taylor notes that, significantly, Owenite women tended to quote Shelley's views on women's social position, rather than on sexuality.[14]

Perhaps unsurprisingly, given these concerns, an alternative discourse on sexuality embraced chastity as a feminist issue [**148–55**]. This followed the earlier insistence of feminists such as Mary Wollstonecraft that passion should be vanquished by the power of reason.[15] These two ideological strands were not always neatly dissevered however, and there was often ambiguity or fluctuation between the promotion of chastity and the desire for less constricted sexual mores. Indeed, although contemporary commentators tended to stereotype the views of all sexual radicals as advocating free love and the dissolution of marriage; only a small minority adhered to such theories.[16] In practice, individual positions were far more complex. There was fairly broad consensus amongst such groups as the Owenites, radical unitarians and Godwinians that divorce should be freely available once couples no longer felt affection for one another. Nonetheless as Barbara Taylor has noted in the Owenite context, Robert Owen's original 'line' on the issue, 'began to dissolve into a range of positions' [**132–6**]. Indeed, many Owenites went on the defensive, assuring their audience that they did not anticipate wide-sweeping marital reform in the existing condition of society.[17] Numerous authors, particularly within radical unitarian circles, sought to take the sting out of their message, by implying that they did not wish to overthrow marriage, merely to make divorce more accessible [**137–40**].[18]

By the mid-1840s many of those in bohemian and radical literary culture were finding still more oblique ways to condone heterodox sexual attitudes. Instead, progressives tended to launch broad, if vague attacks upon the construction of 'respectable' mores. The promotion of the novels of the French writer, George Sand – who lambasted the sexual double standard and insisted on putting feelings before conventions – provided just such a platform. As one popular radical publication explained, 'She believes, and we must declare we think justly, that the codes that govern modern civilised societies as they are termed, tend more to destroy than to enlarge the naturally noble impulses of our nature. ... True delicacy cannot be shocked; though false will be outraged.'[19]

Radical discussions upon marriage and female sexuality did, by their very nature, establish the female body as a site of discussion. These debates could also spiral into other, perhaps less expected, terrains. J. H. Lawrence's celebration of free love, for example, included an endorsement of nudism [**158**]. This received some interest amongst those progressive contemporaries who wished to free women, men and children from social restraints. Similar concerns were evident in the related issue of dress reform, which also drew upon a desire to give women greater autonomy over their own bodies [**156–7**]. Although only the most radical were prepared to defy convention and to exchange the restrictive dresses of the early nineteenth century for the comfort and practicality of trousers, more modest gains might be wrought by rejecting stays (boned corsets).[20]

Within radical reforming culture there were initiatives to provide women with physiological education as part of a wider project to improve women's access to health and enhance control over their own bodies. Intermittent attempts were also made to challenge orthodox and popular medical theories concerning women's constitutional frailty. Thus, we see sporadic interventions insisting that women's physical vulnerability, as well as their disposition towards mental illness, was actually a product of their restricted environment. Consequently, some authors called for such measures as improved diet and exercise [**159–61**].[21]

A small minority urged that women might be further empowered (and their health improved), by access to birth control or at least, family limitation. (Although the methods advocated, which included a brisk walk after intercourse, were unlikely to emancipate women from the demands of biology!) [**139**, **144–7**]. This was, however, a highly controversial step. The issue of family limitation was extremely sensitive during this period. Many political radicals rejected any such moves, fearing that they formed part of a Malthusian agenda hostile to the labouring classes.[22] Those that did promote birth control were far more likely to situate their arguments within economic debates as to its implications for improved standards of living; moral objectives concerning the values of restraint, and the greater possibilities it might yield for family life and education.[23] To ally ideas of female liberation with those of family limitation was highly contentious.

Debates on marriage, sexuality and female bodies were, then, particularly rich and varied during these years. Early feminist ideas penetrated far beyond the consideration of liberal reforms to recast the very nature of sexuality and the treatment of the female body itself. Whilst some issues, for example, polygamy, nudism and 'nairism' flared and then died, other discussions, such as dress reform, divorce, the reform of the marriage laws and so on, became enmeshed into a longer, if fractured, feminist discourse.[24]

Notes

1 Martin (1850), p. 3.
2 For contrasting discussions of the implications of women's legal position and economic status see Berg (1993) and Davidoff and Hall (1987), pp. 209–13, 275–9.
3 Holcombe (1983), ch. 2.
4 See for example *The Laws Respecting Women* (1777), Clancy (1819), Barrister of the Middle Temple (1837), Macqueen (1849). Such approaches also intruded upon other considerations of marriage. Lady Augusta Hamilton's edition of the *Marriage Rites, Customs and Ceremonies of all Nations of the Universe* (1822) also provided an opportunity to protest against the restricted nature of British divorce laws (although Hamilton insisted that British women were in an otherwise favourable position) – see pp. 168, 392–3.
5 Southwell (1840), p. 16.
6 For a fine excavation of Wollstonecraft and Godwin's views and life see Tomalin (1974).
7 Godwin himself (who was, of course, Shelley's father-in-law) did become slightly more conservative on issues of sexual politics in the early nineteenth-century, nevertheless his inspiration remained critical. Both Godwin and Wollstonecraft, and Shelley and Mary Godwin did themselves marry for expediency. For full details see St. Clair (1989).
8 Gittings and Manton (1992), p. 56. See p. 125 n below.
9 *New Moral World* (22 August 1840), vol. 8, no. 8, p. 114.

10 Godwin, Owen and Shelley had met for intellectual discussions when Shelley was in his early twenties: St. Clair (1985), pp. 350–1.
11 For a good overview, see Davidoff (1990), especially p. 90.
12 Hindmarsh (1822), p. 193. See also the attitudes of William Blake, himself a Swedenborgian: Ackroyd (1995).
13 Taylor (1983), pp. 212–16.
14 Taylor (1983), pp. 148, 297, n. 88.
15 Wollstonecraft (1792), especially ch. 2.
16 A notable exception is the Fourierite phalanstery established by Mary Florimel Gliddon and Thornton Hunt (son of Leigh Hunt). See Blainey (1985), pp. 100–1, 176.
17 Taylor (1983), pp. 208–9. Some activists claimed that the present marriage system was 'better than no system', 'Love and Marriage', *Social Pioneer* (13 April 1839), p. 42.
18 In practice the interminable legal processes and enormous costs required to secure a divorce in early nineteenth-century Britain (not to mention the social stigma it occasioned) prohibited it to all but the most wealthy (and desperate).
19 *Douglas Jerrold's Weekly Newspaper* (23 January 1847), no. 28, pp. 85–6. See also Gleadle (1995), pp. 60–2.
20 Geraldine Jewsbury suggested that the wearing of stays was already going out of fashion [19]. Dress reform was a common feature of radical networks. The women at the Owenite community Manea Fen wore trousers, for example: Taylor (1983), p. 255, as did Frances Wright: Lane (1972), p. 3. Catherine Barmby was also insistent on its importance: Bellamy and Saville (1982), vol. 6, p.13.
21 See also documents **18–22**.
22 McLaren (1978), especially chs 2 and 3.
23 Francis Place, for example, maintained that the practice of birth control would lead to the 'increase of comfort, of intelligence, and of moral conduct, in the mass of the population'. Place (1822), p. 165.
24 Many of the activists who campaigned for the repeal of the Contagious Diseases Acts were in favour of dress reform: Walkowitz (1980), p. 129. For later debates on divorce and marriage reform see Bland (1995) and Shanley (1989).

6
Reforming Marriage

'I am a free human being'

The lexicon of slavery and liberty permeated dissentient perspectives on marriage.

110. We call the Greeks and easterns barbarians; and our bond-slaves – women – think they are free and the former in bondage – whereas the reverse is the case – at least in that which to women is the life of their lives – marriages I mean. In Greece and Turkey – particularly in the former – a mutual consent is sufficient cause of divorce[1] – without the degradation of pains and penalties heaped on the weaker head; - a mistake here in the way of marriage is fatal – there it is a transitory evil – easily remedied – and as we are not all gifted with forecasting minds – this is wise ...

Edward Trelawny to Claire Clairmont[2] (23 March 1836)
in Forman (1910), p. 196

111. *Charlotte Brontë's first published novel,* Jane Eyre, *rings with the language of slavery and liberation as the heroine, Jane Eyre struggles to exert her autonomy and insists on her equality with Mr. Rochester.[3] The novel was, fumed* Blackwood's Magazine, *'a wild declaration of the Rights of Woman'.[4]*

... I had wholly forgotten – the letter of my uncle, John Eyre, to Mrs. Reed: his intention to adopt me and make me his testatrix. 'It would, indeed, be a relief,' I thought, 'if I had ever so small an independency; I never can bear being dressed like a doll by Mr. Rochester, or sitting like a second Danae[5] with the golden shower falling daily round me. I will write to Madeira the moment I get home, and tell my uncle John I am going to be married, and to whom: if I had but a prospect of one day bringing Mr. Rochester an accession of fortune, I could better endure to be kept by him now.' And somewhat relieved by this idea (which I failed not to execute that day), I ventured once more to meet my master's and lover's eye; which most pertinaciously sought mine, though I averted both face and gaze. He smiled; and I thought his smile was such as a sultan might, in a blissful and fond moment, bestow on a slave his gold and gems had enriched: I crushed his hand, which was ever hunting mine, vigorously, and thrust it back to him red with the passionate pressure – 'You need not look in that way,' I said: 'if you do, I'll wear nothing but my old Lowood frocks to the end of the chapter. ...'

He chuckled; he rubbed his hands: 'Oh, it is rich to see and hear her!' he exclaimed. 'Is she [not] original? Is she piquant? I would not exchange this one little English girl for the grand Turk's whole seraglio; gazelle-eyes, houri forms and all!' The eastern allusion bit me again: 'I'll not stand you an inch in the stead of a seraglio,' I said; 'so don't consider me an equivalent for one: if you have a fancy for anything in that line, away with you, sir, to the bazar [*sic*] of Stamboul without delay; and lay out in extensive slave-purchases some of that spare cash you seem at a loss to spend satisfactorily here.'

'And what will you do, Janet, while I am bargaining for so many tons of flesh and such an assortment of black eyes?'

'I'll be preparing myself to go out as a missionary to preach liberty to them that are enslaved – your Harem inmates amongst the rest. I'll get admitted there, and I'll stir up mutiny; and you, three-tailed bashaw[6] as you are, sir, shall in a trice find yourself fettered amongst our hands: nor will I, for one, consent to cut your bonds till you have signed a charter, the most liberal that despot ever yet conferred.'

Charlotte Brontë, *Jane Eyre* (1847), pp. 240–2

112.   *Anne Brontë's* The Tenant of Wildfell Hall *has been described as 'one of the most outspoken portrayals of male oppression in the period'.[7] It described the plight of Helen Huntingdon, forced to flee from her boorish and dissolute husband.*

You might as well sell yourself to slavery at once, as marry a man you dislike. If your mother and brother are unkind to you, you may leave them, but remember you are bound to your husband for life.

Anne Brontë, *The Tenant of Wildfell Hall* (1848), p. 380

113.   *This letter indicates the problems incurred by those women who attempted to forge new independent lives free from the bonds of custom:*

Hitherto I have never suffered my actions to be shackled by the tyranny of *custom* – the consequence is, I have but *one* friend, *few* acquaintances and *no* lover – men in general prefer tameness in a woman (which they dignify, or rather *burlesque* with the name of sensibility) to the noble sentiment of *independence* – you – *you* are different . . .

Miss Lexington to William Godwin (3 November 1800)
in St. Clair (1989), p. 145

114.   *Sophia Galton, a middle-class woman from Birmingham, here illustrates the association some made between marriage and the loss of liberty.*

I am arrived at that desperate age *36*. Now you may expect to hear of my committing some desperate folly & for why? – to change those 6 letters GALTON but on the other hand I must lose others to which I am greatly attached viz LIBERTY – seven against six must carry the day.

Sophia Galton to John Howard Galton (4 March 1818), Galton
Papers, MS 306 /28,[8] Birmingham City Library

'Wives *obey* your husbands'

As the preceding passages indicate, the right of women to an independent will within their marriages was a common refrain within progressive discussions. In particular, many commentators focused upon the fact that women vowed to obey their husbands upon marriage.

115.   *This author (possibly Anne Knight[9]) steeped her analysis with biblical scholarship in lengthy footnotes.*

Is it any proof of their [men's] superiority to exult in their privileges, and to triumph over the victim of their power? Did you never observe a cat playing (as it is called) with a wounded mouse? What a despicable spirit does the cat display! Is this done lest the wife should forget who it is that possesses (not the superior mind surely) but superior privileges? Would not that king be thought a fool who thus acted with his subjects? Is there a single passage of scripture that proves the woman to be inferior in the scale of beings? The term 'weaker vessel', applying only to the body; which, probably, one part of the sentence of the fall contributed to weaken.

The wife is recommended to render submission; but is the husband anywhere authorised to consider it a *duty* to *exact* it?...

Submission from the wife ought at any rate to be voluntary, not exacted; the word *obey**, in our marriage service, ought therefore to be expunged, it being an additional effort of their own, ungenerously, binding the curse upon the wife, by a bond of their own manufacturing.

*The society called Friends impose no such word on their wives.

Desultory Queries and Remarks (1828), pp. 4, 6–7

116.   *Anna Jameson spent several months in Canada (1836–7). She used the experience to observe the country's culture and people. As contemporary reviewers were quick to note, Jameson concluded that the condition of women in modern Britain was, in many respects, inferior to those of native Canadians. 'What a dismal picture does this lady give of the condition of all women in civilized life,' lamented* Tait's Edinburgh Magazine, *'and of their sexual relations, whether legitimate or illegitimate! The condition of her Indian squaws seems enviable in the comparison'.*[10]

He [the native Canadian male] neither swears before God to love her till death – an oath which it depends not on his own will to keep, even if it be not perjury in the moment it is pronounced – nor to endow her with *all* his worldly goods and chattels, when even by the act of union she loses all right of property; but apparently the arrangements answer all purposes, to their mutual satisfaction.

Mrs Jameson, *Winter Studies and Summer Rambles* (1838),
vol. 3, pp. 241–2

117.   We agree at once that woman is bound to obey; but only when obedience does not contradict her own convictions of duty. So that evidently her obligation as a rational and responsible creature – to judge for herself – goes before her duty as a woman to obey her husband in all things not contrary to her own conscience.

Marion Reid, *A Plea for Woman* (1843), p. 67

118.   ... it is unquestionable, that nowhere can we meet with more kind-hearted, happier and more *intelligently* contented women, than among those who from different motives have *chosen* to remain single, instead of encountering the arduous task, the unceasing toil and anxiety, which attend the votaries of Hymen. ...[11]

The unmarried woman is *somebody*; the married, *nobody*! The former shines in her own light; the latter is only the faint reflection of her husband's, in whom both law and public opinion suppose her 'to be lost'. She can have no will in her half-sort of existence, is utterly without power, a mere derivative, scarcely held responsible for her own actions! ...

Woman not being permitted by our present social arrangements and conventional rules, to procure a livelihood through her own exertions, *is compelled* to unite herself with some one who can provide for her; therefore in contracting matrimony she thinks principally of this necessary requisite. I fear I annoy the vanity of man in saying this, but I cannot help it, for it is the truth. Man, on the other hand, being educated to regard woman as a something made merely for his benefit, with which he can do as he pleases, amusing himself with the toy the one moment, and neglecting it, if he chooses, the next, seeks to find in his wife, a sort of upper servant, or female valet, who is to wait upon him, attend to his wants, instinctively anticipate his wishes, and study his comfort, and who is to live for the sole purpose of seeing him well-fed, well-lodged, and well-pleased! Companionship, friendship, neither of them bargain for. As long as the female looks pretty, dresses well, and waits assiduously upon her liege lord, he is polite and attentive enough; but if from the multiplicity of her cares and petty annoyances, she smiles less frequently, and finds little time to adorn herself – except on state occasions, then the manner begins to change somewhat on the part of the once devoted admirer. ...

Nothing, however, seems at present to be known [in the marriage relationship] than the one rule of 'Wives *obey* your husbands!' no matter how silly, how absurd – nay, indeed, in many instances, how ruinous the command may be. The duty of the wife *means* the obedience of a Turkish slave, while the husband believes himself empowered to be of a like imperiousness with the follower of the turbaned prophet. It is a curious fact, that we never hear the faintest echo of that equally distinct command, 'Men, love and *honour* your wives!' ... Woman, chained and fettered, is yet expected to work miracles. Man, however, deems himself free to do as he likes; to spend his money and time as he pleases, and to scold his *patient Griselda*,[12] should she dare to remonstrate about extravagance, waste, indolence, or idleness. *Her* business is to love! suffer!! and obey!!! the three articles of woman's creed.

> Anne Richelieu Lamb, *Can Woman Regenerate Society?* (1844),
> pp. 108–9, 122–3, 124–5

The Marriage Laws

119.   *Whilst most radical writers focused upon the inequity of the married women's property laws, Lucy Aikin indicates that other aspects of the common and criminal laws were also a subject of concern.*

... born champion of my sex as I may almost call myself – I say deliberately, on good knowledge and careful consideration, that there are only two points in which it seems to me that our laws bear hard on women. The first is, in the want of a stricter hand against the inveiglers of girls for wicked purposes; the second, in the full power which the father is still allowed to retain over his children when his offences have compelled an innocent wife to obtain a divorce from him ...[13]

On carefully comparing the Code Napoleon with ours, I am convinced that we have the advantage of French women. Yet, understand me, not as admitting that we have nothing to complain of. Society wrongs us where the laws do not. ...

One of our legal exemptions signally offends me. It is that which grants impunity even for felony committed by a wife in [the] presence and under control of her husband. Has a married woman, then, no moral freedom? Must her vow of obedience include even crime? Surely this disgraceful exemption ought now, at least, to be withdrawn, when that immoral vow is no longer an essential of the marriage rite.

Lucy Aikin to W. E. Channing[14] (18 April 1838),
in Le Breton (1864), pp. 368–9

120.   *Following Enlightenment histories, many radical writers believed the modern era to privilege the power of mental reason over bodily might. Consequently the common law was described as a remnant from a former epoch, in which the superior physical strength of males was enshrined in the legislature.*

This idea was further elaborated in Lady Morgan's Woman and Her Master *– a work which attracted considerable attention. However, in common with other reviewers, Charlotte Brontë was uneasy at Morgan's apparent wish to elevate women at the expense of men.[15] As* Tait's Edinburgh Magazine, *in its review of* Woman and her Master, *explained, 'Not content with asserting the moral and intellectual equality of the sexes, the eloquent champion of woman insists upon female superiority, and goes back to Paradise for proofs of their social equality.'[16]*

If, in the first era of society, woman was the victim of man's physical superiority, she is still, in the last, the subject of laws, in the enactment

of which she has had no voice – amenable to the penalties of a code, from which she derives but little protection. While man, in his first crude attempts at jurisprudence, has surrounded the sex with restraints and disabilities, he has left its natural rights unguarded, and its liberty unacknowledged. Merging the very existence of woman in his own, he has allowed her no separate interest, assigned her no independent possessions: 'for,' says the law – the law of man – 'the husband is the head of the wife, and all that she has belongs to him.'*
Even the fruit of her own labour is torn from her, unless she is protected by the solitary blessedness of a derided but innocent celibacy, or by an infamous frailty. Thus, (to adopt the barbarous jargon of these barbarous laws,) as *femme sole*, or *femme couverte* [*sic*], she is equally the victim of violence and injustice, those universal and invariable attributes of the law of the strongest.

But there is still a more terrible outrage committed against all that is most dear to her nature; she may be deprived of the possession of her own child ... her infant may be torn from her while it is still drawing its nourishment from her breast ...

... and if, even while these lines are tracing, a scanty measure of partial and reluctant amelioration has been wrung from the legislature,[17] the exceptional fact has only been made an occasion for the sterner assertion of the outrageous principle.

*'The very being or legal existence of the woman is suspended during the marriage, or, at least, is incorporated or consolidated into that of the husband, under whose wing, protection, and cover, she performs every thing (and is therefore called, in our law-French, a feme coverte, or covert Baron, or, under the protection and influence of her husband, her Baron, or Lord; and her condition during her marriage is called her coverture).' – *Blackstone*.

Lady Morgan, *Woman and Her Master* (1840), vol. 1, pp. 11–13

121a.   ... verily she [Lady Morgan] has told the truth in her opening chapter [of *Woman and Her Master*]. You know it has long been my opinion that women were nearly as much slaves in this *soi-disant* free land of England as the blacks were in the West Indies, and that their character was accordingly debased, as must always be the case where intellectual beings are debarred from the due exercise of their faculties. If, then, when everybody else is to be emancipated, women begin to kick and rattle their chains a little, it is not very wonderful, though some good gentlemen may be as much astounded as when Oliver Twist 'asked for more'. ...

I can see no crime that women have committed which debars them from the common rights of citizenship – *i.e.*, a right over the property which comes to them by descent ...

> Caroline Cornwallis to John Platt (12 June 1840)
> in Cornwallis (1864), p. 217

121b.   I want to have the great principle established, that in a free country every one ought to have the rights of a free citizen, and that sex can never defeat those rights. The deprivation of property is a penalty, and a penalty should not be inflicted on the innocent. There might be a plea – the general good of society – for tying up property for the children of a marriage, but none whatever for giving it to the husband, for the law allows itself to be defeated every day by all sorts of settlements to prevent the husband from getting hold of the wife's property, and no unhappiness or evil to society is the consequence; but if a father is careless of his daughter's interests, and she is inexperienced, she suffers for this a penalty amounting to the loss of her whole property. Society has no right to claim a greater sacrifice from any citizen than that of so much of his liberty or property as may be conducive to the general good, and therefore to his in the long run, as one of that society; but when a law is eluded without damage, and even with an advantage, then that law should be repealed ... I want to see the laws respecting women treated on the ground of *great principles*.

> Caroline Cornwallis to David Power (17 May 1841), ibid., pp. 227–8

122.   *Alexander Walker was disdainful of what he called the 'imprudent advocates of the rights of woman';*[18] *and followed Rousseau in analysing women's potential for dominion in terms of their sexual power. Contemporary feminists dissented from his patronizing comments regarding women, but welcomed his analysis of their legal situation.*[19] *Here Walker expounds with vehemence upon women's legal oppression.*

The fate of women is, indeed, different in different countries; but in all, they are more or less slaves ... half civilized man has performed the operation which he calls legislating, for woman; and, accustomed to feel the foot of the princely or priestly despot upon his own neck, he has planted his foot upon the neck of woman. Difference of intellect is no better a reason for this than it is for the enslavement of the negro ...

The wife may, before marriage, put her fortune into trustees' hands, and so secure it for her own use, provided this be done with the consent of her intended husband; – but young women are very ignorant of points in law, and their inability to use means to guard against falsehood on their husband's part, and confidence in the man they love, prevent their employing that precaution. It has, moreover, seldom been of service to those employing it, because the husband has so entirely the disposal of the wife's person, that he can easily influence her. Hence it was a saying of an English judge, 'that he had hardly known an instance, where the wife had not been kissed or kicked out of any such previous settlement.'

Having no property, it certainly is necessary that they should be so exempted [from imprisonment in civil causes]; and it is accordingly decreed, that the husband, who possesses the wife's property, shall be answerable for her debts. But this makes no amends for the thefts described.

... the whole scheme of robbing, which has been described, is founded in base covetousness and flagrant injustice; and I submit to intended wives and still more to their parents, that the husband's infidelity should be visited in the same way in which it has been proposed to visit the wife's – that her jointure should be increased thereby, and that the wife's fortune at least should always be restored to her ...

Thus, wives in England are in all respects, as to property, person and progeny, in the condition of slaves. Thus has man made woman a slave, and himself at once a tyrant, and his slave's companion, not less degraded than she is. Exercising jealousy, surveillance and sometimes cruel severity, for errors which he hourly commits with impunity, he has had dissimulation, deceit and ridicule for his reward. There can be no other relation between tyrant and slave.

Alexander Walker, Woman Physiologically Considered (1839),
pp. 147, 153–4, 155, 160, 169

123. *In her novel* Cleone, *Mary Leman Grimstone evoked the plight of impoverished working-class women suffering from the abuse of brutal and feckless husbands. It was such arguments, rather than the abstract principle of women's rights, that was eventually to triumph in projects of legislative reform. The use of temperance arguments fits into a recurring pattern of feminine public discourse, which privileged moral reform in the project of social regeneration.*[20]

'I wish,' said Mrs. Howell, and the tears came into her eyes as she spoke, – 'I wish there was not such a thing as spirituous liquor, or intoxicating drink of any kind, in the world! ... O, that poor women had some protection from such idiot husbands – some independent

source of industry, and a security that their earnings would not be torn from them! Many a poor woman must not be industrious, because the sure consequence would be, to make her husband lazy: he could live on her exertions, and, if she refused him her earnings, abuse and ill-treat her, because he has a strong arm and savage laws on his side.'
Mary Leman Grimstone, *Cleone* (1834), vol. 1, pp. 200–1

Domestic Violence

Mary Leman Grimstone's concern with the darker shades of contemporary marriage was not unique. Many texts discoursed with passion upon the iniq-uities of domestic violence. Feminists and reformers were outraged by the widespread assumption that it was legal for a husband to beat his wife with a stick, provided it was no thicker than his thumb. Although, as Anna Clark has intimated, many women attempted legal recourse against their violent husbands, the courts were reluctant to convict the perpetrators of domestic violence. Widespread alcohol abuse in many plebeian communities appears to have exacerbated the occurrence of domestic violence in working-class neighbourhoods. However, the painful histories of individuals, such as Caroline Norton, illustrate all too plainly that male violence was prevalent in all sectors of society.[21]

124.   Were I to attempt an enumeration of the various laws which serve to harass and injure helpless woman, I should have to encounter a difficulty as far beyond my powers as my purpose; and as 'a great book is generally a great evil,' it is my wish to confine my observations within the narrowest limits of which the subject will allow. But there is one glaring instance of impolicy and cruelty to which I desire to call the public attention, in the hope of its utter abolition; I mean the power allowed to men (limited as it may be) of personally chastising their wives; a practice truly repugnant and disgusting to every well-constituted mind, and at variance also with their own professions of bravery and of protection to the weaker sex; for the poor victims are but too well aware that any attempt to retaliate is followed by a most fearful retribution, and an increase of punishment too dreadful to contemplate. It is indeed high time that the legislature interfered with its enactments to explode every vestige of a power so arbitrary and so unworthy the Christian or even the human character ... why, oh why, has the genius of reform halted in its sweeping career, without apply-ing its besom[22] of destruction to this as well as to other abuses?
A Philanthropist, *Domestic Tyranny* (1841), pp. 26–7

125. *This extract comes from one of a series of articles on domestic violence which Harriet Taylor and John Stuart Mill published in the* Morning Chronicle, *demanding legislative reform to stamp out the scourge of male domestic violence.*[23]

That there should be a slavery in civilized life, from which the most savage maltreatment, judicially proved, cannot liberate the victim would be scarcely credible, if it were not notoriously true; and such a state of things cannot, we hope, be much longer tolerated, unless existing laws are deemed more sacred than the primary ends for which all laws profess to exist.

This evil might be removed without interfering with existing institutions on any other point, or raising discussion on any more general question. All that would be requisite is a short Act of Parliament, providing that judicial conviction of gross maltreatment should free the victim from the obligation of living with the oppressor, and from all compulsory subjection to his power – leaving him under the same legal obligation as before of affording the sufferer the means of support, if the circumstances of the case require it. We earnestly recommend this subject to the attention of those philanthropists who desire to signalize themselves by an eminently useful contribution to the work of mitigating the sufferings and raising the moral condition of the poor and the dependent.

Morning Chronicle (31 May 1850), in Jacobs and
Payne (1998), p. 119

Notes

1 Edward Trelawny had himself secured a divorce from his early teenage, Greek wife in 1827. St. Clair (1977), p. 127.
2 Claire (originally Jane) Clairmont (1798–1879) was the daughter of Mary Jane Clairmont, the second wife of William Godwin. In 1814, she accompanied her stepsister Mary Shelley, on her elopement. She had a child with the poet Byron, and may also have had a physical relationship with Shelley. Clairmont appears to have held more radical views on the woman question than her stepsister. Gittings and Manton (1992); Tomalin (1982).
3 See for example, Brontë (1847), vol. 1, ch. XIV and vol. 2, ch. VIII.
4 Quoted in Rendall (1985), p. 217.
5 Danae was kept locked in a bronze tower by her father, the King of Argo. She gave birth to a son, Perseus, after Zeus descended on her in a shower of gold.
6 A Turkish pasha, or governor.
7 Blain, Clements and Grundy (1990), p. 141.

 8 The Galton family are mentioned, *passim*, in Davidoff and Hall (1987).
 9 *Desultory Queries* was published in Anne Knight's home town, Chelmsford. It was evidently written by a Quaker of considerable biblical learning. In the Anne Knight papers, at Friends' House (Temp. MSS, 725/5), Knight has used the back of a title-page from a copy of this work to jot down notes.
10 'Mrs Jameson's Winter Studies and Summer Rambles in Canada', *Tait's Edinburgh Magazine* (February 1839), vol. 6, pp. 69, 71.
11 Hymen is the god of marriage.
12 Griselda, the patient wife, endured a series of trials imposed upon her by her husband to test her devotion. She features in Petrarch's *Decameron* and Chaucer's *The Clerk's Tale*.
13 For the limited reform to this problem see documents **102–4.**
14 William Ellery Channing, an American Unitarian minister, very popular in British Unitarian circles.
15 Charlotte Brontë to W. S. Williams (? 9 November 1849) in Smith (2000), vol. 2, p. 756.
16 'Lady Morgan's "Woman and her Master"', *Tait's Edinburgh Magazine* (June 1840), vol. 7, p. 392.
17 Infant Custody Act (1839), see documents **102–4.**
18 Walker (1839), p. 68.
19 G[eorge] J[acob] H[olyoake], 'The Rights of Women', *People's Press* (May 1847), vol. 1, no. 4, p. 118.
20 For women and the temperance movement see Rendall (1985), pp. 254–6; Tyrell (1980), pp. 219–21.
21 Clark (1995), especially ch. 5. For Caroline Norton's story see Chedzoy (1992).
22 A broom made of twigs.
23 Reform did not come until 1878, when magistrates were empowered to grant 'fast track' separation orders to victims of domestic violence.

7
Divorce and Sexual Radicalism

'Nairism'

126. *James Henry Lawrence's* Empire of the Nairs *evoked the cultural and sexual mores of the Nair cast on the coast of Malabar – a matrilineal society in which women lived independently of men.*[1] *This gave Lawrence the opportunity to rehearse his own views on marriage.*

Marriage is a prison that confines both man and wife; but, as, in a jail, one prisoner may exercise over an other the functions of a turnkey, so the husband is the most favored of the two: but would they not be happy in making their escape together? Can the authority of a turnkey reconcile any prisoner to his detention? ...

Let every female live perfectly uncontrolled by any man, and enjoying every freedom, which the males only have hitherto enjoyed; let her choose and change her lover as she please, and of whatever rank he may be. At her decease, let her possessions be divided among her children. Let the inheritance of her daughters descend in like manner to their offspring; and the inheritance of her sons fall, at their decease, to their sisters, and to their sisters' children.

James Lawrence, *The Empire of the Nairs* (1811), pp. viii, xvii

127. *These themes were further developed by James Lawrence in his poetry – as in his 'Love and Marriage' in which marriage is compared to a feast at which the guests are only permitted to taste one dish; and 'On Matricide' which associated marriage with domestic violence. Lawrence was to further maintain in a later pamphlet that his views were consistent with biblical teaching.*[2] *In this extract from* Love: An Allegory, Hymen, *the god of marriage, is likened to a jailer.*

Then frequently a tender pair
Begg'd leave to visit Love in Hymen's cell.
Long as they found their old acquaintance there,
In her society they pass'd their time so well
They n'er wish'd to return, or change the air;
But Love at last contrived to break her chain,
And fled her fellow prisoners knew not where.
They wish'd not longer to remain,
When Hymen, to their great vexation,
Refused to let them out again.
In vain they seek an explanation;
In vain they cry, 'We came to visit Love:
She being gone, we have no business here.'
Hymen lent them a deaf ear,
Or gave them an uncivil shove,
Would not or could not tell the reason,
But call'd their opposition treason.
Moreover, what we never can excuse,
The jailor, sore afraid his fees to lose,
Still has the effrontery to declare
That Love remains confided to his care,
And that all folks who have the whim
To know his prisoner, must apply to him.
And now and then, whatever books may say
That men grow wiser every day,
Still he finds dupes, who in a rage
May beat their wings against their cage,
When they perceive too late that Love is flown away.

James Lawrence, *Love: An Allegory* (1802), pp. 16–17

'Even love is sold'

Lawrence's ideas were much discussed in the circle of Percy Bysshe Shelley. Shelley himself wrote to Lawrence in 1812, referring both to The Empire of the Nairs *and* Love: An Allegory *explaining his concurrence in his views.*[3] *Shelley's subversive views on marriage and gender relations emerge in a number of his works, such as* The Revolt of Islam *and* Epipsychidion.[4] *In the following footnote to his extraordinary poem,* Queen Mab, *Shelley provided the most famous elaboration of his philosophy. Always a central poet for socialist writers, radical journalists were still quoting from this extract in the late 1830s.*[5]

128. Not even the intercourse of the sexes is exempt from the despotism of positive institution. Law pretends even to govern the indisciplinable wanderings of passion, to put fetters on the clearest deductions of reason, and, by appeals to the will, to subdue the involuntary affections of our nature. Love is inevitably consequent upon the perception of loveliness. Love withers under constraint: its very essence is liberty: it is compatible neither with obedience, jealousy, nor fear: it is there most pure, perfect, and unlimited, where its votaries live in confidence, equality, and unreserve. How long then ought the sexual connection to last? what law ought to specify the extent of the grievances which should limit its duration? A husband and wife ought to continue so long united as they love each other: any law which should bind them to cohabitation for one moment after the decay of their affection, would be a most intolerable tyranny, and the most unworthy of toleration. How odious an usurpation of the right of private judgment should that law be considered, which should make the ties of friendship indissoluble, in spite of the caprices, the inconstancy, the fallibility, and capacity for improvement of the human mind ...

But if happiness be the object of morality, of all human unions and disunions; if the worthiness of every action is to be estimated by the quantity of pleasurable sensation it is calculated to produce, then the connection of the sexes is so long sacred as it contributes to the comfort of the parties, and is naturally dissolved when its evils are greater than its benefits. There is nothing immoral in this separation. Constancy has nothing virtuous in itself, independently of the pleasure it confers, and partakes of the temporizing spirit of vice in proportion as it endures tamely moral defects of magnitude in the object of its indiscreet choice. Love is free: to promise for ever to love the same woman, is not less absurd than to promise to believe the same creed ...

I conceive that, from the abolition of marriage, the fit and natural arrangement of sexual connection would result. I by no means assert that the intercourse would be promiscuous: on the contrary, it appears, from the relation of parent to child, that this union is generally of long duration, and marked above all others with generosity and self-devotion.

P. B. Shelley, *Queen Mab* (1813, 1990 reprint), pp. 144–5, 147, 151

129. *The ideas of Shelley and Lawrence were debated at length in Richard Carlile's publication, the* Lion.[6] *The following is taken from a lengthy letter* *from a Bristol reader, who complained that Lawrence's views did not consider the needs of the family, as mothers required the support of their children's fathers. (Lawrence himself was to reply to the journal, explaining that the state, rather than the father, would take on the responsibility for child maintenance.)*[7]

The voluptuary may be enamoured with his plan, as the soldier is with plunder, and its effects would be alike destructive; but to the man of honour and rectitude – to the philosopher – to the man who seeks for real happiness, it must be most abhorent [*sic*], to say little of the necessity of a wife for our domestic comforts, or the reliance we place on her fidelity and attention to our concerns, of the great share she has in the rearing and education of our children, the comforts of our home, her attention in our illness, and the happiness of our lives. I will meet your author on his greatest point, the gratification of our passions, in which I think his plan most completely deficient – the mere sexual enjoyment puts us only on an equality with our rival the goat, in which he beats us. ...

Why then are we to shun matrimony? the birds couple till their young are full grown and able to provide for themselves, and it takes the major part of a long life, before the youngest child is able to provide for itself. If a bird left the nest for a fresh mate, the consequence would be the destruction of the young, and if man to gratify his passions leaves his home, the result is the misery of all dependent on him; he must then, as a child of nature, submit to nature's laws. ... if he is that unprincipled villain to discard the woman who has placed all confidence in his vows, because he has enjoyed her, and leave the produce of his love to misery and want, he must be bound by laws; as well might we suffer the tiger to go unchained among our young, as to suffer the monster man to enjoy his passions uncontrolled. ...

That there are evils in the marriage state, I admit, and some couples so unfortunately yoked, that their lives are miserable in consequence; and I admit, that laws ought to be made in such cases, to unbind their fetters; but with all the faults of the present system, the plan of the Nairs would be a thousand times worse. ...

'A Child of Nature', *Lion* (19 December 1828),

vol. 2, no. 25, pp. 778–80

130.   *The* Newgate Monthly Magazine *was published from Newgate prison, by a group of radicals who were imprisoned for selling blasphemous works from Richard Carlile's shop. This extract is taken from one of a series* *of articles upon Peter Annet's* Social Bliss. *Annet, who was strongly influenced by John Milton, was a leading deistical writer of the eighteenth century.[8] Despite an apparent desire to emancipate women, and an innovative proposal for legally binding pre-marital agreements, in other aspects this essay splintered into male-centred discursive currents. The article began, for example, by insisting that in the case of divorce, 'all children by right should belong to the father'; it also put forward suggestions for the state regulation of prostitution.*

It is our firm conviction that separations and abandonments would be less frequent than they now are, if the liberty of divorce were easy and generally allowed. The mere dread of such an event would operate strongly to prevent it: and would to a moral certainty render more enviable the general state of matrimonial life. As it now exists, we court, we please, we win, we secure, and then – leave the object of our pursuit to pine under a state of neglect or indifference. We have made her our property, as we would a chair or a book, to be rested on or shelved according to our pleasure. We cease to view her as an intellectual being possessing every endearing and gratifying accomplishment, but as a tie, a burthen, which an imperious law has fixed upon us. – Woman! This is an unnatural state, and as inconsistent with your happiness as with our own. Proclaim yourself an equal in the race of mankind, and assist us to break the fetters which experience has shewn us to be injurious. As you understand your own interest you will render your assistance in producing the desireable, the necessary change. If you require for your countenance the authority of great and good men, call to your assistance the names of MILTON, GODWIN, SHELLEY; men who have dared to give utterance to the dictates of reason; and of your own sex, that of your right-defending Wolstencroft [*sic*]. ...

In the absence of legislative enactments, it would be wise in persons who are entering the state of matrimony to make a private agreement of separation in case circumstances should warrant such an event. This would have the same effect with them as if the law publicly acknowledged it. It would guide their conduct towards each other, and in case of disapproval neither party would have just cause to complain. Make it satisfactory to the parties uniting, and no third party would have any ground for interference. ...

There cannot be too much information thrown among the people on those subjects, by which they are individually more or less affected, and it is better to run the risk of having some bad, than losing any that is good. It is under this view more especially that we are gratified in perceiving the exertions of those political economists who are increasing the information, if not destroying some of the evils attendant on married life. ... there are but few who would not prefer the comfortable association of one woman to the disgusting association of numbers. Remove the evils which have been allowed to attend upon marriage, and the number of single persons of either sex will be greatly diminished.

W. C.,[9] 'Annet's "Social Bliss"', *Newgate Monthly Magazine*
(May 1826), vol. 2, pp. 409–11

131.   *Eliza Sharples entered into a common-law or 'moral' marriage with Richard Carlile (who was already married) in 1832. This arrangement aroused widespread censure among radical circles, but Sharples gave a spirited defence of their decision.*

There are those who reproach my marriage. They are scarcely worth a notice; but this I have to say for myself, that nothing could have been more pure in moral, more free from venality. It was not only a marriage of two bodies, but a marriage of two congenial spirits; or two minds reasoned into the same knowledge of true principles, each seeking an object on which virtuous affection might rest, and grow, and strengthen. And though we passed over a legal obstacle; it was only because it could not be removed, and was not in the spirit of a violation of the law, nor of intended offence or injury to any one. A marriage more pure and moral was never formed and continued in England. It is what marriage should be; though not perhaps altogether what marriage is in the majority of cases. They who are married equally moral, will not find fault with mine; but where marriage is merely of the law or for money, and not of the soul, there I look for abuse. My spirit was wedded to the spirit of my husband before I had spoken to him. My soul craved him on the love of good political principle, and for his endurance of its martyrdom, through many years of imprisonment. I have not yet repented. We fairly won the bequeathed flitch of bacon to a year's happy marriage. And long may it continue! We remembered that we were human, and have not fallen into the error of pledging love for life, hoping, in the absence of that pledge, to make it last the longer.

Eliza Sharples, 'Preface', *Isis* (1834), pp. v–vi

Owenism and the 'system of moral evil'

Robert Owen's Lectures on the Marriages of the Priesthood of the Old Immoral World, *delivered in 1835, were a defining moment for the Owenite movement. The lectures were lambasted by horrified commentators for their bitter attack upon conventional marriage and sexual relations. The ensuing furore raised the priority of marriage reform on the Owenite agenda. It became a common topic on the movement's lecture circuit, being guaranteed to attract wide audiences and considerable publicity. However, in doing so it may have alienated potential female supporters, who were suspicious of the overtones of male libertinism many detected within Owenite declarations.*[10]

132.   ... the present marriages of the world, under the system of moral evil in which they have been devised and are now contracted, are the sole cause of all the prostitution, of all its incalculable grievous evils, and of more than one half of all the vilest and most degrading crimes known to society. And that, until you put away from among you and your children for ever, *this accursed thing*, you will never be in a condition to become chaste or virtuous in your thoughts and feelings, or to know what real happiness is. For now almost all who are in the married state are daily and hourly practising the deepest deception, and living in the grossest prostitution of body and mind; and misery is multiplied by it beyond any of your feeble powers, in your present irrational state, to estimate; for it extends directly and indirectly through all the ramifications of life. Yes! your fathers, mothers, brothers, sisters, husbands, wives, and children, are one and all suffering most grievously from this opposition to nature; from this ignorance of your own organization; from this unnatural crime; which destroys the finest feelings and best powers of the species, by changing sincerity, kindness, affection, sympathy and pure love, into deception, envy, jealousy, hatred and revenge. It is a Satanic device of the Priesthood to place and keep mankind within their slavish superstitions, and to render them subservient to all their purposes ...

Robert Owen, Lectures on the Marriages of the Priesthood of the
Old Immoral World (1840), p. 7

The next four passages are indicative of the contrasting tone and approaches to divorce and marriage within Owenite circles.

133.   *Adorable Sisters!* – Permit a brother, who worships you above all Gods, real or imaginary, in earth or in heaven, to address *you* – the sacred, omnipotent, and love-inspiring source of our existence, and primary cause of all that is good, useful, and beautiful upon earth …

I will now introduce you to that degrading mark of your subjugation, the Ring; which will remind you of those soul-chilling promises, 'honour and obey'. It would appear, from the innumerable atrocities perpetrated in consequence of the priest-coin'd establishment of matrimony, – from the murder of wives by their husbands, and husbands by their wives; wives, husbands, and lovers, destroying themselves and each other … the degrading prostitutions, high and low; the intrigues, the dissimulations, the frauds, the falsehoods, together with the secret and deadly plottings, attendant upon the violation of the immutable law of nature, in furtherance of the cruel law of custom called marriage, – from these circumstances, we may infer that the male is not more happy in his usurpation than the female is in her chains. …

Let it not be supposed that my objections are confined to the *legal ceremony*; I war with the entire system, because it cannot be denied that human nature is ever varying in its likes and dislikes – that the affection of to-day may be the antipathy of to-morrow; and that the feelings of every individual are moved by circumstances over which they have no control – therefore every male and female should be independent each of the other; as it is absolute insanity to declare unceasing affection for another, seeing that the individual has no power over the reception or rejection of ulterior impressions.

'Moral Marriage and Priestly Marriage: 'Agrarius' [George Petrie] to
the Female Portion of the Family of Mankind', *The Man* (September
1833), vol. 1, no. 13, pp. 97–8

134.   In a rational state of society, the necessity which ignorance creates for an artificial law like that of marriage, will be superseded. Woman will be brought upon an equality with man; she will be placed aloof from the fear of want and poverty. … The laws of the community will be formed on a pure and rational basis, so as to afford to all, without distinction or exception, equal protection, privileges, and immunities; so that you see the advantages being reciprocal, what inducement can there be for one individual to wrong another? and what interest can a man have in deceiving a woman whose happiness is associated with his own? My friends, the fatal and fundamental error on which [the] old society has been built (and which will ultimately subvert the whole fabric,) has been the means of bringing into hostile collision an infinite variety of human interests, and the consequence is, that envy, hatred and malice, strife, contention and eternal warfare reign throughout the land. That this has likewise been the fruitful source of all the calamities that have befallen the female sex, will, I think be readily admitted; for, owing to the general thirst for the acquisition of money, woman has been made a mere commodity of trade, and the fountain of love has either been choked, or its course directed into the channel of worldly ambition. But in community, money will not be known, neither will the want of it be dreaded, for all that can minister to the comforts of life will be had in abundance; there will, therefore, be no need of this 'deadly foe to human weal'. If two individuals entertain an affection for each other, there will be no necessity to conceal those pleasing emotions which draw them naturally together, as there will be no distinction in rank, so there will be neither condescension on the one side nor obligation on the other, which ever has, and ever will, constitute a serious drawback on the conjugal felicity of the old immoral world. We shall hear of no heart-rending seductions, abductions, elopements, crim cons[11], &c. which stain the annals of the marriage system, as by christian law established; neither shall we hear of those unhappy instances of inconstancy, which cause so much family disturbance among all classes of society. There will be no marrying for convenience merely (a very cold word), but real affection will be inspired by real and known worth on both sides.

Frances Morrison, *The Influence of the Present Marriage System* (1838), pp. 10–11

135.   *Charles Southwell here addresses the Bishop of Exeter, who had exco-riated the Owenites for their views on marriage and divorce.*

Mr Owen has done nothing more than endeavour to apply for the benefit of mankind the doctrines advocated by – Helvetius, Hume, Pope, Shelley, Milton, Bolingbroke, Montesquieu, Dryden and other[s]....[12] in fact, Mr. Owen has not proposed the abolition of marriage, but simply an alteration in the law of divorce, but you or your party cannot or will not see this, and thus day after day are denouncing that which has no existence save in your own imaginations...

Charles Southwell, *An Essay on Marriage* (1840), p. 2

136.   *Joanna Southcott's teachings defy simple categorization, and she was certainly more interested in spiritual affairs than tackling temporal abuses.[13] However, as this extract illustrates, notions of a female messiah* *blurred into other progressive movements, often on the fringes of Owenism. Consequently, worldly reform was often promoted in her name.*[14]

She [Joanna Southcott] plainly declared herself the Bride – the Woman of the Gentile Church; but she also said, she was only the herald of another that would succeed her; and still there are many laying claim to this title, and predicting great things of themselves. Believers in modern prophecy differ in their opinions of this free woman who is coming, according to the different degrees of knowledge and liberality which they possess, and the number of prophecies they acknowledge; but many say that she will put an end to marriage, and introduce an entirely new era in the social and domestic system; others, that she will perfect love and marriage, which is the same thing; for what is love, but the marriage of nature? Thus you see how fanaticism – ultra-fanaticism, which is despised by the learned and the wise, is just at the very verge of an union with ultra-liberalism ...

'Mr. Smith's [James Elishama Smith] lecture on Education,
Charlotte St. Institution', Crisis (31 August 1833),
vol. 2, no. 35, p. 276

'To make woman what she ought to be': radical unitarians and the divorce debate

Despite the considerable overlap in Owenite and radical unitarian debates on divorce, within Owenite discourse, divorce was more commonly situated within broader schemes for a reform in the sexual relations of society. In radical unitarian arguments, divorce was more likely to be suggested within the context of married women's poor legal status, and related to specific proposals to reform women's position.[15]

137.   To make woman what she ought to be, and might be, marriage should be rendered a civil contract, capable of being dissolved like any other contract ... Let me not be misunderstood. I am no advocate of light love, or changing affections. I believe that constancy between the sexes is more productive of human happiness than any other condition, and it is only because I would ensure, as far as possible, that constancy, that I would wish to sever the unnatural unions whose only result is misery, both to parents and offspring.

[William Bridges Adams], Junius Redivivus, 'On the Condition of
Women in England', Monthly Repository (1833), vol. 7, pp. 228–9

The following two extracts are taken from the private essays which John Stuart Mill and Harriet Taylor wrote for one another.

138. ... it is absurd to talk of equality while marriage is an indissoluble tie. ... The husband can ill-use his wife, neglect her, and seek other women, not perhaps altogether with impunity, but what are the penalties which opinion imposes on him compared with those which fall upon the wife who even with that provocation retaliates upon her husband? It is true perhaps that if divorce were permitted, opinion would with like injustice, try the wife who resorted to that remedy by a harder measure than the husband. But this would be of less consequence: Once separated she would be comparatively independent of opinion: but so long as she is forcibly united to one of those who *make* the opinion, she must to a great extent be its slave.

J. S. Mill, 'Essay' (1832), in Rossi (1970), pp. 83–4

139. At this present time, in this state of civilization, what evil could be caused by, first placing women on the most entire equality with men, as to all rights and privileges, civil and political, and then doing away with all laws whatever relating to marriage? Then if a woman had children she must take charge of them, women could not then have children without considering how to maintain them. ... All the difficulties about divorce seem to be in the consideration for the children – but on this plan it would be the women's *interest* not to have children – now it is thought to be the woman's interest to have children as so many ties to the man who feeds her.[16]

Harriet Taylor, 'Essay' (1832), in Rossi (1970), p. 86

140. In no country, I believe, are the marriage laws so iniquitous as in England, and the conjugal relation, in consequence, so impaired. Whatever may be thought of the principles which are to enter into laws of divorce, whether it be held that pleas for divorce should be one, (as narrow interpreters of the New Testament would have it;) or two, (as the law of England has it;) or several, (as the Continental and United States' laws in many instances allow,) nobody, I believe, defends the arrangement by which, in England, divorce is obtainable only by the very rich. The barbarism of granting that as a privilege to the extremely wealthy, to which money bears no relation whatever, and in which all married persons whatever have an equal interest, needs no exposure beyond the mere statement of the fact. It will be seen at a glance how such an arrangement tends to vitiate marriage:

how it offers impunity to adventurers, and encouragement to every
kind of mercenary marriages [*sic*]; how absolute is its oppression of the
injured party: and how, by vitiating marriage, it originates and aggra-
vates licentiousness to an incalculable extent. ...

It is clear that the sole business which legislation has with marriage
is with the arrangement of property; to guard the reciprocal rights of
the children of the marriage and the community. There is no further
pretence for the interference of the law, in any way. An advance
towards the recognition of the true principle of legislative interference
in marriage has been made in England, in the new law in which the
agreement of marriage is made a civil contract, leaving the religious
obligation to the conscience and taste of the parties. It will be probably next perceived that if the civil obligation is fulfilled, if the children
of the marriage are legally and satisfactorily provided for by the
parties, without the assistance of the legislature, the legislature has, in
principle, nothing more to do with the matter.

Harriet Martineau, *Society in America* (1837), vol. 3, pp. 123–5

Notes

1   The work was originally published in German, in 1800; it was then rewrit-
ten in French and finally published in England in 1811. See also document
158. The Nairs evoked considerable interest in progressive circles, Godwin
went to visit a 'Nair man' in London in 1819: St. Clair (1989), p. 422.

2   Lawrence (1828), pp. 171–86; Laurence [*sic*] (1833).

3   P. B. Shelley to J. H. Lawrence (17 August 1812) in Ingpen (1926), vol. 9,
pp. 17–18. The letter was later reprinted in the *Lion* (28 November 1828),
vol. 2, no. 23, pp. 717–18.

4   For excellent contextualization of Shelley's thought and life see St. Clair
(1989) and Tomalin (1982).

5   See for example, *National* (1839), p. 132.

6   See for example the *Lion* (21 November 1828), vol. 2, no. 21, pp. 653–72;
and (13 March 1829), vol. 3, no. 11, pp. 346–9.

7   The *Lion* (16 January 1829), vol. 3, no. 3, pp. 84–89; see also Carlile's own
intervention into the debate: the *Lion* (19 December 1828), vol. 2, no. 25,
pp. 780–1.

8   For further discussions of Annet's ideas see *Newgate Monthly Magazine*
(February 1826), vol. 2, pp. 270–9; (March 1826),vol. 2, pp. 301–14; (April
1826), vol. 2, pp. 344–50.

9   The author was probably William Campion – one of the editors of the
magazine.

10   Taylor (1983), pp. 183–92.

11   Criminal conversation – a legal action in which a husband could claim
damages against a man who had committed adultery with his wife.

12   Claude Adrien Helvétius (1715–71), French philosopher; David Hume

(1711–76), philosopher and historian; Alexander Pope (1688–1744), poet; Percy Bysshe Shelley (1792–1822); John Milton (1608–74), poet, parliamentarian during the English Civil War; Lord Bolingbroke (1678–1751), Tory politician; Baron de Montesquieu (1689–1755), influential French philosopher; John Dryden (1631–1700), poet and playwright. Whilst all these writers mention divorce in their work (particularly with regard to anthropological contexts, or philosophical insights), they were not necessarily champions of it. Milton probably has the best claim for being considered as a staunch advocate of the measure. See Hill (1977), pp. 119, 123–4.

13 See also documents **48a** and **48b**.

14 This was particularly true of Zion Ward, who proclaimed sexual libertarianism and a whole-scale reorganization of society in Southcott's name: Taylor (1983), p. 166.

15 In practice, many of the leading couples in radical unitarian milieux, such as W. J. Fox and Eliza Flower, Thomas Southwood Smith and Margaret Gillies, and John Stuart Mill and Harriet Taylor were personally affected by the strict divorce laws. See Gleadle (1995), p. 112.

16 See also document **80**.

8
Female Sexuality and the Female Body

'What is adultery?'

Behind the radicals' calls for the right to divorce, lay the assumption that women, as well as men, may feel sexual love and attraction for men other than their husbands. Many radical works sought to normalize a view of female sexual love.

141.   *T. Bell's work contained detailed anatomical explanations of sexual organs and intercourse. An advocate for liberalization of the divorce laws, he insisted on the need for variety in sexual pleasure, especially for men, but also suggested that sexual love was essential to women's health:*

Considering, then, sexual pleasure, without any reference to moral and political consequences, it is ridiculous to assert, that there is any more crime in two persons of opposite sex mixing together two drops of albumen in the sexual embrace, than there would be in their mixing together two drops of saliva by spitting on the same spot of the ground, or in their smelling a bouquet composed of more than one species of flower.

... in modern times, and in our own country, there are innumerable instances in which men and women have indulged in temporary and evanescent loves, without ever having seriously neglected their wives, husbands or families. There are few men, indeed, and far fewer women than is commonly imagined, who have not indulged irregular pleasures; and, if the number of abandoned, ruined or neglected families were as great as the number of husbands or wives who have sinned in this respect, this sin would undoubtedly be the most extensive, and this calamity the heaviest, that England ever had to endure.

T. Bell,[1] *Kalogynomia* (1821), pp. 277, 289

142.   For a woman's having loved another man besides her husband does not unhumanize her; it does not make her a wild beast, to be beaten, and pelted, and hunted, and mangled.

> [W. J. Fox], 'Politics of the Common Pleas', *Monthly Repository*
> (1836), vol. 10, p. 397

143.   *When W. J. Linton learnt that the prominent French socialist, Pierre Leroux had proposed that convicted adulterers should be ineligible as members of the French legislative assembly he was outraged. Much of his response, as indicated here, went beyond these specific political circumstances, to contest the very meaning of adultery.*

What is adultery? If a woman has the right to possess her own person, if she ought to be sovereign of herself, in virtue of her independent nature, her distinct individuality, who shall gainsay her liberty of connecting herself with whom she pleases, when and where she will? She may be careless of her own person, and go lightly esteemed; but her right remains unquestionable. Her wantonness is an offence against herself principally, also against good manners, in neither case cognisable or corrigible by statute.

> W. J. Linton, 'Adulterers Ineligible: On the Motion of Pierre
> Leroux', *The Reasoner* (1849), vol. 6, no. 146, p. 167

Birth control

To advocate birth control did not necessarily imply sympathy with radical views on women. Nevertheless, many evidently considered its far-reaching implications for women's health and happiness.

144.   *In this touching letter, Mary Shelley hints to her friend Marianne Hunt (the wife of Leigh Hunt, the radical essayist and poet) that they have produced too many children, too quickly, with consequent ill-effects for both Marianne and her offspring.*

before I leave the subject of your *cares* my dear, let me advert to your *health* – Bessy says in her letter that Percy from a sickly infant is grown a fine stout boy – he appears to have been in the same case as Swinburne & I am afraid from the same cause – I could say a great many things to prove to you that a woman is not a field to be continually employed either in bringing forth or enlarging grain – but I say only, take care of yourself …[2]

> Mary Wollstonecraft Shelley to Marianne Hunt (24 March 1820),
> in Bennett (1980), vol. 1, p. 136

145.   *Robert Dale Owen's* Moral Physiology *was well received in publications such as W. J. Linton's journal, the* National. *(The* National *was highly critical of British doctors who withheld contraceptive information, and fumed that to force a woman to have children against her will was akin to murder[3]).*

She it is who bears the burden, and therefore with her also should the decision rest. Surely, it may well be a question whether it be desirable, or whether any man ought to ask, that the whole life of an intellectual, cultivated woman, should be spent in bearing a family of twelve or fifteen children, to the ruin, perhaps, of her constitution.

Robert Dale Owen, Moral Physiology (1831), p. 31

146.   *Richard Carlile's* Every Woman's Book *contained explicit contraceptive information, recommending in particular the use of a damp sponge. It was based upon an essay, 'What is Love', which first appeared in the* Republican. *The book was printed with a striking cover portraying a naked Adam and Eve, designed to represent nature and truth. It was partly financed by Godfrey Higgins, a wealthy gentleman from the West Riding, who in common with other correspondents to Carlile's paper, situated their support for birth control within a broader agenda of reform to women's position. It aroused considerable controversy in the working-class press.[4]*

... it is a barbarous custom, that forbids the maid to make an advance in love, or that confines that advance to the eye, the fingers, the gesture, the motion, the manner. It is ridiculous. Why should not the female state her passion to the male, as well as the male to the female? What impropriety can there be in it? What bad effect can it produce? Is it immodest? Why is it immodest? Is it not virtuous? Why is it not virtuous? Equality and the right to make advances in all the affairs of genuine love are claimable for the female. The hypocrisy, the cruelty that would stifle or disguise a passion, whether in the male or female, is wicked and proper to be detested. Young women! Assume an equality, plead your passion when you feel it and to those to whom it may apply.

Richard Carlile, Every Woman's Book (1826) reprinted in Bush
(1998), pp. 83–4

147.   Had much interesting conversation with Mrs. H[ennell] on a great variety of topics. She thinks that before we can make any great moral progress there must be some restraint on the number of children born, which I think impossible absurd and unnecessary. She thinks our sexual relations are very conventional, and that though pure monogamy is the ideal, it will only be reached thro' a previous age of general licence! I don't agree with her that such a mud bath is at all necessary.

Entry from John Chapman's[5] diary (26 June 1851),
in Haight (1969), p. 184

'Chaste as the icicle'

Throughout heterodox discussions on sexuality, ideas concerning the social and personal virtues of chastity remained a provocative skein of thought.

148. It is against the rude gusts and storms of passion we have to guard, which, when rising to a hurricane, wreck even the soul, and engulph it in a dreadful abyss. In the divine faculty of reason only, an efficient power can be found to oppose their violence and impetuosity …

Miss S. Hatfield, *Letters on the Importance of the Female Sex* (1803),
p. 56

149. Cleone was 'chaste as the icicle on Dian[a]'s temple'[6]; from no sickly factitious rule of convention – from no principle of specious propriety, which social usage substitutes for the principle of truth – but *from the perfection of her reason.*

Mary Leman Grimstone, *Cleone* (1834), vol. 2, p. 79

150. Let no woman call that man her friend, who has one rule of morality for her, and another for himself. The longer she tolerates such a false and pernicious system, the longer unquestionably does she retard the progress of the whole race. Why should the vicious among men be deemed fit companions, while the vicious among women are shunned with a more than pious horror? as if an angel had become a demon, instead of a weak ignorant human being having committed precisely the same fault, and walked in the same path as those whom she is perpetually told are her superiors in wisdom and knowledge …

Anne Richelieu Lamb, *Can Woman Regenerate Society?* (1844), p. 42

151. *Whilst socialist feminists were usually hostile to the bastardy clause of the Poor Law Amendment Act (1834),[7] which (until its repeal ten years later) made illegitimate children the sole responsibility of their mothers, in*

this passage Anna Jameson praises it for restoring responsibility to women
for their own actions.

You remember the outcry which was raised against that provision of
the new poor law act, which made women solely answerable for the
consequences of their own misconduct – misconduct, into which, in
nine cases out of ten, they are betrayed by the conventional license
granted to the other sex; but I, as a woman, with a heart full of most
compassionate tenderness for the wretched and the erring among my
sister women, do still aver that the first step towards our moral emancipation is that law which shall leave us the sole responsible guardians
of our own honour and chastity; it may seem at first view most pitiable
that not only the ban of society, but also the legal liabilities, should
fall on the least guilty; and hard indeed will be the fate of many a poor,
ignorant delinquent, for the next few years, unless those women who
take a generous and extended view of the whole question, be prepared
to soften the horrors that will ensue by individual help and acts of
mercy; but let the tendency of such an enactment, such a public
acknowledgment of the moral and legal responsibility of women, be
once understood, let it once be brought into action, and I am sure the
result will be the general benefit and elevation of the whole sex; it
brings the only remedy to this hateful mischief which can be brought;
the rest remains with ourselves. The best boon we could ask of our
masters and legislators is, to be left in all cases responsible for our own
actions and our own debts.

Mrs Jameson, *Winter Studies and Summer Rambles* (1838),
vol. 1, pp. 155–6

152.   *Manea Fen (whose publication the* Working Bee, *is quoted here),*
was an Owenite community which occasioned much scandal because of
what was commonly thought to be the practice of 'free love' doctrines.[8]

The union of the sexes will necessarily assume a different character
upon the full establishment of Communities ...

Intercourse will only take place when there is affection, and can only
be chaste under such circumstances. It is a false, and unnatural, idea,
that the union of two parties to each other, without outward infidelity, but without affection, is a moral union: it is both unchaste and
immoral. Real chastity and real virtue will consist in intercourse, with
affection as the basis of the union.

This idea of sexual union, it will be seen, is at variance with polygamy, promiscuous intercourse, and prostitution, and can only be realized in a state of society such as we have alluded to, where due provision will be made for the offspring, where equality of condition will exist, and where truth and sincerity will govern the conduct of all.

'Marriage and Divorce', *Working Bee* (31 October 1840), vol. 1, no. 22, p. 169

153. *John Stores Smith expressed clearly the unease many felt at the glorification of female sexuality. Charlotte Brontë wrote approvingly to Smith of his work, believing his views expressed a particular rectitude.*[9]

There have been no lack of female souls who have seen into this injustice [the sexual double standard], and who, in their books and in their lives, have flung up an indignant protest against it. Latterly they have multiplied, and with George Sand for their Penthesilea,[10] are, in all manner of shapes, denouncing the iniquitous treatment of woman. But, alas! all who have yet spoken seek to right woman at the cost of social purity, at the expense of the nobility of the human family. ... They seek, in a word, for woman the licence man at present claims and takes.

John Stores Smith, *Social Aspects* (1850), p. 106

154. *For radicals influenced by transcendentalism and the work of Margaret Fuller, chastity formed part of a wider ideological framework which sought to elevate marriage to a peculiar spiritual and symbolic significance.*

Freedom, peace, salvation, cannot be expected for woman while she permits herself to be the instrument of man's lowest gratifications, and tolerates a degree of unchastity in him, which in her he would utterly condemn. It is for woman to bar the door against licentiousness, and thereby both herself and man will cease to be its victims. Self denial is the only hopeful means for any improvement, whether moral or physiological, and woman must not expect so great a work as her salvation to be wrought by any easier process.

C[harles] L[ane], 'A Chaste and Honourable Book' [M. Fuller's *Woman in the Nineteenth Century*], *Herald of Freedom* (5 September 1845), in Fuller (1998), p. 229

155. *For Charles Lane and his associates, only couples who obeyed the dictates of the 'love law', that is, who were pure in body, soul and spirit could hope to fulfil the divine possibilities of human union.*[11] *For J. P.*

Greaves, their mentor, this also meant that women should be empowered to decide when physical intercourse might take place. Adherents to these circles believed that limiting sexual intercourse to but one act every two or three years would also produce healthier children.

The man and the woman ought to be betrothed, and live together until the prothetical union is consolidated, as well as the metaphysical; and at a given state, when the woman demands it, not the man, the physical marriage should take place.

J. P. Greaves to Alexander Campbell[12] (23 February 1840),
in Campbell (1843), vol. 1, p. 32.

'Knowledge is power'

156.   *Many radicals believed it essential to empower women to have greater control over their own bodies. Thomas Jefferson Hogg, a close friend of P. B. Shelley, gave the following account of a feminist lecture, on the evils of stays, that he attended in the early years of the century. Normally female-only events, the bemused Hogg was permitted to attend as the organizer (whose drawing room had been fitted up as lecture hall) believed him to be sympathetic to their views.*

She addressed herself first to the casts, and, laying her hands upon them, expounded at length [on] what may be called the upper works of woman. She then directed our attention to the deceased rabbit, pointing to different portions of the lungs, and explaining, or attempting to explain, the whole economy of respiration. She proved likewise, exceedingly well, that stays on the body of a rabbit would interfere with and impede its movements, and would be inconvenient and uncomfortable. Bundles of stays of different kinds were handed to her; these she successively applied to the plaster-casts, and demonstrated how grievously they offended against every principle of anatomical science; launching forth into an animated invective against busks, which, whether they were of wood, of whalebone, or of steel, found no quarter. She then exhibited pictures of crooked shoulders, distorted spines, contracted chests, and manifold deformities, painful to behold. She assured us, that all these calamities, and many others, were occasioned solely by the pernicious pressure of stays.

Thomas Jefferson Hogg, *The Life of Shelley* (1858; 1906 edn), p. 437

157.   *The young Barbara Leigh Smith was strongly influenced, as were* *many in her networks, by the ideas of George Combe. Combe, a leading phrenologist, expounded a philosophy of moral and physical well-being which depended upon following certain natural laws. Health reform advocates drew heavily upon his work and ideas.*[13]

Beautiful and appropriate dress is a charming thing for the eye to behold; the body is the temple of the soul, and should be well cared for; such care procures us the respect of others and ourselves; but when a false standard, injurious to health, prevails – when those vilest of torture-engines, *stays*, are worn, and it is thought elegant to diminish the graceful and *ample* waist of nature – when the heart, liver, and lungs are compressed into half their natural space – when the beautiful foot is cramped into disease, and the delicate person exposed where it should be wrapped in flannel; then the dress is not *lovely*; the standard is that of our petty nineteenth century, not that of an artist – and conformity is absurd as well as *wrong*.

Knowledge is power: medical science gives us the mastery of ourselves; teaches us the will of God and the conditions of our healthy, happy existence. ... Many of these things it is deemed improper for a woman to study; they are to be the passive instruments of serious duty, not the intelligent performers thereof. ...

Why should we sacrifice our freedom and our birthright, as heirs of Christian liberty, for the whims of a society composed of an aggregate of individuals whom, taken singly, we perhaps despise? Let us be sufficiently free to judge by our *own* standard of right in these matters; and life, redeemed from idleness and ill health, and given to the performance of duty and the enjoyment of innocent pleasures, will become deeper and more beautiful every day.

[Barbara Leigh Smith], Esculapius,[14] 'Conformity to Custom',
Hastings and St. Leonards News (7 July 1848), p. 4.

158.   *James Lawrence went so as far as to offer a defence of female nudism, suggesting that this would give women a sense of ownership over their own bodies. Nudism was practised by some of the more extreme radicals in Shelley's circle, such as the de Boinvilles, as well as a tiny and eclectic mixture of other progressives.*[15] *In this passage from Lawrence's tale of life among the Nairs on the Malabar coast, the Countess of Raldabar explains to the chief protagonist, Walter De Grey, that their elderly leader, Samorina, will appear naked before her people, in an annual ceremony. This is to commemorate the actions of Samora, the founder of their empire, who quelled a rebellion, by remonstrating with the dissidents straight from her bath!*

The singularity of this institution, so contrary to your European ideas, may strike you; but accuse not that great woman of a puerile vanity, desirous to perpetuate the memory of her own intrepidity. No, her motives proceeded from a nobler source; she saw the state of slavery in which the neighboring nations held their women, whom they obliged to veil themselves from head to foot, and whose bodies they considered private property, which they were entitled to conceal as a miser would hide his treasures. Samora saw that a false modesty was the first pretext toward the humiliation of her sex, and being herself revered as a prophetess, she wisely confirmed their liberties by the authority of religion, and cut at once at the root of the evil, by ordering the first woman in the empire to appear naked before the eyes of the whole nation.

James Lawrence, *Empire of the Nairs* (1811), vol. 1, p. 101

159.   *Female midwives and physicians were frequently to be found in the radical subculture of the day.*[16] *Many, as this advertisement for the Owenite Emma Martin, indicates, were insistent upon the need to enlighten women as to the workings of their own bodies.*

LECTURES ON THE PHYSIOLOGY OF WOMAN
Delivered (to Females only) by Mrs. Martin, Accoucheur. . . .
In the general onward march of intelligence, Women have longed to understand something of the laws of their own nature – to become acquainted with the interesting mysteries of the source of life, and to be able to judge of the causes of health and disease in themselves and offspring. Their modesty revolts from obtaining this knowledge from the other sex, and, until lately, it was in vain to seek it from their own. Thus a natural and becoming delicacy, while it is one of the best preservatives of morals, has unfortunately been a cause of considerable suffering.

This most important knowledge may now be obtained from one of their own sex, in a series of familiar conversational lectures, accompanied by such illustrations as may completely inform the mind respecting the maternal functions, conditions, and duties, and many are gladly availing themselves of so great an advantage.

The Reasoner (17 June 1846), vol. 1, no. 3, p. 48

160.   *Thomas Beddoes was a trenchant critic of boarding-school culture. He blamed the poor diets and the lack of encouragement given to physical exercise in these institutions for the prevalence of mental health problems in women later in life.*

The greater part of the movements of girls at boarding schools, no one, who has any regard to propriety of language, will characterize by the name *exercise*: and if we reckon upon them as such, we shall grossly impose upon ourselves. The hours, allotted for parading two or three abreast, must be deducted from the account of time, set apart for health. ... in the tolerably robust, to pace in solemn procession along the sides of a square, or through a public walk, would be a very hopeless expedient for exciting that chearfulness [*sic*] and glow, which can be the only rational purpose in sending young people abroad. – Playgrounds are usually too confined to allow of interesting amusements; and the majority of girls, with whom I have conversed, preferred staying within doors during the free hours.

Thomas Beddoes, *Hygëia*[17] (1802), vol. 1, Essay 3, pp. 42–3

161.   *Benjamin Parsons's 1842 work provided one of the most substantial defences of women's intellectual equality to be published in this period. Although he adhered to particularist gender notions, believing women to be 'instinctively kind' [45], the book was, as he later admitted, regarded as 'utopian' by some. It nevertheless received extremely favourable reviews in both the radical and nonconformist press.*[18]

... girls are supposed to need less exercise than boys, and therefore are early doomed to confinement. But no reason can be assigned for this difference of training. The lungs and the circulation in both sexes have the same offices to perform, and therefore exercise in the open air is just as requisite for females as for males. Talk of women having originally inferior minds! before we come to any conclusion on this head, we ought to inquire whether proper means have been used to give them healthy physical frames; for if we weaken the body by improper treatment, we must of necessity, injure the intellect. Were the soul of an archangel penned up in the body of a modern tight-laced, dyspeptic, hysterical, boarding school lady, it would struggle in vain to exercise its seraphic powers. Before we taunt women with being weaker in intellect than men, we must inquire whether or not they have had their physical energies duly cultivated; and as fact demonstrates that this is never the case in our country, we have a sufficient reason for any supposed mental inferiority. Bad as the physical education of males is, we know that that of females is in every particular a great deal worse, and therefore we have used all the likeliest methods to fetter the mind and enfeeble its moral powers.

Rev. Benjamin Parsons, *The Mental and Moral Dignity of Woman*
(1842), pp. 112–13

Notes

1   According to M. L. Bush, the author was probably Alexander Walker: Bush (1998), p. 35.
2   'Bessy' was Elizabeth Kent, Marianne Hunt's sister. Percy, the Hunts' son, born in 1816, was named after Shelley; his brother, Swinburne, born a year later, died in 1827.
3   *National* (1839), p. 365.
4   It was based upon an essay, 'What is Love', which first appeared in *The Republican*. These details are taken from the superb Bush (1998).
5   John Chapman (1821–94) a progressive book-seller and publisher, and editor of the *Westminster Review* from 1851–94. His mistress, Elisabeth Tilley lived in his household with his family. He was attracted to both George Eliot and the young Barbara Leigh Smith. Haight (1954), vol. 1, pp. lix–lxi. For Hennell, see the Biographical Notes, below.
6   Diana, the goddess of nature, was a virgin.
7   For example, in the *Pioneer* (28 June 1834), no. 43, p. 423.
8   See Taylor (1983), pp. 253–8 for the story of Manea Fen.
9   Charlotte Brontë to J. Stores Smith (25 July 1850), Smith (2000), vol. 2, p. 429.
10   Penthesilea was a young queen of the Amazons during the Trojan War.
11   See for example Wright (1840), p. 3.
12   Alexander Campbell (1796–1870) was a leading Scottish Owenite, trades unionist and founding editor of the *Spirit of the Age*. He came under the influence of J. P. Greaves in the late 1830s and spent some time at Greaves's community, the First Concordium. His distinctive contribution to the Scottish cooperative movement was to insist upon the importance of female participation. Fraser (1996).
13   See Cooter (1984); Combe (1828) Hirsch (1998), pp. 34, 36–7.
14   Aesculapius: the Roman god of healing and medicine.
15   Ackroyd (1995), p. 154; Harrison (1979), p. 18; for the de Boinvilles see St. Clair (1989), pp. 263 ff.
16   Gleadle (2002).
17   Hygëia: the Greek goddess of health.
18   Parsons (1845), pp. 21, 48–9.

Part IV

Political Rights and Public Power

Though the *rule of the sex* you so amply pourtray
O'er the milder dominion of life:
We had rather, believe me, our characters play
In the national drama of strife.[1]

Introduction

Women's access to public political activity, and their appropriation of the language of rights, is often conceptualized as intrinsic to the whole feminist project. However, not all feminists of the early nineteenth century would have agreed. For example, those influenced by socialist theories were sceptical that the assignation of political rights was any guarantee of wider cultural gains for women [36].[2] Furthermore, we should be wary of assuming that female political rights were somehow the crowning glory of a feminist agenda. Contemporary positions were far more muddied. Arguments for women's suffrage could, for example, be coolly dissevered from calls for female employment, autonomy within marriage, or even a belief in the equal intellectual capacities of the sexes [173–4]. Female political rights should not, then, be seen as the ultimate 'test' of a feminist identity. Furthermore, even those who positioned themselves as radicals on the woman question could have complex, nuanced views of female suffrage. Emma Martin, the Owenite lecturer, for example, intimated that women should be the recipients of better education before they were enfranchised.[3] Samuel Smiles announced that it was ridiculous to claim that women were politically represented given their legal oppression, and urged for a rational inquiry into the constitution – but he did not give an open endorsement to female suffrage.[4] Moreover, as in the later period, strategic and political arguments also raged as to whether the suffrage should be extended to all women, or confined to spinsters and widows. [5]

Equally, it would be wrong to assume that the suffrage was necessarily perceived as the insuperable barrier to women's right to engagement with the political nation. As many of the contributors in this section note, the concept of female suffrage was already diffused throughout the polity. As shareholders of the East India Company women had influence over imperial policy; they could exercise economic muscle as shareholders of the Bank of England; and in many areas of local government they were, it was suggested, permitted to vote [**169, 174, 181, 185–6, 191**].[6] Furthermore, in a move prescient of later suffrage campaigners,[7] historical narratives were constructed of women's ability to vote in Anglo-Saxon England [**164, 166b**]. (Such arguments negate the views of historians of radical politics, who have assumed that the constitutionalist idiom made it difficult for women to stake a claim for political representation.[8]) Hence many polemicists were arguing not that a revolutionary insight be granted – of women's right to vote – but rather that rights women already held (or had held) might be merely extended.

If women's existing political rights gave discursive legitimacy to calls for the parliamentary suffrage, then a further matrix of opportunities was opened up by contemporary debates over widening the franchise per se. In particular, popular demands for franchise reform in the late 1810s [**162–4**], the agitation surrounding the 1832 Reform Act [**166–9, 182–3**], and the Chartist movement [**170–7**][9] all provided obvious focal points for feminist discussion. This was not, of course, an automatic move – female political identities were multilaterally constituted. Female political discourse frequently hinged not upon liberal concepts of the sovereignty of the individual, but rather upon pre-existing forms of plebeian political engagement. These derived their authority variously from concepts of community welfare, or from feminine subjectivities which privileged women's social responsibility as wives and mothers. Consequently, the majority of female activists purported to be seeking the suffrage purely for their menfolk, as the best way to promote the interests of their class.[10] Indeed, those who prised apart the masculinist language of liberal rights and sought to apply its theoretical insights to women were as likely to be men as women. For male reformers, female suffrage could form a potent part of their political imaginary, evoking a post-reform world of an inclusive citizenship, based upon stable and harmonious domestic relationships [**173–5**].

Nevertheless, the practice of politics could in itself develop or fracture assumptions of the political self. In the process of intense politicization which involvement in the reform societies or Chartist movement afforded, women might explore or express new dimensions to their political engagement. Accordingly, a small minority within such movements unsettled the official agenda of male suffrage by positing questions of female political rights [**171–2**].

Similarly, middle-class women could also find that their engagement in public activities complicated or disturbed orthodox gender divisions. Most dramatically, gender tensions within the anti-slavery movement burst sharply asunder when American female delegates were excluded from the 1840 World Anti-Slavery Convention. Furthermore, as Anne Knight pointed out, the cultural dynamics of women's social action could alter their very psyche, as they emerged from passive to active agents in the cause of philanthropic reform [**189–92**]. Others drew attention to women's role in nationalist movements and the importance of female patriotic identities, hinting that such commitment to the state should also legitimize a greater political role for women [**101, 169**].

It would be mistaken to construe demands for female enfranchisement as arising only within unique historical moments – such as the Reform Act, or debates concerning the Charter, when historical circumstances crystallized particular ways of exploiting discursive 'gaps' or silences. Throughout this period we find attempts to rethink intellectual languages – in particular utilitarianism and liberalism – through a feminist optic. Needless to say, this process was further modulated by varying agendas concerning class and gender. For example, many writers insisted that (middle-class) women might be far superior as political actors to lower-class men. Another recurring argument (particularly within utilitarian debates) was to dwell upon the particular contribution that women might bring to the polity by dint of their unique, female qualities [**180–8**].

Arguments for the suffrage, then, were complex and multi-faceted. They drew upon, whilst also subverting, existing political discourses in many varied ways. Whilst female suffrage did not carry the same symbolic weight as it did to later Victorian suffrage campaigners (and this should not surprise us, given that only a minority of men enjoyed the franchise during this period) the issue of enfranchisement nonetheless provoked heated and sustained debate which foregrounded the concept of female political identities.

Notes

1 'Rights of Women,' Answer to Florio, *Black Dwarf* (14 October 1818), vol. 2, no. 41, p. 665.
2 See also Catherine Barmby's reply to Anne Knight's request that she support a female suffrage campaign. Taylor (1983), p. 55.
3 *London Social Reformer* (May 1840), vol. 1, no. 1, p.1.

4 See Tyrell (2000), pp. 194–5.
5 These issues emerge, passim, throughout Chapters 9 and 10. But compare, for example documents **173–4** with **177**.
6 Little research has been done on women as shareholders or as voters in local elections in the early nineteenth century. For the earlier period see Susan Staves, 'Investments, votes, and "bribes": women as shareholders in the chartered national companies', in Smith (1998), pp. 259–78 and Amanda Vickery, 'Introduction' in Vickery (2001), pp. 6–8. The extent of women's local franchise was probably very limited and confined to partic-ular local circumstances. The author of document **187** is under the impression that women do not have local political rights.
7 For the later period see for example Holton (1998).
8 See Epstein (1994), p. 23. For a stimulating analysis of gender and the populist idiom see Rogers (2000), especially ch. 1.
9 See also pp. 188–91 regarding the activities of Anne Knight.
10 For useful discussions see Clark (1995), chs 9, 12–13; Hall (1992), ch. 6; Thomis and Grimmett (1982), chs 5–6; Schwarzkopf (1991).

9
Female Rights, Popular Politics and Electoral Reform

Female rights and radical reform in the 1810s

162. *Women played a major role within the radical revival of the late 1810s, forming numerous societies to participate in the work of their male colleagues.[1] Samuel Bamford accorded himself a central role in sanctioning progressive attitudes towards female political participation![2]*

With the restoration of the Habeas Corpus Act,[3] the agitation for reform was renewed ...

Numerous meetings followed in various parts of the country, and Lancashire, and the Stockport borders of Cheshire, were not the last to be concerned in public demonstrations for reform. At one of these meetings, which took place at Lydgate, in Saddleworth, and at which Bagguley, – Drummond, – Fitton, – Haigh, – and others, were the principal speakers;[4] I, in the course of an address, insisted on the right, and the propriety also, of females who were present at such assemblages, voting by shew of hand, for, or against the resolutions. This was a new idea; and the women, who attended numerously on that bleak ridge, were mightily pleased with it, and, the men being nothing dissentient, – when the resolution was put, the women held up their hands, amid much laughter; and ever from that time females voted with the men at the radical meetings.

Samuel Bamford, *Passages in the Life of a Radical* (1841),
vol. 1, pp. 164–5

163. *Most female reformers argued that their political activities arose from a desire as wives and mothers, to salvage the fortunes of their families. Nevertheless, discussions as to the propriety of female political involvement* *could occasionally spark more radical claims to women's political engage-ment. At a meeting of female reformers in Stockport, the president, Mrs Hallworth, having requested the men present to withdraw, pledged herself to work for reform, 'until we fully possess those constitutional liberties and privileges which are the birthright of every English man and woman'.*[5]

In the Black Dwarf, *a radical paper edited by Thomas Wooler, the contiguity between women's political activities and female claims for their own political rights, was often alluded to, although frequently with satire and sometimes sarcasm. The following article elicited a number of facetious replies, although one poem, 'The Rights of Women', firmly reasserted the case.*[6] *The article quoted here swings uneasily, and at times ironically, between these various registers. It uses an Enlightenment device, frequently employed in this journal, of analysing Britain through the eyes of an oriental observer.*[7]

I was about to retire – to embark again for Japan – and among *professed slaves* forget the follies and absurdities of *pretended freemen*! When lo! I was assailed by a new cry. My ears were astounded by a declaration of the RIGHTS OF WOMEN, in every key of female expression. Venerable wearer of the yellow garb, what am I to do? Thou who hast been the husband of seven wives, teach me how to act. Their arguments are very forcible. They say that since *the men* abandon the cause of freedom, they will support it. They say *freedom* was a woman, and therefore every woman ought to be free. Man, they add, has shamefully deserted his post: – and has no right to control woman: – since he has lost the power of defending himself: – that the grovelling slaves of Oliver and Castles are not proper masters for freeborn woman – that woman can expect no protection from the cowards that cannot protect them-selves! And they demand *Universal Suffrage* in its fullest extent. They say they are not so mercenary, so deceitful, or so silly as the great body of the lords of the creation:- that they would never have appointed such an administration as the present. ...

The wiser part of the male creation propose already terms of accommo-dation. They offer a participation in the government; but men are proverbially such dangerous allies to women, that I yet hesitate whether I shall advise a compromise. ... No! no! ladies. Trust them no further. Proceed in your heroic resolution to conquer the difficulties before which they have fallen, or from which they have retreated. Erect the banner of female independence, since man has confessed himself a slave.

'From the Black Dwarf in London, to the Yellow Bonze at Japan. Rights of Women', *Black Dwarf* (9 September 1818), vol. 2, no. 36, pp. 574–6

164.   *The Peterloo Massacre (1819), in which the Manchester yeomanry killed eleven people as they attempted to disperse political reformers, further stimulated public debates as to the propriety of female political involvement. Radicals dwelt, indignantly, on the suffering of innocent women at the hands of the Manchester yeomanry. Samuel Waddington's intervention, which put an interesting slant upon the prevalent discourse of popular constitutionalism,[8] came in the midst of such discussions.*

… when the inhabitants of the northern regions descended south, they appear to have rejected, or escaped the oriental refinements which overran Greece and Italy: and in the Saxon and Danish conquests, it seems that the *natural equality of the sexes* was preserved inviolable. So far from immuring women in seraglios, and otherwise degrading them, the northern tribes, and especially the whole of Germany, reverenced the female sex, as if possessed of superior intelligence, and *deliberated with them in national emergencies.* Tacitus says, they believed that their women were endowed with a divine and prophetic spirit, so that they always consulted them, and never neglected their oracular responses.[9] … By Hicks's Thesaurus, we find that women among the Saxons retained separate property, could bequeath legacies even during the life of the husband; and other women besides Abbesses, who sat and decided in county courts … were in equal numbers with the men, *and, capital punishments were extremely rare. …*

Our British establishment presents a strange inconsistency in allowing women to wield the sceptre, without being entitled to hold any subordinate situation. We should not, however, forget that our Queen Boadicea headed our troops, and made the last great effort against Roman tyranny; or the actions of the four succeeding Scandinavian heroines; or our Elizabeth, and Anne; or those of the reigns of Elizabeth and Catherine of Russia, so tremblingly alive are women to the preservation of the human species, read this, ye Manchester savages! During their time, *not one Russian subject fell by the hand of the public executioner*!

May we not then infer from all this, that women have possessed *coequal power*? And that it materially tended to assuage the malignant and brutal passions of men? Does not every succeeding *male* parliamentary session present further acts of power, from the fountain of a more sanguinary description? Could such have been enacted, if the benevolent and compassionate female had held equal sway?

S. Ferrand Waddington, 'Vindication of Female Political Interference',
The Republican (10 September 1819), vol. 1, no. 3, pp. 44–5

The Queen Caroline affair

165. *In 1820, the attempt of King George IV, to divorce his wife, Caroline, so as to deprive her of her position as royal consort, created a national furore. In the massive populist response which ensued, the Queen was depicted as the victim of a corrupt political system.[10] The affair also sparked isolated defences concerning women's right to a central role within the government of the political nation.*

> Woe be to the age wherein WOMEN lose their influence,
>   and their judgments are disregarded.
> Reflect on glorious and virtuous Rome. It was there that the
> WOMEN honoured the exploits of renowned Generals.
> All the Grand Events were brought about by WOMEN.
> Through a WOMAN Rome obtained Liberty.
> Through WOMEN the mass of the People acquired the rights of
>   the Consulship.
> A WOMAN put an end to the oppression of the *ten Tyrants.*
> By means of *WOMEN,* Rome, when on the brink of destruction,
>   was screened from the resentment of an enraged and
>   victorious outlaw.
> France was delivered from her Invaders and Conquerors,
>   In the fourteenth century, by a WOMAN.
> It was a WOMAN that brought down the bloody tyrant, Marat.
> A WOMAN nailed the tyrant, Sisera, to the ground.
> A QUEEN caused the cruel Minister, Haman, to be hanged
>   on a gallows
>   Fifty cubits high, of his own erecting.
> And a QUEEN will now bring down the corrupt
> Conspirators against the Peace, Honour, and Life of the Innocent.[11]

'Glorious DEEDS of WOMEN!' (1820)

1832 Reform Act

The Reform Act of 1832 was a landmark in British political history. It extended the franchise to wide sections of the middle class, particularly with the new £10 householder franchise in the boroughs. This legislation has rarely been linked to feminist demands, yet as the following examples demonstrate, the widespread political unrest and debate occasioned by the passage of the Act, led many to question its gendered basis. (And, as subsequent extracts illustrate, the Reform Act came to form a common source of reference for feminist arguments in the years to come.[12])

166a. *This impassioned letter, declaiming against the corruption of the political establishment, was published in Richard Carlile's radical publication the* Prompter *during the height of the reform agitation.*

At such a momentous crisis as the present, the 'press' of this country is naturally teeming with discussions on the sacred 'Rights of Man' – good – the more discussion we have on *all* subjects, and the more free and unshackled it is, the greater is the probability of our arriving at a correct and just conclusion. But whence comes it that these stern and uncompromising champions of *their own* liberties, while nerving the arms of prostrate millions to strike down tyranny, and cleave the front of the 'hydra' to its poisoned jaws;[13] whence comes it, I ask, that in the plenitude of these ardent aspirations, for what, in fact, ought to be common to all, they totally overlook the mental and bodily degradation in which so large a portion of our fair countrywomen is enthralled, and a 'domestic tyranny', alike the most odious and humiliating, consecrated by the brand of 'serf', which 'tyrant custom' has too long stamped on the brow of female excellence and loveliness? ...

Spirit of *Francis Wright*, of *Mary Wolstonecraft*, and *De Staël*,[14] your varied brilliancies of genius, and powerful originalities of thought, will alone rescue the capabilities of your sex from obloquy, and cover such puny libellers of feminine worth and talent with undying and merited scorn! Let us search history, ancient and modern, and *both* will not fail to furnish us with examples, that where the prerogatives of women have been held most sacred, where their opinions have been allowed the most influence, and where their smiles and approbation have been most courted, public virtue has *there* been most pre-eminent, and *men* have been irresistibly spurred to deeds of purest chivalry and unflinching heroism. ... Unless a greater scope is afforded for a less restricted system of association betwixt the sexes, the *great and glorious era* which is now breaking to realize our wildest dreams of bliss cannot but be retarded, and the *crested* and *hooded* reptiles which lie with such a paralyzing weight on our poor dreaming species, and fatten on its corruptions, and agonizing sweets, will *partially* retain our *reason* and our *riches* in their harpy fangs!

John Beechcroft Dixon, Citizen, 'Letter to editor', Prompter
(9 April 1831), no. 22, pp. 373–5.

166b. *This is Carlile's response to John Dixon's letter:*

Will the new Reform Bill allow *women*, who are householders, to vote for members of the House of Commons? I have just thought of this matter; but have not the bill at hand, to be sure that there is no exception. If no express exception be made, female householders will be entitled to vote. In some boroughs, where the vote is in a burgage tenure, I have known a woman vote.[15] And what existing law is there to reject a woman, if she were returned to Parliament? I have no such high opinion of men, as to think them intellectually superior to women. There are not a hundred men in England to be matched with Frances Wright; and I know none superior. *That* woman is qualified to be a member of the English House of Commons. We shall not make this leap at once; but I am sure it will come to this. Women will claim and exercise the elective franchise, and sit in parliament. In ancient times, such was the case in this country. Noble women have sitten in parliament and have acted as Sheriffs; and there is not now any express law on the subject to prevent it. If a woman were returned, it would bother the House to decide on the merits of that return. In law, woman is *homo*, or man; thus, if a woman be killed, it is called *man-slaughter*. There are some instances in which the man is, and the woman is not, liable, such as serving in the militia, in the navy, on juries, etc., but these are not sufficient objections to the qualifications of women for other offices. I would have them put on a perfect equality with men, as far as their states of health will permit ... I can see no evil in a parliament of women, or in a mixture of women with men in public offices. I see that much good would arise, in the stimulus that would be given to female improvement in spirit.

Richard Carlile, 'Freedom and Franchise of Women', *Prompter*
(9 April 1831), no. 22, pp. 357–8

167. *The* New Charter *was one of the many pamphlet contributions to the* Reform Bill *debate. Eliza Sharples was critical of the author's highly complex and stratified proposals for legislative reform, but fully supported its feminist dimensions. (Sharples suggested that if men were not prepared to grant women their rights they should retaliate by means of 'passive resistance' and refuse to live with them.)[16]*

The mental capabilities of both sexes being equal they shall enjoy in every respect, the same civil rights.

In the absence of bodily strength females have an additional claim to such a political existence as would give them the power of protecting themselves against the possible injustice or neglect of their near connections. It is not the interest of either sex that one should be reduced to a state of helplessness, or of complete dependence upon the other. When the sexes cease to be equals the bond of sympathy between them is weakened and often broken. Females shall not be incapacitated by marriage from acquiring, or holding property in their own right. In this charter, the term man or men, and the masculine pronouns are designed only to except females in that part which relates to the appointment of a civil and military force ...

Every adult individual, male and female, shall have a voice in the election of a representative.*

*We know there are few persons yet prepared for an extension of the elective franchise to females, and yet no one appears startled at the appointment of the Duchess of Kent to the office of regent, or at the prospect of the Princess Victoria one day becoming queen. Are women capable of wielding sceptres, and yet not capable of choosing a representative to protect their interests? It is said, that a woman's best protector is her husband; but do we never hear of husbands against whom women are compelled to claim the protection of the laws? Or are women, because kindly treated, to have no independence of mind or action, no thought but of obedience and unreserved submission? Again, all women have not husbands, and a widow or a spinster holding lands or houses is not exempted from the payment of rates and taxes; and upon what ground is it assumed that she ought to have no voice in the management of the funds to which she is compelled to contribute? Is Miss Edgeworth or Miss Mitford[17] intellectually less capable of exercising the elective franchise than Sir Walter Scott? The only serious objection to extending the elective franchise to women is that which arises from the desire not to expose females to the rancorous spirit and riotous proceedings of elections as they have hitherto been conducted; but the character of elections would be completely changed by the graduated system which we propose, and vote by ballot.

The New Charter (1831), pp. 6–7, 12–13

168. *In 1832 the radical orator, Henry Hunt, presented the first petition for women's suffrage to the House of Commons. Little is yet known about the petitioner, Mary Smith, a wealthy Yorkshire woman. Hunt was later gibed at by the press for failing to realize the anti-democratic sentiments which underpinned Smith's petition.[18] The event was recorded thus in Hansard:*

[RIGHTS OF WOMEN.] Mr. *Hunt* said, he had a petition to present which might be a subject of mirth to some hon. Gentlemen, but which was one deserving of consideration. It came from a lady of rank and fortune – Mary Smith, of Stanmore, in the county of York. The petitioner stated that she paid taxes, and therefore did not see why she should not have a share in the election of a Representative; she also stated that women were liable to all the punishments of the law, not excepting death, and ought to have a voice in the making of them; but so far from this, even upon their trials, both judges and jurors were all of the opposite sex. She could see no good reason for the exclusion of women from social rights, while the highest office of the State, that of the Crown, was open to the inheritance of females, and, as we understood, the petition expressed her indignation against those vile wretches who would not marry, and yet would exclude females from a share in the legislation. The prayer of the petition was, that every unmarried female, possessing the necessary pecuniary qualification, should be entitled to vote for Members of Parliament. Sir *Frederick Trench* said, it would be rather awkward if a jury half males and half females were locked up together for a night as now often happened with juries. This might lead to rather queer predicaments. Mr. *Hunt* well knew that the hon. and gallant Member was frequently in the company of ladies for whole nights, but he did not know that any mischief resulted from that circumstance.

Sir *Frederick Trench*: Yes, but not locked up all night.

Petition laid on the table.

> *Parliamentary Debates*, third series (3 August 1832) vol. 14, p. 1086

169.   *Mary Smith's petition also featured in William Johnson Fox's article 'A Political and Social Anomaly'. Despite the cautious tone struck at the end of this passage, the article was an important intervention in the feminist debate. Harriet Taylor, for example, was prompted to write her own essay after reading the article.*[19]

In the common opinion of common statesmen, the fitness of woman to vote for an individual's elevation to the temporary dignity of a legislator in the House of Commons, is a mere joke: yet her naming scores of persons legislators for life, and all their heirs legislators too, through all generations, is an essential portion of that perfection of ancestral wisdom under which we live. ...

There are sundry little clubs and dignities, about the country, in selecting for which a woman's judgment, if she possess property, may be legitimately exercised. She may have her portion of parochial representation in the vestry. She is perfectly competent to pronounce on the skill of a physician who may save or sacrifice life, on a large scale, in the county hospital. She helps to elect the sovereigns of India, who hold their august sittings in Leadenhallstreet. All this is reasonable and constitutional; but – vote for a Member of Parliament – preposterous!

What makes this matter yet more odd is that a man does not vote because he is a man, still less because he is an honest man, or a wise man, but because he is a ten pounder or upwards. There, and there alone, is his qualification. But though the woman be a fifty-pounder and upwards, and both honest and wise into the bargain, yet it availeth not. Truly it is very mysterious.

So thought one Mary Smith, who thereupon petitioned the Legislature that female householders, possessing the requisite property qualification, might be included within the enfranchising provisions of the Reform Act.

This petition, which we have not been able to see, is said to have contained some very foolish things, and some very disgusting ones. It may be so; but we cannot imagine that it contained anything so foolish, or so disgusting, as the conversation which followed its presentation in the House of Commons. Many newspapers declined to publish what we will not insult the poor by calling pot-house ribaldry.

Who or what Mary Smith is, we neither know nor care; nor have we a word to say on behalf of the judiciousness of her petition, or of her selection of an advocate; nor are we offering any opinion on the expediency of granting, or even attending to its prayer: but we must say that its reception was most disgraceful; and that the distinction against which she petitioned is a very curious anomaly in our social institutions. Be not alarmed, gentle reader; nor suppose that we are about to pen an eulogy on woman, or an assertion of her political rights. We are not going to descant on domestic virtues, and Cornelia the mother of the Gracchi, and Dorcas, and Mrs. Hutchinson, and the patient Grizzle.[20] We shall not talk of patriotism either, nor celebrate the peasant girls of Uri and Unterwalden, who died in the ranks in the memorable fight against French invasion;[21] or the noble ladies of Warsaw, who gave their golden trinkets to be melted and coined into ducats for the pay of the Polish army in the late righteous rebellion.[22] We will say nothing against the common horror of female politicians. Our only purpose is to mention, and merely to mention, a few particulars in which there is great room for improvement in the condition of women.

[W. J. Fox], 'A Political and Social Anomaly', *Monthly Repository*
(1832), vol. 6, pp. 638–9

Anti-Poor Law movement

The Poor Law Amendment Act (1834) abolished outdoor relief and instituted the separation of families in the hated workhouses. Many communities

*reacted with hostility to its threat to the stability of working-class families.
On rare occasions, as in this meeting of women gathered to protest against
the Act in Elland, Yorkshire, such anger fuelled the articulation of feminist
sentiments.*

170.   Mrs. Susan Fearnley having been voted into the chair, opened
the business of the meeting by exhorting the females present to *take
the question of a repeal of this Bill into their own hands,* and not to rely
on the exertions of others, least of all *on the House of Commons,* but at
once to assert THE DIGNITY AND EQUALITY OF THE SEX ... The
worthy chairwoman went on to recommend her sisters, the equal sex,
'to resist the enforcement of the cruel law *unto death.'*
    British and Foreign Quarterly Review (1838), vol. 7, no. 13, p. 354n

Chartism

*Despite the self-positioning of many Chartist women as supportive wives
and mothers, female activists (particularly at their own meetings) could
display far more belligerent political identities. Moreover, whilst the movement as a whole may be characterized by its conservative views of women's
position, there was nonetheless, a significant, if diverse, minority of feminist
views.*[23]

171.   *The Ashton Female Political Union, under the leadership of Mrs
Williamson, acknowledged that there was a proud tradition of women acting
as auxiliaries in political causes; but as they point out here, such an agenda
did not preclude the possibility of female enfranchisement:*

Join with us, dear Sisters, in pointing out to our husbands and friends,
the necessity of uniting in the strictest bond of unity, to wrest from
those merciless villains those privileges – those political rights they
have so long been deprived of, and we do not despair of yet seeing
intelligence, the necessary qualification for voting, and then Sisters,
we shall be placed in our proper position in society, and enjoy the elective franchise as well as our kinsmen.
    'Address of the Ashton Female Political Union to the Women of
        Britain and Ireland', *Northern Star* (2 February 1839), p. 3

172.   *At a lively, good-humoured meeting of the Sheffield Radical Female
Association, the chairwoman, Mrs Barker, rose to suggest the importance of
female political rights:*

After the company had been suitably addressed by Messrs. Boardman, Andrews, Bradwell, Gill, Otley, Harvey and several other friends, Mrs. Barker read the Address of the Female Radical Association; after which she made some excellent remarks on the necessity of the admission of the female portion of society into political existence.

The Charter (27 October 1839), p. 629

173. *The Chartist, John Watkins, located women firmly within the 'domestic sphere'; he also criticized women for their shallow understanding. Yet, as we see here, he was supportive of the political rights of single women.*

So far from being excluded from taking a part in politics, women ought to be allowed to vote; not wives – for they and their husbands are one … but maids, and widows. They pay rates, cesses, and taxes; they participate in the prosperity or adversity of the state. They have an equal stake in the land they live in. Why should the law exclude them? I do not know that they would make better laws than men make: they could scarcely make worse. They would be more likely to seek the true interests of their children, for the husband who does this, cannot consult a better judge than a good wife.

John Watkins, 'Address to the Women of England', *English Chartist Circular* (April 1841), vol. 1, no. 13, p. 49

174. *R. J. Richardson's* The Rights of Woman, *which also argued for extending the franchise to single women, was the most famous Chartist disquisition upon the rights of women. Despite his argument that women deserved enfranchisement because of their contribution to the economy, much of this sizeable tract dealt with the iniquities of women's working conditions, and the need to restore women to the domestic environment.*

… I conceive Woman has a political right to interfere in all matters concerning the state of which she is a member, more especially as applied to Great Britain, for the following reasons:

1st – Because, by the ancient laws of the English constitution, she is admissable to every executive office in the kingdom, from the monarch upon the throne to the parish Overseer,[*] or the village sexton,[†] or the responsible office of post mistress, which is still common in small towns.

2d. – Because, by the present law of tenures, of powers, of contracts, of bargains and sale, of inheritance, of wills, and every other matter or thing touching the rights of property and transfer, woman (except in *femme covert* [*sic*],[24]) is qualified to be, and therefore, is admissable, as a contracting party, save during her minority or a ward in chancery, then her affairs are managed by trust.

3d. – Because, woman is responsible in her own person for any breach of contract, for any offence against the peace and laws of the land. In the church, by the penalties of imprisonment, excommunication, and premunire[25]; in the state, by fine, imprisonment, banishment, and death.

4th. – Because, she is taxed in the same degree with others for the maintainance of the state and its appendages under all circumstances.

5th. – and lastly, because, she contributes directly and indirectly to the wealth and resources of the nation by her labour and skill.

On these five reasons I found my opinion upon the great question, 'Ought woman to interfere in the affairs of the state?' and to that question I again answer Yes! emphatically YES!

To the first of these reasons I will add, if a woman is qualified to be a queen over a great nation, armed with power of nullifying the powers of Parliament or the deliberate resolutions of the two estates of the realm, by parity of reason, a woman in a minor degree ought to have a voice in the election of the legislative authorities. If it be admissable that the queen, a woman, by the constitution of the country can command, can rule over a nation, (and I admit the justice of it,) then I say, woman in every instance ought not to be excluded from her share in the Executive and legislative power of the country.

To the second reason I will add further, if a woman can exercise the powers of a contractor, or vendor, or become heiress, testatrix, executrix or administratix, and act in such important capacities over matters and things daily arising out of transactions with real and personal property, I say that it perfectly justifies my opinion that woman is not only qualified, but ought by virtue of such qualifications, to have a voice in the making [of] those laws under which the above transactions take place.

The third reason I will illustrate by saying, that, if woman be subject to pains and penalties, on account of the infringement of any law or laws, – even unto death, – in the name of common justice, she ought to have a voice in making [of] the laws she is bound to obey.

The fourth reason is next in importance to the last, so long as the legislature claim and levy a portion of the worldly income of a woman for the support of the state, surely it is not presumption in woman to claim the right of electing that legislature who assume the right to tax her, and on refusal, punish her with pains and penalties; it is unjust to withhold from her her fair share of the elective power of the state, it is tyranny in the extreme, and ought to be properly resisted.

The fifth reason is equal in importance to the last, and in support of which, I shall extend my arguments. It is a most incontrovertible fact, that women contribute to the wealth and resources of the kingdom ...

To the women I say, endeavour to throw off the degradation of predial[26] slavery, return to your domestic circles and cultivate your finer feelings for the benefit of your offspring ...

I think, nay I believe, that God ordained woman 'to temper man.' I believe, from this reason, that she ought to partake of his councils, public and private, that she ought to share in the making of laws for the government of the commonwealth, in the same manner as she would join with her husband in the councils of his household. It is a duty she owes to herself, to her husband, to her children, to posterity, and to her common country.

* See Bott on the Poor Laws.
† Lucy Turner was many years parish clerk of Eccles, Lancashire.

R. J. Richardson, The Rights of Woman (1840; 1986 edn),
pp. 12–14, 21

175. *The National Association, a Chartist organization which depended heavily upon the support of middle-class radicals, many of them sympathetic towards feminism, epitomized William Lovett's 'new move' Chartism, with its strong emphasis upon the education of the people.*[27]

... how much of men's happiness depends upon the minds and dispositions of women, how much of comfort, cheerfulness, and affection their intelligence can spread in the most humble home – how many cares their prudence can prevent, and their sympathy and kindness alleviate, it ought to redouble our anxiety to promote *the education* and contend for *the social and political rights of women.*

'The Female Members of our Association', National Association
Gazette (8 January 1842), no. 2, p. 11

176. The political emancipation of woman first demands our attention. This can only be acquired by her possession of the suffrage equally with man. The means for obtaining this are similar to the means adopted by the men. There is now being agitated an electoral document, entitled the PEOPLE'S CHARTER, advocating a general masculine suffrage. Women must, before they give it their support, insist upon the insertion of clauses advocating general feminine suffrage as well; so that the document becomes a requirement for the universal adult franchise; and thus advocates the electoral rights of the man and the woman together.

> Catherine Barmby, 'The Demand for the Emancipation of Woman, Politically and Socially', *New Tracts for the Times* in Taylor (1983)

177.   *The* National *was a journal conducted by W. J. Linton – a pivotal figure within contemporary radical movements and a committed campaigner for the rights of women. Unlike Watkins and Richardson, Linton and his associates envisaged the enfranchisement of married, as well as single women.*

… some of the provisions of the Charter [are] open to improvement. The suffrage should be extended to every adult (whether male or female) of the community. Now, the unmarried woman has no political existence: often standing proudly in her loneliness, independent and perhaps depended upon, surely she has a right to be heard. And though the interest of the married woman may be that of her husband – what then? Shall the voice of the couple have no more weight than that of a single person. Nor do we believe that such a measure of justice would create the confusion anticipated by many consciencious, but timorous reformers. For a long time, few women would avail themselves of their right: and what harm could those few do? Certain persons seem very much afraid of their 'inferiors'.

> 'One of the People', 'Political Suggestions', *National* (1839), p. 359n.

Notes

1 Thomis and Grimmett (1982), ch. 5.
2 Bamford's subsequent claim that such practices were critical in encouraging female philanthropic activity has little basis. For a discussion of Bamford and the gendered nature of radical reforming activity see Hall (1992), ch. 6.
3 Habeas Corpus, protecting citizens from unlawful imprisonment by the state, had been suspended following the Pentrich Rising of 1817. It was reimposed in 1818.
4 John Bagguley, a teenage apprentice, was a Stockport radical; as was Samuel Drummond, a reedmaker. William Fitton was an activist from Oldham. Epstein (1984), p. 243. I have not been able to trace the identity of Haigh.
5 Rogers (1998), p. 241.
6 Compare for example, 'Rights of Women', *Black Dwarf* (30 September

1818), vol. 2, no. 39, pp. 618–20 and Roderick Random, 'An Ode to the Ladies on their Alleged Rights', *Black Dwarf* (14 October 1818), vol. 2, no. 41, pp. 655–6, with 'Rights of Women, Answer to Florio', *Black Dwarf* (14 October 1818), vol. 2, no. 41, p. 665. (See the epigraph for this section.)

7 Epstein (1994), p. 38.
8 For popular constitutionalism see Epstein (1994), ch. 1.
9 For a different treatment of Tacitus see Rendall, 'Writing History for British Women: Elizabeth Hamilton and the *Memoirs of Agrippina*', in Orr (1996), pp. 79–93.
10 For a clear, if provocative, analysis of the affair, see Clark (1995), pp. 164–74.
11 In tracing the public and political significance of women, from the battles of Ancient Rome; through to Joan of Arc and Charlotte Corday (murderer of the French Revolutionary leader, Jean Paul Marat); as well as including biblical figures such as Jael (who assassinated Sisera, leader of the Canaanites) and Queen Esther (who ordered the execution of Haman and his ten sons), this text provides a particularly bellicose history of women. See the documents in Chapter 1 for a comparative approach.
12 For socialist radicals, such as Alexander Campbell, the reform agitation provided a moment to challenge the importance of the male suffrage, arguing that such measures as free trade, the separation of church and state – and female political rights, should also form a part of the reform agenda. Fraser (1996), pp. 35–9. See also documents **182–3, 185, 187**.
13 The hydra, a mythical beast, was a sea serpent with nine heads.
14 Germaine de Staël (1766–1817), highly esteemed French author who was a significant voice in the development of European nationalism. Document **166b** also championed Frances Wright.
15 See Elaine Chalus, 'Women, Electoral Privilege and Practice', in Gleadle and Richardson (2000), pp. 19–29 for women's electoral rights.
16 'Review of "The New Charter"', *Isis* (14 April 1832), no. 10, p. 159.
17 Maria Edgeworth (1767–1849), novelist and celebrated educationist; Mary Russell Mitford (1787–1855), a popular writer.
18 Belchem (1985), p. 261.
19 Jacobs and Payne (1998), pp. 12–13.
20 For Cornelia see document **2** and note. Dorcas was the charitable woman of Joppa [Acts 9: 36–42]. Lucy Hutchinson, a parliamentarian during the English Civil War, is famous for the memoir she wrote of her husband, Colonel Hutchinson. Grizzle is Griselda – an unlikely feminist icon, see document **118** and note.
21 Presumably a reference to the French invasion of Switzerland in 1798, which led to the establishment of the Helvetic Republic (1798–1803).
22 The November Rising of 1830, which sparked the Russo-Polish War (1830–31).
23 For excellent discussions see Schwarzkopf (1991); Jones (1983); and Thompson (1984), ch. 7.
24 That is, married women. See document **120**.
25 The forfeiture of goods.
26 Literally, of the land. In this context, Richardson presumably means 'serf-like'.

27 For further discussion see Gleadle, '"Our Several Spheres": Middle-Class Women and the Feminisms of Early Victorian Radical Politics', in Gleadle and Richardson (2000), pp. 140–3.

10
Middle-Class Reform Projects

'Terrible battles of wits'

The question of women's right to vote prompted vigorous debate in the drawing-rooms of middle-class dissenters throughout these years.

178.   I remember too the first time it broke upon me that a woman was debarred from voting for M.P.s. It struck me like a great blow and I argued it out with my sisters who being more used to the fact could not at all sympathise with my boiling indignation.

> Julia Smith, 'Memoirs of Julia Smith', William Smith Papers, Add MS 7621, Cambridge University Library

179.   This day fortnight Mr. Smyth[1] arrived, and, with his gay good humour, rendered Allerton itself more gay and more animated. We had terrible battles of wits, however, all the time he was with us, for the professor was rash enough, the very first evening, to give utterance to two of his fusty college notions, which brought all us ladies out in array against him. The first was that no woman is fit to govern a kingdom; the second, that the true art of tea-making is a mystery too deep for female comprehension. I charged him boldly on the first of these heretical propositions, all the females following me, and Mr. Roscoe[2] gallantly cheering us on, and a glorious victory we gained.

> Lucy Aikin to Dr Aikin (28 August 1814), in Le Breton (1864), p. 93

Utilitarianism

The famous 'Essay on Government' by utilitarian James Mill had argued that women did not need the vote, as their political interests were already

represented through their male relatives. This evoked the ire of early social-
ists, William Thompson and his collaborator, Anna Wheeler, who were
themselves deeply influenced by Jeremy Bentham and the theoretical argu-
ments of utilitarianism.[3] *In one of the most extensive and comprehensive*
treatments of the subject, Thompson and Wheeler's Appeal *exploded what*
they held to be the intellectual fallacies of Mill's position. In a sustained
attack, they asserted that women's legal, sexual, economic and personal
subjection to men highlights the fallacy of assuming that an 'identity of
interests' (as Mill had put it) can exist between the sexes.

180.   The 'Article' [by James Mill] asserts, 'therefore, political rights
are superfluous to women, their happiness being so impartially
guarded by men without them.'

I assert, 'therefore, all women, and particularly women living with
men in marriage and unavoidably controlled by their superior
strength, having been reduced, by the want of political rights, to a
state of helplessness, slavery, and of consequent unequal enjoyments,
pains, and privations, they are *more in need* of political rights than any
other portion of human beings, to gain some chance of emerging from
this state.' ...

Is it possible to conceive that legislative power lodged exclusively in
the hands of women, without force, the weaker half of the race, could
have produced atrocities and wretchedness equal to those with which
exclusive male legislation has desolated the globe? Is there no hope
that under the exclusive legislation of women, some at least of these
palpable and avowed evils would have been obviated or lessened?

There is the strongest ground for hope, amounting almost to a
certainty, that the exclusive legislation of women would have been
much more beneficent – less beneficent it is almost impossible to
conceive it to be capable of being – than that of men has absolutely
been; because the sympathies of women for the whole race, for all
those liable to be affected by their regulations, must, from the fact of
their inferior physical strength, have been much more active than
those of men, and much more inclined to promote impartially the
happiness of all.

William Thompson [and Anna Wheeler], Appeal (1825),
pp. 107, 131–2

181.   *The* Westminster Review, *a journal established and run by utilitar-*
ian radicals, was an early supporter of female suffrage.

If the mode of election was what it ought to be, there would be no more difficulty in women voting for a representative in parliament, than for a director at the India House. The world will find out at some time, that the readiest way to secure justice on some points, is to be just on all; – that the whole is easier to accomplish than the part; – and that whenever the camel is driven through the eye of the needle, it would be simple folly and debility that would leave a hoof behind.

'Article on Mill's Essays on Government', *Westminster Review* (July 1829), vol. 11, no. 21, p. 266.

182. *Unlike James Mill, the utilitarian political economist Samuel Bailey moved decisively from Bentham's caution regarding the supposed inappropriateness of female electors. Bailey's intervention became one of the most discussed texts on female enfranchisement amongst contemporary radical intellectuals. Henry Brougham, for example, concluded his own proto-feminist pamphlet with an extensive quotation from it. Bailey's work was also discussed in such journals as the* Monthly Repository *and the* London Review.[4]

The legitimate object of all government – namely, the happiness of the community – comprehends alike male and female, as alike susceptible of pain and pleasure; and the principle, that power will be uniformly exercised for the good of the parties subject to it only when it is under their control, or the control of persons who have an identity of interests with themselves, is equally applicable in the case of both sexes. The exclusion of the female sex from the electoral privilege, can therefore be consistently contended for only by showing two things; first, that their interests are so closely allied with those of the male sex, and allied in such a manner, as to render the two nearly identical; secondly, that the female sex are incompetent, from want of intelligence, to make a choice for their own good, and that on this account it would be to the advantage of the community, on the whole, to leave the selection of representatives to the stronger part of the human race, the disadvantages arising from any want of perfect identity of interests being more than compensated by the advantages of that superior discernment which the male sex would bring to the task. Let us examine, for a moment, the force of these allegations. The interests of the female sex are so far from being identified with those of the male sex, that the latter half of the human species have almost universally used their power to oppress the former. By the present regulations of society, men wield over women, to a certain extent, irresponsible power; and one of the fundamental maxims on which representative government is founded is, that irresponsible power will be abused. The case before us presents no exception: the power of man over woman is constantly misemployed; and it may be doubted whether the relation of the sexes to each other will ever be placed on a just and proper footing, until they have both their share of control over the enactments of the legislature. ...

There is no truth, then, in the argument, that the interests of the female sex in the regulations of the state are identified with those of the male; and even if the allegation were true it would furnish no reason for excluding women from the elective franchise, unless it could be shown, that, from their general want of intelligence, they are incapable of making a good choice, or that (it may be added) they labour under some other disqualification. If it were alleged, that, inasmuch as all persons who inhabit houses at the rent of ten pounds a-year have an identity of interests in political affairs, one half may be excluded from the elective franchise without infringing the true principles of representation, it would be quite as sound an inference, as that women ought to be excluded because their interests are the same as those of men. There must be not only proof of an identity of interests, but also a specific ground of exclusion from the privilege to be exercised.

The specific ground urged in the case of women, is incompetency from ignorance – the same ground which is urged in the case of the poorer classes of the community. It cannot, however, be urged with the same justice. Though the female sex may be allowed, in all existing societies, to be on the whole inferior in intelligence to the men, yet the higher classes of females are superior in this respect to the lower classes of the males. Women, for instance, possessing five hundred a-year, are generally superior in information to men of fifty pounds a-year, although not perhaps equal to men of five hundred. If this is a true statement, the obvious expedient is, not to exclude women, but to place their pecuniary qualification higher. Even the necessity of such a higher qualification may be doubted, inasmuch as in that peculiar intelligence which is requisite for a judicious choice of persons to fill public offices, females are in some respects greater proficients than men of the same station.

Female tact, in the discrimination of at least certain qualities of character, is universally admitted; and it can scarcely be questioned, that such coadjutors would be highly useful in the selection of representatives, were their minds fully brought to bear on the merits of the candidates by their having a voice in the decision. With regard to any other disqualification under which the female sex may labour, if any exists, it has not hitherto been brought into discussion. The inconsistency of the exercise of a valuable political privilege with female delicacy, will scarcely be alleged. Were a proper method of taking votes adopted, and such other appropriate measures employed … to disencumber elections of what at present renders them scenes of rudeness and riot, the exercise of the elective franchise would be compatible with the most scrupulous refinement of feelings and habits.

On this subject, doubtless, abundance of sneers will be indulged in, and a thousand sarcasms uttered; but when the happiness of human beings is concerned, and as in this case that of half of the human race, the subject is rather too important and sacred to be sacrificed to the fear of ridicule. If the exclusion of women is to be maintained, let it at all events be placed on some plain and rational ground.

Even Mr. Bentham, bold as he was in the free expression of his opinions, scarcely ventured to do more than hint his views on the subject of female electors. After justly remarking, that the propriety of disqualifying women for being members of the legislative assembly, and of disqualifying them for being electors, stand on very different grounds, he maintains, that, although there might possibly be some inconvenience in giving them the franchise, there would be no absurdity. 'Everywhere,' he continues, 'have females possessed the whole power of a despot; everywhere but in France without objection. Talk of giving them, as here, the smallest fraction of a fraction of such a power, scorn without reason is all the answer you receive. From custom comes prejudice. No gnat too minute to be strained out by it, no camel too great to be swallowed' [*Radical Reform Bill*, p. 56].

In the English Reform Act, a very small concession, without disturbing the legal relations in which the sexes stand to each other, would have saved the appearance of injustice to females. No evil, in fact, could have arisen from placing men and women on such an equality, in regard to the franchise, as the present system of law would admit. Wives and sisters and daughters, living under the same roof with their husbands and brothers and fathers, and not having independent possessions, would have been excluded, not on the ground of sex, but on account of not being householders; sharing, in this respect, the condition of sons residing with their fathers, and of other mere lodgers. It would have been only widows or single women keeping house, or possessing the requisite amount of property, that could have been entitled to vote; and it is difficult to conceive the shadow of a reason why they should be debarred from the privilege, except the tumultuous proceedings which are the unruly progeny of unskilful arrangements.

Samuel Bailey, The Rationale of Political Representation (1835),
pp. 236–42.

183.   *Despite Bailey's generally warm reception in radical circles, Margaret Mylne, a contributor to the* Westminster Review, *was disappointed with what she judged to be the limitations of Bailey's feminism. (The* Morning Star *was also critical of Bailey, arguing that he revealed a lack of awareness of women's wider social subjection.[5])*

Ever since the Reform Bill – that era of better hope – it has appeared to us a needless, if not prejudicial inequality, to exclude women altogether from representation. ... While they contribute to its support, and are not exempted by the weakness of their sex from paying taxes, it seems to us a plain case that they should have a voice in the management of the revenue, or at least be able, like other loyal subjects and citizens of the same grade in society, to 'lay this flattering unction' to their souls; and we agree with Mr Baillie [*sic*] that it might be made quite consistent with female delicacy to register and go to the poll; as consistent, at any rate, as to go to the cess office, or to receive the visits of the tax-gatherer or rate collector. ...

We do not expect that the greatest legislators, or most profound politicians, will be found among female householders, after the elective franchise has been extended to them. The Reform Bill, however, does not proceed on the supposition that the knowledge or wisdom of a statesman is required in an elector, but on this, that within certain limits of intelligence, and opportunities of instruction, every one understands his own interests best, and has a right to let them be known by the fittest deputy he can find. ... granting between a lady and her coachman an original difference of capacity (in favour of the latter for the affairs of government) we think it is making too much account of it in its undeveloped state to give him the right, and withhold it from his mistress. ...

What a poor remedial expedient is suggested by Mr Baillie himself: how little would the slender voices of a few old maids and widows avail to 'represent' their sex's peculiar interests!

[Margaret Mylne], 'Woman, and her Social Position', Westminster Review (1841), vol. 35, pp. 37–41

Liberalism[6]

Writers such as Harriet Martineau applied classic liberal arguments in their demands for the vote. Martineau used the American Declaration of Independence as an intellectual vehicle on which she might elaborate her case. In common with Marion Reid, her defence of women's political rights also involved an onslaught on conventional formulations of women's sphere.

184. One of the fundamental principles announced in the Declaration of Independence is, that governments derive their just powers from the consent of the governed. How can the political condition of women be reconciled with this? ...

The question has been asked, from time to time, in more countries than one, how obedience to the laws can be required of women, when no woman has, either actually or virtually, given any assent to any law. No plausible answer has, as far as I can discover, been offered; for the good reason, that no plausible answer can be devised. The most principled democratic writers on government have on this subject sunk into fallacies, as disgraceful as any advocate of despotism has adduced. ...

Some who desire that there should be an equality of property between men and women, oppose representation, on the ground that political duties would be incompatible with the other duties which women have to discharge. The reply to this is, that women are the best judges here. God has given time and power for the discharge of all duties; and, if he had not, it would be for women to decide which they would take, and which they would leave. ... The English Tories feel the hardship that it would be to impose the franchise on every artizan, busy as he is getting in his bread. The Georgian planter perceives the hardship that freedom would be to his slaves. And the best friends of half the human race peremptorily decide for them as to their rights, their duties, their feelings, their powers. In all these cases, the persons thus cared for feel that the abstract decision rests with themselves; that, though they may be compelled to submit, they need not acquiesce. ...

I, for one, do not acquiesce. I declare that whatever obedience I yield to the laws of the society in which I live is a matter between, not the community and myself, but my judgment and my will. Any punishment inflicted on me for the breach of the laws, I should regard as so much gratuitous injury; for to those laws I have never, actually or virtually, assented. I know that there are women in England who agree with me in this – I know that there are women in America who agree with me in this. The plea of acquiescence is invalidated by us. . . .

I cannot enter upon the commonest order of pleas of all; – those which relate to the virtual influence of woman; her swaying the judgment and will of man through the heart; and so forth. One might as well try to dissect the morning mist. . . .

The truth is, that while there is much said about 'the sphere of woman,' two widely different notions are entertained of what is meant by the phrase. The narrow, and, to the ruling party, the more convenient notion is that sphere appointed by men, and bounded by their idea of propriety; – a notion from which any and every woman may fairly dissent. The broad and true conception is of the sphere appointed by God, and bounded by the powers which he has bestowed. This commands the assent of man and woman; and only the question of powers remains to be proved.

That woman has power to represent her own interests, no one can deny till she has been tried. The modes need not be discussed here: they must vary with circumstances. The fearful and absurd images which are perpetually called up to perplex the question – images of women on woolsacks in England, and under canopies in America, have nothing to do with the matter. The principle being once established, the methods will follow, easily, naturally, and under a remarkable transmutation of the ludicrous into the sublime. The kings of Europe would have laughed mightily, two centuries ago, at the idea of a commoner, without robes, crown, or sceptre, stepping into the throne of a strong nation. Yet who dared to laugh when Washington's super-royal voice greeted the New World from the presidential chair, and the old world stood still to catch the echo?

The principle of the equal rights of both halves of the human race is all we have to do with here. It is the true democratic principle which can never be seriously controverted, and only for a short time evaded. Governments can derive their just powers only from the consent of the governed.

> Harriet Martineau, *Society in America* (1837), vol. 1, pp. 199–207

185. *Lucy Aikin objected to Harriet Martineau's views on divorce and marriage but was fully in favour of her views on female enfranchisement:*

With regard to her notions of the political rights of women, I certainly hold, and it appears to me self-evident that, on the principle that there should never be taxation without representation, women who possess independent property *ought* to vote; but this is more the American than the English principle. Here it is, or was rather, the doctrine that the elective franchise is a trust given to some for the good of the whole, and on that ground I think the claim of women might be dubious. Yet the reform bill, by affixing the elective franchise only, and in all cases, to the possession of land, or occupancy of houses of a certain value, tends to suggest the idea that a single woman possessing such property as unrestrictedly as a man, subject to the same taxes, liable even to some burdensome, though eligible to no honourable or profitable, parish offices, ought in equity to have, and might have without harm or danger, a suffrage to give. I vote for the guardians of the poor of this parish by merely signing a paper, why might I not vote thus for members of parliament?

Lucy Aikin to W. E. Channing (14 October 1837),
in Le Breton (1864), pp. 362–3

186.   *Marion Reid's* A Plea For Women *received glowing reviews in feminist-leaning journals such as* Tait's Edinburgh Review.[7] *(Nonetheless her assurance that she was not insisting upon women's right to sit as Members of Parliament infuriated Anne Knight who noted in her own copy of the work, 'The point at issue must be equalization of human privilege if my brother have a right to sit, then his sister has the same right[,] give it up to her pay your debts ye dis "honourable men".[8])*

No taxation without representation, is the great motto of the British constitution. Does the tax-gatherer pass the door of the self-dependent and solitary female? Do the various commodities she consumes, come to her charged only with the price of their production and carriage to her? Or is a fourth, or even a third, added to that price, which goes into the public treasury? If she must pay, why cannot she also vote?

A little inquiry will show, that there must be some very curious and inconsistent ideas prevalent about the civil duties for which women are fit or not fit, – for they are by no means even at present excluded from all civil privileges. The necessary property qualification admits her to vote for an East India Director; nor have we heard the faintest hint of any inconvenience resulting from the practice. What great and obvious difference there is between voting for the governors of India and those of England – so great and so obvious as to make the one a matter of course for women, the other an absurdity which cannot be so much as named without exciting the most contemptuous laughter – we confess we do not very clearly see. Nor is it alone in the government of that foreign country that women, equally with the other sex, are allowed a voice. In the local governments of our own country we often see women invested with a vote for some one or other of the public servants. Now, since no practical inconvenience has been found to result from allowing her to vote, for instance, for a commissioner of police – and since, in theory, it seems no more than justice – why not allow her right of voting for other local authorities, or any authorities whatever? ...

It sometimes happens that a merchant, manufacturer, or shopkeeper, runs mad with politics, and leaves his own business neglected, that he may have leisure to attend to that of the nation; yet, to prevent more mishaps of that kind, nobody proposes to take away the civil rights of merchants, manufacturers, or shopkeepers. Now, the domestic duties of woman being so much more closely, or at least more immediately, bound up in the affections than the business duties of man, there is much less risk of her ever falling into such an error. Is it to be so much as imagined, that any political excitement will be so apt to make a woman forget her children as to make a man forget his counting-house, counter, or spinning-jennies? Every heart, worthy of the name, answers distinctly, and at once, No. ...

We have no wish whatever to see women sitting as representatives; but, in saying this, we must not be misunderstood; for neither do we think it just to prevent them by law from doing so. There is very little prospect of women becoming very willing to accept the duties of legislators, and still less of bodies of electors becoming willing to accept them as representatives: so that there is no need of any law restraining them in this matter. In fact, in this as in every other respect, the natural restraints are enough: few women would consent to be chosen, and few electors would like to choose them; but still, if any individuals of the softer sex are able and willing to overleap the natural barriers,[9] we see neither justice nor utility in opposing artificial ones to their progress.

Marion Reid, *A Plea for Woman* (1843), pp. 58, 60–1, 79, 146–7

187.   *This article, advertised in advance by its publishers, attracted considerable publicity. Conservative observers, believing it to be written by Caroline Norton, fumed that it was 'a female manifesto against the whole human race of male tyrants'.*[10]

... amongst our hereditary legislators, are there many who might not be equalled or surpassed by women taken from their own or other classes of society? I imagine no one will controvert this: and if women are capable of exercising the functions of legislators, as well or better than those to whom the execution of such responsible duties is confided, it is not too much to presume that they are equally well qualified to fill the lower offices in the state, and ought therefore to be invested with the minor privileges of citizens, which no *man* is thought too mean or too ignorant to possess, and which the more earnest reformers assert to be the right of every one but a criminal. Surely it requires no great genius to fulfil the duties of an overseer, of a member of the vestry, of a parish clerk, of a guardian of the poor, of a burgess, or of a parliamentary elector? When we see the hands into which these offices and trusts are thrown, we cannot suppose it is from incapacity, but from jealousy, that women are excluded from them.

Let us take, for example, the generality of electors both in towns and in the country. The electors in many towns (with few exceptions) were, until recently, all but paupers, grossly ignorant, and utterly regardless of their privilege, excepting as it gave them a title to indulge in all manner of excess during an election, at the expense of one of the candidates, and also afforded an easy way of gaining money by the sale of their votes. The Reform Bill has introduced a more respectable class of persons into the constituency; but events continually show that many of the ten-pound householders are totally uninformed regarding their political duties, and are directed in the exercise of their prerogative solely by caprice or interest. In the country the case is just as bad. The farmers, to whom the Reform Bill gave votes, in general neither know nor care anything about politics; they vote to please their landlords; and many whose landlords do not take any decided political part – and therefore do not compel their tenantry to do so – will not ride a few miles to attend a polling-place, and in numerous instances will not even allow their names to be placed on the register! The forty-shilling freeholders are commonly of the poorest class. Many a small proprietor may be seen working on the roads, many are employed as menial servants, and it not unfrequently happens that a woman of ability, possessing a large stake in the country, and devoted to her political party, is subjected to the mortification of seeing the privilege denied to herself, confided to uneducated and unenlightened men in her own household.

Many ladies possess large property in towns, but not a voice have they in any schemes of local improvement. They can neither give their vote for the levying of a rate or a local tax; for the appointment of a town councillor, an alderman, or any other officer. The select vestry is closed against them, so are the hustings – they may neither appear at one place nor the other.

It is sometimes suggested, that women are adequately represented by their fathers, brothers, and husbands; and – passing by the cases in which a woman has no relation who can represent her interest – the suggestion has a slight show of plausibility, until we recollect that points are frequently discussed by the legislature, which affect women not only in their quality as citizens, but also in their distinctive character as females.

Did women constitute a portion of the senate, would not the unjust laws respecting property be abolished? would they continue after marriage in a state of perpetual tutelage? Still less, would acts have been allowed to pass which exonerate one sex from burdens which are heaped tenfold on the other?[11]

When we reflect on these things, it will not require any extraordinary sagacity to discover that women are *not* represented by men.

'An Outline of the Grievances of Women', *Metropolitan Magazine*
(May 1838) vol. 22, no. 85, pp. 17–19

188.   *As recent research has illustrated, middle-class women made a vigorous and multi-faceted contribution to the Anti-Corn Law campaign.[12] As in other movements involving women's public political participation, the question of their own right to the franchise could occasionally crack through the complex discursive layers of women's engagement. Richard Cobden delivered the following speech on free trade, at Covent Garden, London on 15 January 1845.*

There are many ladies, I am happy to say, present; now, it is a very anomalous and singular fact, that they cannot vote themselves, and yet that they have a power of conferring votes upon other people. I wish they had the franchise, for they would often make a much better use of it than their husbands. The day before yesterday, when I was in Manchester (for we are brought up now to interchange visits with each other by the miracle of steam in eight hours and a half), a lady presented herself to make inquiries how she could convey a freehold qualification to her son, previous to the 31st of this month; and she received due instructions for the purpose. Now, ladies who feel strongly on this question – who have the spirit to resent the injustice that is practised on their fellow-beings – cannot do better than make a donation of a county vote to their sons, nephew, grandsons, brothers, or any one upon whom they can beneficially confer that privilege.[13]

Richard Cobden in Bright and Rogers (1908), vol. 1, p. 132

The World Anti-Slavery Convention, 1840

The World Anti-Slavery Convention held in London in 1840 created a furore when the British and Foreign Anti-Slavery Society refused to allow the female delegates from the United States to address the Convention. For many British activists this moment was like a lighted match to dry kindling as the right of (middle-class) women to full participation in public political events was debated extensively for, perhaps, the first time.[14]

189.   This was a convention met together on the principles of universal benevolence, and they ought to welcome all who came there for the purpose of carrying those principles into effect; and from such a meeting assembled on such principles they were now about to exclude the women of America, and this they called acting on principles of universality. They professed to act on principles of universality, and were about to commence their proceedings by disfranchising one half of creation. Women were as competent as men to understand, and to guard everything connected with Christianity, and to bring forth the best qualities of our nature ...

The anti-slavery cause was under the greatest obligation to the exertions of women, and yet they were going to begin their first Convention by disfranchising their constituency as they did one-half of creation. [cheers]

> William Ashurst speaking at the World Anti-Slavery Convention, reported in *The Liberator* (24 July 1840), p. 119.

190.   It is highly gratifying that in such an assembly as the Anti-Slavery Convention, the right of woman to take an active part in the administration of public affairs was brought into discussion, and that that discussion, was full, animated and yet temperate, which is not usually the case when a prejudice or a custom is first assailed.

> *Leicestershire Mercury* cited in *The Liberator* (31 July 1840), p. 122

191.   *Daniel O'Connell, in this letter to Lucretia Mott (the most prominent of the American delegates) reveals that he, like many others, was forced to re-examine his own position on women's rights, thanks to the events of the convention.[15]*

My mature consideration of the entire subject convinced me of the right of the female Delegates to take their seats in the Convention, and of the injustice of excluding them. ...

My reasons are, *first,* That as it has been the practice in America for females to act as Delegates and Office-Bearers, as well as in the common capacity of members, of Anti-Slavery Societies, the persons who called this Convention ought to have warned the American Anti-Slavery Societies to confine their choice to males. ...

Secondly, The cause which is intimately interwoven with every good feeling of humanity, and with the highest and most sacred principle of Christianity, the Anti-Slavery cause in America, is under the greatest, the deepest, the most heart-binding obligation to the females who have joined the Anti-Slavery Societies in the United States. . . .

Thirdly, Even in England, with all our fastidiousness, women vote upon the great regulations of the Bank of England, in the nomination of its Directors and Governors, and in all other details, equally with men. That is, they assist in the most awfully important business, the regulation of the currency of this mighty empire, influencing the fortunes of *all* commercial nations.

Fourthly, Our women, in like manner, vote at the India House – that is – in the regulation of the Government of more than one hundred millions of human beings.

Fifthly, Mind has no sex; and, in the peaceable struggle to abolish Slavery all over the world – it is the basis of the present Convention to seek for success by peaceable, moral, and intellectual means alone, to the utter exclusion of physical force or armed violence . . . . We rely entirely on reason and persuasion, common to both sexes, and on the emotions of benevolence and charity – which are more lively and permanent amongst women than amongst men. . . .

... women have the same duties, and should, therefore, enjoy the same rights with the men, in the performance of these duties.

Daniel O' Connell to Mrs Lucretia Mott (20 June 1840) Glasgow Emancipation Society, *Sixth Annual Report* (1840), pp. 33–4

Anne Knight

192.   *Anne Knight's letter to Lucretia Mott, published (like O'Connell's) by the Glasgow Emancipation Society, formed a furious defence of women's right to political engagement. Knight's cousin, William Allen, although professing to be 'a strong advocate for the rights of women' was deeply disturbed by this vociferous letter, fearing that it would endanger both Knight's own reputation and that of the Quakers.[16]*

I believe they cannot deny the equality of talent as well as worth of their wives, sisters, and daughters. These ideas, discussed often among us, are helping the cause. We tell our opponents, in the beginning, that they must take off their grandmothers' night caps, and throw them to the 'things that love night;' they good naturedly comply, and entertain the subject with a smile. We tell them we are not the same beings as fifty years ago; no longer 'sit by the fire and spin,' or distil rosemary and lavender for poor neighbours; but appoint visiting Committees for them, and sit in Mission and Bible Societies reporting to the men, sitting in their public meetings, and uniting with them in association Committees. Then comes the great and mortal conflict. The dreadful monster *Slavery* must be grappled with; and who is sent out to do it? Not man – not the stronger vessel … No! weak, tender, untrained for the work – modest woman!

We have a far superior claim to the men, – the claim of our ensan-guined battle-field, – the claim of our trophies, our captives; and can they much longer dare to hold up the puny cry of *custom* and dread of ridicule, in their confused jargon and strife of tongues – their darken-ing of counsel by words without knowledge – while the veterans sit without, in silent contempt of their rhodomontade?[17] Surely, the folly is hastening to an end; it cannot withstand the light of truth. Tacitus relates that the Germans always called the women to their war-coun-sels, because they had something divine in them;[18] and do not your Indians have their conferences unitedly? The scientific Congresses of France are composed of men and women, – myself being a member, and having addressed them, *a Leige aux Blois* [*sic*], on the subject of Slavery. Our own Society invites its men and women in mission and conference; and if we may handle the holy things, is it for our sect, to raise its voice opposing our secular and moral engagements? Forbid it, common sense, and thou, my dear friend, cease not to cry aloud and lift up thy voice like a trumpet; for surely, if Indian women, if German women, if the women of France may hold colloquy with men, the women of England, not less Christian, and not less qualified than they, must, ere long, 'what is dark illumine.' … I wish it were practi-cable that, continuing the subject now begun, the cause of humanity might be extended, so that by the time of a *second* Convention, it would be more deserving the name of a *World's* Convention.

Anne Knight, Glasgow Emancipation Society, *Sixth Annual Report*
(1840), pp. 48–9

Anne Knight was one of the most assiduous campaigners for female suffrage. She embarked upon a massive campaign – writing letters to anyone and everyone, whom she believed might support the measure. Widely read in contemporary feminist literature, she carefully adapted her arguments to each person canvassed.[19] A political radical, she seized upon the Chartist movement to further her objectives, and was to establish a women's rights association in Sheffield in the early 1850s.[20] This is the text of a little women's suffrage leaflet, written in a male persona, that Anne Knight sent (in bulk!) to Matilda Biggs[21] in April 1847.

193a.   NEVER will the nations of the earth be well governed, until both sexes, as well as all parties, are fairly represented, and have an influence, a voice, and a hand in the enactment and administration of the laws. One would think, the sad mismanagement of the affairs of our own country, should, in all modesty, lead us MEN to doubt our own capacity for the task of governing a nation, or even a State, alone; and to apprehend that we need other qualities in our public councils – qualities that may be found in the female portion of our race. If woman be the complement of man, we may surely venture the intimation, that all our social transactions will be incomplete, or otherwise imperfect, until they have been guided alike by the wisdom of each sex. The wise, virtuous, gentle mothers of a State or nation, might contribute as much to the good order, the peace, the thrift of the body politic, as they severally do to the well-being of their families, which for the most part, all know, is more than the fathers do.

In a letter accompanying the leaflets she wrote,

193b.   I wish that talented philanthropists in England would come forward in this critical juncture of our nation's affairs and insist on the right of suffrage for all men and all women unstained with crime ... and take the liberty of requesting thy opinion as well as hearty co-operation in the demand for justice to us all, whether gowned or coated, in order that all may have a voice in the affairs of their country at a time when all interests are roused and it is important that 'every man should do his duty, and every woman also'.

Cited in Helen Blackburn, *Women's Suffrage* (1902), p. 19

194.   *Knight also used the radical press to publicize the cause:*

It is my right equally with my brother to the Suffrage, because I pay taxes as well as he ...

Why not Universal Adult Suffrage ... There are twenty public men who have acknowledged that our claim is just, but they are mute in public. Is that which is right in the parlour *not* right in the hall? Why not demand it at Exeter Hall,[22] at places of political resort? Of all your publications, Thomas Cooper[23] goes the farthest – 'The indubitable right of every human being to the Suffrage,' but says nothing of co-legislation – our right too; and he has confessed all this to me. You powerful men could soon 'subdue the world's dread laugh', and you ought. Pray, then, write a strong article *urging the claims of all.*

Anne Knight, 'The Rights of Woman', *The People* (1850),
vol. 2, no. 92, p. 315

Notes

1 William Smyth (1765–1849), professor of modern history at Cambridge.
2 William Roscoe (1765–1849) historian and promoter of Italian literature, was a well-known unitarian radical in Liverpool and champion of women's rights. Watts (1998), pp. 65, 93.
3 Dooley (1996), ch. 3.
4 [Brougham], Lydia Tomkins (1835), pp. 57–8; *Monthly Repository* (1835), vol. 9, pp. 408–9 and 627–8.
5 'The Dawn of Female Dignity', *Morning Star* (13 January 1841), no. 10, pp. 78–80.
6 See also documents **167–9**.
7 Review of Mrs. Hugo Reid's 'Plea for Woman', *Tait's Edinburgh Magazine* (1844), vol. 11, pp. 423–8.
8 Anne Knight, MS vol. s495, p. 146, Friends House Library. Knight's copy of Marion Reid's *A Plea For Woman* is full of notes and enclosures on other contemporary feminist authors, including William Thompson and Samuel Bailey.
9 Anne Knight was stung by the phrase 'natural barriers' declaring in her copy of Reid's work, 'What natural barriers? She has none but those placed equally before men how stupid these sentimentalisms!' Anne Knight, MS vol. s495, p. 146.
10 *British and Foreign Quarterly Review* (1838), vol. 7, no. 13, p. 398. See Chapter 2 above, n.2.
11 A reference to the bastardy clause of the Poor Law Amendment Act. See document **151**.
12 Simon Morgan, 'Domestic Economy and Political Agitation: Women and the Anti-Corn Law League, 1839–46', in Gleadle and Richardson (2000), pp. 115–33.
13 For other methods by which some women could confer votes upon men in a slightly earlier context (pre-1832) see Elaine Chalus 'Women, Electoral Privilege and Practice in the Eighteenth Century', in Gleadle and Richardson (2000), pp. 19–38.
14 Midgley (1992), pp. 158–61.
15 My thanks to Clare Midgley for assistance with locating documents **191–2**.
16 He particularly dissented from her argument that women had 'clearer and

diviner instincts' than men. MS letter from William Allen to Anne Knight (19 March 1841), Friends House Library, Temp MSS 725/5/23.

17 Rhodomontade: an extravagant boast.

18 See Chapter 9, n. 9.

19 Knight used scriptural arguments, for example, when approaching the more conservative children's writer, Ann Taylor (24 February 1849), Temp MSS 725/5/35, Friends House Library.

20 Schwarzkopf (1991), p. 254.

21 Matilda Biggs, (*c.* 1823– ?) was the daughter of William Ashurst, and was married to the Leicester radical, Joseph Biggs. She was a committed radical and supporter of women's rights – a pattern her daughter, Caroline Ashurst Biggs, was to follow.

22 Exeter Hall was a central meeting place of Evangelical organizations.

23 Thomas Cooper (1805–92), a leading Leicestershire Chartist. Intensely religious, he was also close to radical unitarian circles (being asked to deputize for W. J. Fox at South Place Chapel during the latter's illness). Cooper (1872).

Biographical Notes[1]

The following notes are restricted to individuals whose writings have been used directly in the main body of the anthology. An asterisk next to an individual's name indicates that they have their own biographical entry. (Where insufficient details have been found on an individual's life, brief information may be found in a footnote following the relevant document.)

Adams, Sarah Flower (1805–48)

Sarah Flower Adams was born in Harlow, Essex, the youngest daughter of radical parents (her father, Benjamin Flower, was the editor of the radical publication the *Cambridge Intelligencer*). Following the early death of their mother, Flower raised his daughters unconventionally, allowing them considerable freedom. They moved to Dalston, near Hackney, in 1820, where they struck up an acquaintance with Unitarian radicals such as Harriet Martineau[*]; and later with the progressive coterie of William Johnson Fox[*] at South Place Chapel in Finsbury. Sarah began to write for the network's radical journal, the *Monthly Repository* under the pseudonym 'S.Y.'; and in 1834 she married William Bridges Adams[*]. After a brief spell as an actress in the late 1830s, she concentrated upon her writing, composing many political poems, as well as essays for the *Westminster Review*. Adams was also a gifted singer and hymn writer (and an accomplished mountain climber!).

Adams's feminism, as her articles for the *Monthly Repository* indicate, was deeply infused with a faith in women's unique qualities. This emerged in her acclaimed dramatic poem, 'Vivia Perpetua' (1841) – an exposition on female heroism.

Bridell-Fox (1894); Garnett (1909); Stephenson (1922)

Adams, William Bridges (1797–1872)

William Bridges Adams came from a prosperous Staffordshire family. Having spent several years in South America, by the 1830s he was moving in radical unitarian circles in London, and writing for the *Monthly Repository*. In 1834

Adams, who had previously been married to Francis Place's daughter, Elizabeth, married Sarah Flower [Adams]*, another central figure in the W. J. Fox* circle. Often writing under the pseudonym, 'Junius Redivivus', Adams wrote widely on contemporary politics and the rights of the poor. As the owner of a railway carriage factory in Bow, Adams was renowned for the extensive facilities he provided for his workers. He was also widely respected as an engineer. He believed (in common with the St. Simonians) that mechanical devices could be used to lighten domestic tasks. This insight was just one strand of a broad feminist philosophy. His article, 'On the Condition of Women in England',[2] may have horrified many Unitarians, but it became a classic essay on the need to reform women's position.

Engineering (26 July 1872); Gleadle (1995)

Aikin, Lucy (1781–1864)

Lucy Aikin was born in Warrington, the daughter of the prominent author, John Aikin and Martha (Jennings), and a niece of the educationist, Anna Laetitia Barbauld. As Unitarians, the family encouraged Aikin's intellectual development and she was to achieve a high reputation as an historian and biographer. Her *Epistles on Women* (1810) indicated a commitment to female emancipation, although her correspondence reveals a more nuanced position. She did not, for example, support plans for marriage reform, although she believed passionately in the need to improve female education and secure female enfranchisement.

Le Breton (1864); Mellor (2000)

Ashurst, William Henry Snr (1792–1855)

William Henry Ashurst, a self-educated solicitor from London, was an affluent supporter of early Victorian radicalism. His home at Muswell Hill formed a key nexus for the reformers active in such movements as Chartism, Owenism and European nationalism. Ashurst and his children were particularly associated with the cause of Italian Emancipation, through their intimacy with Giuseppe Mazzini; but they also forged close transatlantic ties with anti-slavery campaigners. Ashurst financed a number of progressive, left-leaning journals such as the *Spirit of the Age* and *The Reasoner*, all of which published radical articles on women's position. Although Ashurst concurred with certain proscriptions concerning the limits of public female political activity, he encouraged his daughters to be independent and to eschew many of the conventional standards of feminine behaviour.

Gleadle (1995) and (2000)

Bailey, Samuel (1791–1870)

Samuel Bailey was born in Sheffield; his father was a cutler. He was closely involved in the cultural and political life of the city, helping to establish the Sheffield Literary and Philosophical Society, and becoming a town trustee in

1828. Strongly influenced by utilitarianism, he wrote many essays on political economy, finance, psychology, primogeniture and electoral reform. His works attracted considerable attention and debate amongst philosophic radicals.

Bamford, Samuel (1788–1872)

Samuel Bamford, a weaver, was born to radical parents in Middleton, near Manchester. Bamford became closely involved in radical activity from the mid-1810s, being a founder member of the Hampden Reform Club. Despite being prosecuted for conspiracy to incite riot in the wake of the Peterloo Massacre, Bamford himself was opposed to the use of violence. During the 1820s he distanced himself somewhat from the radical movement, and was even to act as a special constable during Chartist disturbances. Catherine Hall has used Bamford's classic account of the Peterloo incident to draw a fascinating portrait of the gendered basis of plebeian politics.

Bamford (1841); Hall (1992)

Barmby, Catherine (? 1817–53)

Catherine Barmby (née Watkins) was a leading socialist, writing numerous articles for the *New Moral World* under the pseudonym 'Kate'. She was later to write for other progressive publications, such as the *People's Press*. In 1841 she married Goodwyn Barmby, and later that year they issued a protest against the Chartists' failure to commit to women's suffrage. The Barmbys were the founding members of the Communist Church, they also established the short-lived Moreville Communitorium in 1843. During the 1840s, the Barmbys became close to radical unitarian feminists, such as William and Mary Howitt[*], and they were members of the coterie's Whittington Club. From the late 1840s, Barmby appears to have suffered from ill health, and her project to establish a woman's journal was never fulfilled. Part of Catherine Barmby's extensive contribution to Owenite feminism lay in two wide-ranging tracts: 'The Demand for the Emancipation of Woman, Politically and Socially' (reprinted in Taylor (1983)) and 'Women's Industrial Independence' (reprinted in Bellamy and Saville (1982)). As a committed socialist Barmby firmly believed in the need for a wider social and political reformation as the only means of securing emancipation for women.

Gleadle (1995); Taylor (1983)

Beddoes, Thomas (1760–1808)

Thomas Beddoes was born in Shifnal, Shropshire. He was educated at Oxford, before training as a doctor and chemist. A radical physician, he was committed to bringing health-care and knowledge to the poor. He wrote a number of self-help medical manuals, as well as radical political pamphlets. Moving in the progressive circles of rational dissent, Beddoes (who married Maria Edgeworth's sister, Anna) was highly sympathetic to progressive formulations of women's role. He gave lectures, for example, to all-female audiences on human physiology. He believed that women were peculiarly suited to domestic duties, but also respected and promoted their need for employment.

Stansfield (1984)

Bodichon, Barbara Leigh Smith (1827–91)

Barbara Leigh Smith Bodichon was the granddaughter of the radical MP William Smith. Her unconventional father, Benjamin Smith (also an MP) caused family controversy by his common-law partnership with her mother, Anne Longden. In her late teens, Bodichon, who was encouraged by her father to be independent, became acquainted with the network of radical unitarians, whose views on religion and social reform appealed to her. In the mid-1850s she began to organize a campaign to petition for reform to married women's legal position, and in 1857 she published *Women and Work* – a resounding demand for women's right and need for employment. A key figure in the Langham Place feminist circle, Bodichon was central to the establishment of the *English Woman's Journal* in 1858. A pioneer of educational reform (she established an innovative co-educational school, Portmann Hall in 1854), Bodichon was a promoter of Girton College for women. As a member of the Kensington Discussion Society in the mid-1860s, she also played a significant role in the formation of the women's suffrage campaign. Bodichon's feminism was equally evident in her private life. As an artist, she was a respected professional in her own right and her marriage to Eugène Bodichon was established on egalitarian lines.

Herstein (1985); Hirsch (1998)

Brontë, Anne (1820–49)

Born in Howarth, Yorkshire, Anne Brontë was the youngest child of Rev. Patrick and Maria Branwell Brontë. Largely educated at home, and intensely religious, Brontë had an isolated upbringing. She worked as a governess for several years, an experience which provided her with material for her first novel, *Agnes Grey* (1847). Charlotte Brontë[*], her sister, was critical of Anne's second novel, *The Tenant of Wildfell Hall* (1848) and many reviewers were shocked by its frank portrayal of drunkenness. Modern commentators, however, focus on its vigorous protest against women's position within marriage.

Brontë, Charlotte (1816–55)

Charlotte Brontë, the best known of the Brontë sisters, was a prolific writer from childhood. She found employment as a teacher and a governess, working for a period in Belgium. Her novel *Jane Eyre* (1847) (written under her pseudonym Currer Bell), attracted considerable attention. The publication of her second novel, *Shirley* (1849), brought her into the orbit of London literary circles. She married Arthur Nicholls, her father's curate, in June 1854, but died the following spring. Charlotte Brontë did not agree with the project of fighting for women's rights, maintaining a belief in the importance of Christian duty and sacrifice; and politically she was conservative. Nevertheless, in *Jane Eyre* she wrote poignantly on women's need for self-determination; and in *Shirley*, *Villette* and *The Professor* she provided subtle disquisitions on women's position within society, and their desire for useful occupation.

Gaskell (1857; 1997 edn); Smith (2000)

Brougham, Henry, 1st Baron (1778–1868)

Henry Brougham was born and educated in Edinburgh, and trained as a lawyer. He was a founder of the *Edinburgh Review* (1802), an influential Whig periodical. His many pamphlets and essays dealt with a wide range of political and current affairs. An MP from 1810, Brougham acted as Chief Counsel for the Queen during the Queen Caroline affair. As Lord Chancellor (1830-4), Brougham was a key figure in the passage of the 1832 Reform Act. Brougham's attitude towards women's rights is ambiguous.[3] However, he was instrumental in the establishment of the National Association for the Promotion of Social Science (1857) which encouraged the participation of women in public debate; and also played a leading role in the passage of the Divorce Act (1857).

Holcombe (1983); Stewart (1985)

Carlile, Richard (1790–1843)

Richard Carlile was born in Devon, into a working-class family. He moved to London in 1813 with his new wife, Jane, where he soon became involved in metropolitan radicalism. He was prosecuted for his publication of blasphemous works and spent six years in Dorchester jail (1819–25). From prison he published his journal *The Republican*, relying heavily upon a network of female and male activists to distribute his works and maintain his business. His religious views also underwent modification during this period and he came to develop an allegorical view of religion. In 1830, Carlile took over the Rotunda, in Blackfriar's Road, London which became an important centre for working-class radicalism. 1831 saw him back in prison for seditious libel. From prison he began to develop an intense relationship with Eliza Sharples*. Their subsequent 'moral marriage' made Carlile a controversial figure for fellow radicals, as did his dismissive attitude towards the political mobilization of the working-classes. Carlile does not appear to have had any sympathy with progressive views on women until the period of his first imprisonment – when, ironically his autocratic treatment of Jane Carlile became particularly apparent. Nonetheless, it was during these years that he began to articulate radical views as to women's political position and sexuality. In particular, closely influenced by Francis Place, he came to advocate birth control. Despite his support of Eliza Sharples's feminist journal, his career was prioritized over hers, and his philosophical commitment to women's rights frequently foundered over his evident personal desire for male domestic control.

McCalman (1980); Weiner (1983); Rogers (2000)

Cobden, Richard (1804–65)

Richard Cobden, the son of a poor Sussex farmer, was trained in the cloth trade, but became a successful businessman in his own right. He became a central figure in the 'Manchester School', promoting free trade and was a founder of the Anti-Corn Law League in 1839. An MP from 1841, Cobden promoted a non-interventionist foreign policy, free trade, national education, household suffrage and cheaper government. In many ways, Cobden typified noncon-formist middle-class radicalism. He was sympathetic to women's involvement in public affairs and, as a pacifist, he believed that the gradual cultural demise of physical force within social and political life would lead to the elevation of women's position. Nevertheless, he could be ambivalent as to women's claims for wider political rights.

Morley (1896)

Cornwallis, Caroline Frances (1786–1858)

Caroline Cornwallis was born at Wittersham, Kent. Her father was the Rev. William Cornwallis and her mother Mary was a theological writer. Despite persistent ill health Cornwallis taught herself several languages, as well as studying philosophy, science, history, law, theology and politics. With a small group of friends she launched, in 1842, an ambitious series of 'Small Books on Great Subjects'. A committed Christian, Cornwallis also wrote on the philoso-phy of Christianity. She published an historical novel, *Pericles* in 1846 and won a prize in 1853 for an essay on juvenile crime. With her extraordinary intel-lectual ability, Cornwallis often resented the lack of academic opportunities for women, and the domestic duties which demanded so much of her time. Although Cornwallis did not move within the networks of female campaigners, and was ambiguous as to women's public activity, she made a significant contribution to early women's rights campaigns with two accomplished articles on married women's legal position which appeared in the *Westminster Review* (1856–7).

Cornwallis (1864); Holcombe (1983)

Epps, John (1805–69)

John Epps came from a wealthy Calvinist family in Kent. After training as a doctor, he became closely involved in metropolitan radical circles, and went on to champion such causes as parliamentary reform and European nationalism. Epps, a homeopath and phrenologist, edited and contributed to a number of health reform journals, including the *Christian Physician and Anthropological Magazine* (1835–9) and the *Journal of Health and Disease* (1845–52). He was pres-ident of the Jennerian Institute. Epps used his position as a popular health reformer to challenge received opinions concerning women's physical and intellectual abilities.

Cooter (1984); Epps (1875)

Fox, William Johnson (1786–1864)

William Johnson Fox came from a humble Calvinist family in Suffolk. Largely self-educated, he trained as a dissenting minister at Homerton Academy in 1806. By 1812 he had declared himself to be a Unitarian, and developed a reputation for the political radicalism of his sermons. In 1824, he became minister of South Place chapel, in Finsbury, London. Already a contributor to progressive publications, such as the *Westminster Review*, Fox began to develop an influential coterie of writers, intellectual and artists. He took over the *Monthly Repository* in 1831, and under his proprietorship it became a leading organ for feminist ideas. In 1834 he separated from his wife and set up home with his former ward, Eliza Flower (the sister of Sarah Flower Adams*), causing many of his congregation to leave in protest. During the 1840s, Fox became increasingly absorbed in political activities, particularly as an Anti-Corn Law League lecturer (a factor which appears to have strained his relationship with Flower, who died in 1846). From 1847–63 Fox was MP for Oldham. Fox persistently championed the rights of women in both his published works and his public lectures. He was not, however, as radical on such issues as gender traits as many of his associates, and many contemporaries noted his insensitive behaviour towards his wife and Flower. Perhaps his greatest contribution to the feminist movement lay in his role as a facilitator. The salon he established with his partner Eliza Flower, and his editorship of the *Monthly Repository*, provided vital forums for feminist discussion and debate.

Garnett (1909); Mineka (1944)

Gillies, Mary (1800–70)

Mary Gillies was the daughter of a Scottish merchant, William Gillies (her Welsh mother, Charlotte, died when Mary was still a child). On the collapse of her father's business, Mary and her sister Margaret (who was to become an accomplished artist) went to live under the guardianship of their uncle, Lord Adam Gillies in Edinburgh. They returned to live in London with their father in about 1819, and later became closely acquainted with the William Johnson Fox* circle. By 1836 Mary Gillies was editing the *Monthly Repository* with Richard Hengist Horne. She subsequently published articles in *Howitt's Journal* and collaborated on literary projects with Horne.

Gillies and her sister lived in a household with the sanitary reformer, Thomas Southwood Smith (Margaret's partner) and Richard Hengist Horne for many years. The precise nature of Gillies's relationship with Horne is not easy to ascertain, although their friendship survived Horne's marriage in 1847 and subsequent separation.

Blainey (1968); Yeldham (1997)

Gillies, Mary Leman, see Grimstone, Mary Leman

Greaves, James Pierrepont (1777–1842)

James Pierrepont Greaves, a London merchant, spent eight years on the continent (1817–25), studying Swiss educational theory, and was a disciple of Pestalozzi. On returning to England he established the Infant School Society. A political radical who moved in Owenite circles, Greaves fostered a progressive intellectual salon from his home in Burton Street, London. His mystical beliefs set him apart from mainstream Owenism, in particular his commitment to the need to cultivate the spiritual in human existence. This was to be achieved by the adoption of an ascetic life-style, which eschewed dietary stimulants (including animal products, alcohol and caffeinated drinks) and encouraged celibacy (Greaves was highly critical of the existing marriage system). His views were practised at the First Concordium community in Ham Common, Surrey.

Harrison (1969); Latham (1999)

Grimstone, Mary Leman (*c.* 1800– *c.* 1851)

Mary Leman Grimstone (née Rede) was from a literary family. As a teenager she wrote verse and contributed to *La Belle Assemblée*. In 1825, she travelled to Tasmania with her sister and brother-in-law (but without the husband whom she had recently married). It was in Tasmania that she began to write novels (a fact which has led to her being championed as a formative influence on Australian literature). By the early 1830s she was back in London and moving in radical unitarian circles. In the mid-1830s, Grimstone (presumably a widow) married William Gillies (the father of Mary Gillies[*]), and her writing career appears to have gone into abeyance until the mid-1840s when she began to contribute to such publications as *Howitt's Journal* and the *People's Journal*. Grimstone was a committed political radical, supporting franchise reform, European nationalism and national education. She also had great faith in the potential of the co-operative system to reform the ills of capitalist society. One of the most quoted feminists of her day, Grimstone wrote passionately and eloquently of the ills of women's position. Her novels, such as *Woman's Love* (1832) and *Cleone* (1834) provided clear expositions of these views. However, it was a feminism designed to placate the wary – as indicated by her beautiful, chaste and morally scrupulous heroines. Indeed, although her articles for journals such as the *Monthly Repository* could wax pertinently on the social construction of gender difference, Grimstone was adept at fitting her message to her audience. In many of her essays she celebrated the importance of maternal love and female moral strength, whilst delivering powerful indictments of women's cultural, political and legal oppression.

Gleadle (1995); Roe (1989); Rogers (2000)

Hamilton, Mrs (*fl. c.* 1830–late 1840s)

Mrs Hamilton came from Paisley, Scotland. During the 1830s she embarked upon many lecture tours across Scotland (and from the 1840s, across England). Announcing herself to be a 'female Reformer' she discoursed upon popular phrenology, women's rights and Owenism.

Cooter (1984)

Hatfield, S. (Miss) (*fl.* 1803–16)

S. Hatfield appears to have been a woman of diverse literary skills. In addition to her feminist writing, she published books on Lincolnshire, and the theology of ancient pagans, as well as a novel, *She Lives in Hope* (1801). Her view of women's liberation was perhaps closer to Mary Astell's Tory feminism, than to the philosophy of Mary Wollstonecraft.

Hays, Mary (1760–1843)

Mary Hays came from a family of rational dissenters in Southwark, London. In 1792 she entered theological controversy by publishing a pamphlet in support of public worship. Two years later in her *Letters and Essays* (which was partly co-authored with her sister, Eliza) she indicated her firm commitment to disestablishment, civic rights, philosophical materialism and feminism. Hays, who was determined to forge an independent career as a writer, wrote for publications such as the *Monthly Magazine*, as well as publishing novels. She moved in the circles of advanced rational dissent, and benefited from the mentorship of William Frend, William Godwin and Robert Robinson. A close friend of Mary Wollstonecraft, Hays's *Appeal to the Men of Great Britain in Behalf of the Women* (1798) was a powerful feminist tract, and her *Memoirs of Emma Courtney* (1796) and *The Victim of Prejudice* (1799) evoked considerable discussion because of their open avowal of female passion. According to Janet Todd,[4] Hays became more conservative in the early years of the nineteenth century. Influenced by the works of Maria Edgeworth and Hannah More, her writings assumed a greater moral didacticism.

Luria (1977)

Hays, Matilda Mary (1820 – *c.* 1866)

Matilda Mary Hays was a novelist and translator who moved in radical literary circles. In the mid-1840s she embarked upon the translation of George Sand's novels, with the assistance of Eliza Ashurst and Edmund Larken. This was seen as an important feminist project by metropolitan radicals. Her own novel, *Helen Stanley* (1846), was insistent upon women's right to earn a living; and in the late 1840s she sat on the council of the progressive Whittington Club. In 1849 Hays began a relationship with the actress, Charlotte Cushman, who coached her in the theatrical profession. They travelled to the United States together and were known for their 'female marriage'. Hays, a cross-dresser, also lived for a time with the lesbian sculptor Harriet Hosmer, in Rome. Hays returned to England in 1858 to take a leading role in the new feminist periodical, the *English Woman's Journal*.

Gleadle (1995); Leach (1970)

Hennell, Elizabeth ('Rufa') Brabant (1811–98)

Elizabeth Hennell came from an intellectual middle-class family. (Her father, Dr R. H. Brabant was the model for Mr Casaubon in George Eliot's *Middlemarch*.)

In 1843 she was married to Charles Hennell at South Place Chapel in Finsbury by W. J. Fox[*]. George Eliot was one of her bridesmaids. Hennell moved in the radical circles of Charles Bray and his family in Coventry, and was close to John Chapman, editor of the *Westminster Review*, and his coterie in London. A gifted intellectual in her own right (George Eliot completed her groundbreaking translation of the German theologian Strauss in 1846), Hennell established a radical school near Regent's Park, following the death of her husband in 1850. She married Wathen Call in 1857, who had recently resigned as an Anglican clergyman.

Hennell, an individualistic radical, was one of the first people to visit George Eliot following her decision to live with a married man, George Henry Lewes. Despite her unorthodox pronouncements on sexual matters, Hennell insisted that it was a wife's role to revere her husband.

Haight (1969)

Hogg, Thomas Jefferson (1792–1862)

Thomas Jefferson Hogg was the son of a Yorkshire barrister. He was expelled, with his friend Shelley, from Oxford in 1811, following the publication of Shelley's *Necessity of Atheism*. He remained close to Shelley, mixing in the same unorthodox circles. Hogg enjoyed the patronage of Henry Brougham[*] who appointed him revising barrister for Northumberland and Norwich in 1841. Hogg's biography of Shelley is a colourful and not always reliable account of the poet's life. Hogg's political views appear to have been far more conservative than those of Shelley, but they shared a scepticism for organized religion, as well as an interest in sexual radicalism. Hogg, for example, encouraged by Shelley, appears to have made advances to Mary Shelley[*]. Hogg was to form a long-term relationship with Jane Williams, whose husband Edward had drowned with Shelley.

Hogg (1858; 1906 edn); Rees (1985)

Howitt, Mary (1799–1888)

Mary Howitt (née Botham) was born in Staffordshire to a strict Quaker family. In 1821 she married William Howitt. The Howitts collaborated on many literary projects, and edited *Howitt's Journal* and the *People's Journal*. Howitt was later to turn to spiritualism and Catholicism, but from the late 1830s to the early 1850s, she and her husband moved in radical unitarian circles in London, their home functioning as a radical salon. Howitt herself was keenly interested in radical politics, supporting the Chartist movement, the Anti-Corn Law League, and the peace and anti-slavery movements. She believed in the importance of domesticity for women, but was nonetheless committed to challenging conventional ideas of womanhood. As editors, Howitt and her husband frequently included feminist contributions in their periodicals, and Mary Howitt's translations of the work of Swedish feminist Frederika Bremer, were widely acclaimed. In the 1850s Howitt was secretary to the committee established by Barbara Leigh Smith[*] to campaign for a reform to married women's legal position.

Howitt (1889); Woodring (1952)

Hughes, Mary (*c.* 1756–1824)

Mary Hughes, of Hanwood in Shropshire, was the daughter of an Anglican rector. Educated by her mother, Hughes became a Unitarian in her late teens. A woman of comfortable means, Hughes was an active and influential Unitarian. She was a frequent contributor to the *Monthly Repository*, writing on a variety of issues, including the peace movement and education. She was a leading member of the Christian Tract Society, writing nineteen of its pamphlets.

Monthly Repository (1821–5)[5]

Hunt, Henry (1773–1835)

Henry Hunt came from a family of prosperous Wiltshire farmers. He appears to have been radicalized by his imprisonment in 1800 (for a duel), which brought him into association with political activists. By 1816, when he joined the Spa Fields demonstrations, he was developing a reputation as a radical orator. Hunt was sentenced to two and a half years' imprisonment following the Peterloo Massacre in 1819. Hunt, an M.P. 1830–3, was known to be an egotistical man, whose attitude toward the working class was frequently condescending. His views on women remain to be fully excavated, although he was clearly supportive of female radical societies.

Belchem (1985)

Jameson, Anna Brownwell (1794–1860)

Anna Jameson (née Murphy) was born in Dublin. She was home-educated and became a governess at the age of sixteen. She married Robert Jameson, a lawyer in 1825. They separated within four years, although she joined him in Canada in 1836–7. Jameson enjoyed friendships with many leading literati, including Mary Howitt[*], the Brownings, Harriet Martineau[*], Lady Byron and the Carlyles. Jameson established herself as a writer in 1826 with *Diary of an Ennuyée*, and went on to develop her reputation with works such as *Memoirs of Celebrated Female Sovereigns* (1831) and the more explicitly feminist *Characteristics of Women* (1832). Jameson, who won a Civil List Pension in 1851, was to be an important inspiration to the next generation of feminists, supporting the Married Women's Property Committee and the Langham Place group. In 1855/6 she delivered two celebrated lectures: 'Sisters of Charity' and 'The Communion of Labour' in the home of Elizabeth Jesser Reid. She did not openly support the fight for women's rights, but issued a potent call for women to play an active, if woman-centred, role in public life. Whilst her feminism may often appear tentative, scholars have noted that her works are infused with a deep and persistent commitment to a reform of women's position.

Johnston (1997); Thomas (1967)

Jewsbury, Geraldine Endsor (1812–80)

Geraldine Jewsbury was the fourth of six children of a Derbyshire mill owner. Her mother died when she was young, and she was largely raised by her sister,

Maria Jewsbury*, before attending boarding school. Jewsbury cared for her father until his death in 1840. Then, until his marriage in 1853, she became a housekeeper for her brother Frank in Manchester, where she moved in radical intellectual circles. Jewsbury, who enjoyed close friendships with the Carlyles and Sydney Morgan* published a number of successful novels from the mid-1840s to the late 1850s, as well as books for children. She was a prolific reviewer for the *Athenaeum* and, from 1858 became a reader for the publishers, Bentley's. During the 1840s, when she was influenced by Saint-Simonism, Jewsbury was known for her heterodox views. Her first novel, *Zoë* (1845) dealt with the sexual passion between a Catholic priest and a married woman; whilst her second book, *The Half Sisters* (1848) formed a radical commentary on the lives of conventionally married women. Cherishing the association between domesticity and femininity, Jewsbury herself could be cynical about those who simply demanded women's rights. Her own vision was of a more organic, complex maturation of female abilities and character.

Clarke (1990); Howe (1935); Ireland (1892)

Jewsbury, Maria Jane (1800–33)

Maria Jewsbury, the elder sister of Geraldine Jewsbury*, was born and educated in Derbyshire. She composed essays and poetry from her teens, becoming the leading writer for the *Athenaeum* in 1831. Often plagued by religious doubt herself, she married a rector, Rev. William Fletcher in 1832. The following spring they travelled to India together where Jewsbury died after contracting cholera. Jewsbury moved in literary circles, and was close to Dora Wordsworth. Despite her ambivalence on the subject of female employment,[6] Maria Jewsbury was keenly alert to the psychological problems created by women's lack of intellectual outlets, and she was particularly concerned with the needs of exceptionally talented girls.

Clarke (1990)

Knight, Anne (1786–1862)

Anne Knight came from a prosperous Quaker family in Chelmsford. She was a tireless campaigner for the anti-slavery cause, and also believed passionately in the peace movement, attending the 1848 world peace conference. From the late 1840s Knight became resident in France, where she developed a close interest in the Saint-Simonian movement. One of the most important feminist campaigners of her day, Knight campaigned ceaselessly on the subject of female enfranchisement employing indignant, impassioned and at times millenarian language.[7] In the early 1850s she was instrumental in the foundation of a women's rights association in Sheffield. Knight did not marry, wishing to maintain her independence.

Malmgreen (1982)

Lamb, Mary (1764–1847)

Mary Lamb was a London dressmaker. In 1796 she stabbed her mother to death and was placed in the care of her brother, the famous writer, Charles Lamb. She completed a number of literary projects with Charles including *Tales from Shakespeare* (1807) and *Mrs. Leicester's School* (1808). Seemingly more radical politically than her brothers, Lamb benefited from an alternative female network which included women such as Sarah Hazlitt and Eliza Fricker. Mary Lamb's biographer, Katharine Anthony, has written sensitively of the tension between Lamb's 'sensitive demeanour' beneath which simmered a sense of injustice at women's subordination. Mary Lamb acted as one of the many conduits between the ideas of Mary Wollstonecraft and Mary Hays[*] and the literary culture of the early nineteenth century.

Aaron (1991); Anthony (1948)

Lane, Charles (c. 1800–1870)

Charles Lane worked in the city during his early career, and was editor of the *London Mercantile Price-Current*. By the 1840s he was moving in Owenite circles, and in 1842 (a year after the breakdown of his marriage) he went to live with the 'sacred socialists' in their vegan community, the First Concordium at Ham Common. Having invited the community's mentor William Bronson Alcott to visit them in 1842, Lane and his young son accompanied Alcott back to the United States. Here, Lane became a founding member of the short-lived, transcendental community, Fruitlands. He also spent several months in a Shaker community before returning to London in 1846. Lane then entered into a permanent relationship with Hannah Bond (a former matron of the First Concordium). Lane was a prolific contributor to contemporary radical journals, both in Britain and the United States. His feminist ideas were close to those of Margaret Fuller, whose life and work he discussed in his journalism.

Latham (1999); Sanborn (1918); Shephard (1937)

Lawrence, James Henry (1773–1840)

James Lawrence came from a wealthy family who were settled in Jamaica. Lawrence himself spent much of his life living on the continent. Eccentric and idiosyncratic, he claimed to be a Knight of Malta, calling himself the 'Chevalier Lawrence'. Lawrence's interest in rank was also made evident in his *On the Nobility of the British Gentry* (1824). Lawrence, an advocate of spelling reform, was best known to contemporaries for his works on the Nair cast, which advocated free sexual unions. In the 1830s, he appears to have moved into Saint-Simonian circles.

Linton, Eliza Lynn (1822–98)

Eliza Lynn Linton was born in Cumberland, the twelfth child of the Rev. James Lynn. In 1845 she moved to London where she became associated with radical circles. She began to establish herself as a writer, producing novels and essays. By the late 1840s she was a paid journalist for the *Morning Chronicle*, and from 1852–4 the Parisian correspondent for the *Leader*. Her 1851 novel, *Realities* demonstrated a familiarity with contemporary feminist ideas, and in 1858 she married the feminist republican William James Linton*. They separated after six years, and Eliza Linton, whose views were becoming increasingly conservative, began to write for the *Saturday Review*. Her famous essays 'The Girl of the Period' and 'Modern Mothers' satirized the manners and shallowness of modern women, berating them for neglecting their family duties. However, Linton supported both the right to divorce and reform to married women's legal position. Indeed, her religious agnosticism, and her decision to write her autobiography in a male persona, are indicative of her complex personal and ideological make-up.

Van Thal (1979)

Linton, William James (1812–97)

William James Linton, a wood-engraver, came from a radical family in Mile End, London. At the instigation of radical literati such as Thomas Wade and Richard Hengist Horne, Linton was brought into the ambit of the *Monthly Repository* circle in the late 1830s. By 1839, Linton had launched his own paper, the *National*, which published a special issue devoted to feminist issues. Linton, a fervent supporter of Chartist and republicanism, went on to become a pivotal figure in early Victorian radical culture. He was particularly active in campaigning for European nationalism; and articulated a republicanism that emphasized the importance of individual moral and spiritual growth. Although he believed firmly in natural gender differences (believing that women were more emotional and lyrical, for example), he reiterated the importance of female suffrage in many of his publications. His unconventionality also extended to his personal life. He had seven children with Emily Wade, the sister of his first wife, Laura. A marriage to Eliza Lynn* in 1858, after Emily's death, was brief and unhappy. He emigrated to the United States in 1866.

Smith (1973)

Lynn, Eliza, see Linton, Eliza Lynn

Lytton, Edward Bulwer (1803–73)

Edward Bulwer-Lytton was the third son of wealthy parents, and was educated at Oxford. In 1827 he married Rosina Doyle Wheeler (the daughter of Anna Wheeler*), but the marriage ended in acrimony in 1836. Lytton evidently engaged in extra-marital affairs, and his wife also complained of his violent and abusive temperament. In 1858 he incarcerated Rosina in an asylum. Lytton enjoyed a high reputation as a novelist, and moved in fashionable literary and radical political circles. He sat in parliament as a radical MP 1831–41; dabbled in alternative medicine; demonstrated a keen interest in utilitarianism and was editor of the *New Monthly Magazine* (1831–2). Inheriting the family seat,

Knebworth House in 1843, he gradually adopted more conservative ideas. When he returned to parliament in 1852 his views were closer to those of a Tory democrat.

Lytton (1948)

Martin, Emma (1812–51)

Emma Martin came from a lower-middle-class Bristol family. In the 1830s Martin, a Baptist, became a lecturer, delivering denunciations of Owenite atheism. She gradually began to alter her views however, and, in 1839, left her unhappy marriage to become one of the most popular Owenite lecturers. A staunch feminist, she also lectured on phrenology and on capital punishment. Although she formed a stable partnership with Joshua Hopkins in the mid-1840s, her life continued to be plagued by poverty. She trained as a midwife to boost her income, and used her medical training to espouse women's right to control over their own bodies.

Taylor (1983)

Martineau, Harriet (1802–76)

Harriet Martineau was the daughter of a Unitarian Norwich cloth manufacturer. She started to contribute to the *Monthly Repository* from 1821 and achieved fame with her *Illustrations of Political Economy* (1832–4). Her reputation as an astute observer of social, cultural and political life was further enhanced by her *Society in America* (1837) (composed after an extended trip to the United States) and her novel *Deerbrook* (1839). Senior Whig politicians, such as Henry Brougham[*], frequently turned to Martineau for advice. In 1844 she announced her faith in mesmerism, and in 1851, her *Letters on the Laws of Man's Nature and Development* (co-authored by Henry Atkinson) created a furore for its views on religion. Martineau wrote for a wide range of contemporary publications, and was the leader writer for the *Daily News*. She is particularly associated with the Lake District, where she lived from 1845, and became a prominent figure in the local community.

Martineau championed the virtues of female domesticity, and was ambivalent as to the role of women's rights campaigners. Nevertheless, the *British and Foreign Quarterly Review* referred to her as one of the 'most notorious' propagandists of sexual equality of the age.[8] She wrote pertinently on the evils of married women's legal position, their right to the suffrage and need of employment. In common with most Unitarians, she believed education to be the key in transforming women's position.

Webb (1960)

Meteyard, Eliza (1816–79)

Eliza Meteyard, the daughter of an army surgeon, was born in Liverpool. She moved to London in 1842 following her father's death and became close to radical unitarian networks (particularly William and Mary Howitt[*]). A struggling writer, she wrote for such publications as *Douglas Jerrold's Weekly Newspaper* and *Eliza Cook's Journal* using the pseudonym 'Silverpen'. Meteyard was a staunch supporter of radical social and political reform, and was particularly associated with the Cooperative League, and the Early Closing Movement. She later became an ardent supporter of Gladstonian Liberalism. Whilst she often had to tone down her feminism for publication, Meteyard was as concerned to reorientate limiting cultural constructions of women, as she was to fight for their rights. Meteyard lent assistance and advice to the emerging women's rights campaigners of the 1850s.

Gleadle (1995); Rogers (2000)

Mill, John Stuart (1806–73)

Mill was the eldest son of the intellectual James Mill, a close associate of Jeremy Bentham. The two men subjected John Stuart Mill to an intensive education, which Mill argued lead to a mental crisis. During the 1830s Mill played a leading role in the *London Review* and the *Westminster Review*. He was associated with the W. J. Fox* circle and developed a close attachment to Harriet Taylor*, who he claimed exerted an enormous influence over his intellectual development. They married in 1851 and Mill signed a marital agreement granting Taylor equal rights in their relationship. Mill's works on political economy and political philosophy, for example, *Essays on Liberty* (1859) and *Considerations on Representative Government* (1861), established him as one of the country's leading political scientists. His *Subjection of Women* (1869) provided a liberal theoretical basis to women's emancipation – a position which many commentators argue underestimates the wider cultural and sexual basis of women's oppression. In 1866 he submitted a women's suffrage bill to parliament, although his high-handed attitude towards the women's suffrage societies was resented by some activists.

Caine (1978); Coole (1993); Hayek (1951)

Morgan, Lady Sydney Owenson (1776–1859)

Sydney Morgan was the daughter of a well-known Irish actor. She married Sir Charles Morgan in 1812. In addition to numerous travel books and essays, she wrote a number of novels. Many of these considered aspects of Irish nationalism, and were highly controversial. The first woman to receive a pension for her literary endeavours (1837), Morgan's *Woman and Her Master* (1840) earned her widespread esteem in the reforming world. *Tait's Edinburgh Magazine* claimed that it began the agitation for women's rights.[9]

Campbell (1988)

Morrison, Frances (1807–98)

Frances Morrison (née Cooper) was a working-class teacher from Surrey. At the age of fifteen she moved to Birmingham with James Morrison*, whom she married four or five years later. The mother of four daughters, Morrison ran a small newspaper shop whilst spending her spare time studying radical politics. She contributed feminist articles under the pseudonym 'Bondswoman' to her husband's paper, the *Pioneer*. After her husband's death she took up teaching and also became well known as an Owenite lecturer, specializing in lectures on women's rights. She published one of these lectures, *The Influence of the Present Marriage System*, in 1838. It is, according to Barbara Taylor, one of the most significant examples of feminist writing to be published by an Owenite woman.[10]

Taylor (1983)

Morrison, James (1802–35)

James Morrison, a house-painter, was born in Newcastle. He was a key member of the Operative Builders' Union and founding editor of its publication, the *Pioneer*, in 1833. A staunch defender of the need for independent working-class political action, Morrison resigned from the Grand National Consolidated Trades Union because of political differences with Robert Owen. As editor of the *Pioneer*, Morrison established an important forum for working-class feminism – the Woman's Page. Nevertheless, despite his penetrating insights into the effects of capitalist organization upon women's private and political lives, Morrison often adopted a patronizing tone towards his female readers.[11]

Taylor (1983)

Mylne, Margaret (1807–92)

Margaret Mylne was the daughter of Professor John Thomson (a radical doctor) and Margaret Millar (daughter of the Scottish philosopher, John Millar). In 1843 Mylne married her cousin, John Millar Mylne. Her feminism evidently sprang from the enlightened liberalism of her background, in which women played a lively and important role in political and social networks. Her significant essay on woman's position, which appeared in the *Westminster Review* (1841), was republished in 1870.

Rendall (2000)

Norton, Caroline (1808–77)

Caroline Norton was the granddaughter of the playwright Sheridan. A committed Whig, in 1827 she married George Norton, a staunch Tory. The marriage broke down irretrievably in 1836, and George Norton removed their three sons from his wife's care. He then (unsuccessfully) took the Prime Minister, Lord Melbourne, to court for adultery.

Caroline Norton's desperate attempts to gain access to her children galvanized her to campaign for legal change. Norton, who already had a literary reputation, published a number of pamphlets to aid her cause. The Infant Custody Act was finally passed in 1839. George Norton softened his own attitude towards Caroline's access to their children, after the death of their youngest son. Norton's private letters reveal a more radical attitude towards women's position than that which she enunciated in her published work. Although never part of a feminist network, her experiences compelled her to make an important contribution to debates on women's position, particularly with her *English Laws for Women in the Nineteenth Century* (1854) and *Letter to the Queen on Lord Cranworth's Marriage and Divorce Bill* (1855).

Perkins (1909)

O'Connell, Daniel (1775–1847)

Daniel O'Connell was born in County Kerry to a Roman Catholic, aristocratic family. He trained as a lawyer and by 1815 had become a leading figure in the movement for Irish emancipation. Opposed to revolution, he promoted democratic suffrage, and urged peasants to join the Catholic Association to help the struggle for their rights. An MP from 1828, O'Connell, who was strongly influenced by Benthamism, supported a range of political and administrative reforms. His policy of compromise with the Whigs over the Irish question proved highly controversial. As a young man O'Connell read the works of Mary Wollstonecraft and William Godwin and declared himself in favour of their feminist programme, although as a politician he prioritized other objects of reform.

Houston (1906)

Owen, Robert (1771–1858)

Robert Owen came from a fairly prosperous background in Newton in Wales. In 1799, having flourished as a drapery merchant in Manchester, he purchased a cotton mill at New Lanark (and married Caroline Dale, daughter of the mill's former owner). At New Lanark, Owen established a reputation as a philanthropist for his innovative treatment of his workers. Increasingly radical, he denounced Christanity and began to develop a critique of the capitalist system. In 1824 he travelled to the United States where he bought the Rappite Community at Indiana, renaming it New Harmony. He established the *New Moral World* in 1834, the leading organ for Owenite ideas. Nevertheless, Owen had a problematic relationship with the Owenite movement, having little faith in the independent political action of the working classes. This attitude led him to be ejected in 1844 from Queenwood Community (the cooperative community) he established in Hampshire) and he subsequently went to the United States where he continued his work as a lecturer. Although he was a persistent advocate of marriage reform, the rights of women do not receive the same sustained attention in his oeuvre as they do in the Owenite movement at large.

Harrison (1969)

Owen, Robert Dale (1801–77)

Born in Glasgow, Robert Dale Owen was the eldest son of Robert Owen[*]. As a teenager he was educated at the progressive Hofwyl Institute. In 1825 he travelled to the United States and joined the New Harmony Community. Two years later he became an American citizen, and began a long political career as a democrat. With Frances Wright[*] he edited the radical feminist paper *Free Enquirer* from 1828 to 1832; and his *Moral Physiology* (1831) established his progressive credentials in such areas as sexual relations. His wife, Mary Robinson, assisted in his work to secure reforms to women's legal position in the legislature of Indiana.

Royle (1974); Taylor (1983)

Parkes, Bessie Rayner (1829–1925)

Bessie Rayner Parkes was born in Birmingham. Her unitarian father, Joseph, was widely known as a radical lawyer. As a teenager she developed an intense friendship with Barbara Leigh Smith* (later Bodichon) and in the 1850s Parkes assisted in her campaign to reform married women's legal position. In 1854 Parkes published her *Remarks on the Education of Girls* and four years later helped to establish the *English Woman's Journal*. Parkes married Louis Belloc in 1867 and spent much of her time in France. Her feminism was more muted and conservative than that of many of her associates.

Hirsch (1998)

Parsons, Benjamin (1797–1855)

Originally a tailor's apprentice, Parsons became a Congregational minister at Ebley in Stroud in 1826. A temperance campaigner, Parsons was also active in promoting 'education Chartism', and exhorting Chartists to eschew physical force. His view of women was strongly infused with a vision of their moral and inspirational potential.

Petrie, George (1791–1836)

George Petrie was born in Western Scotland. A tailor and soldier he was associated with Leicester but moved to London in the early 1830s, where he became a member of the Grand National Consolidated Trades Union and a campaigner for the unstamped press. Strongly influenced by the ideas of Thomas Spence, his views were aired (often under the pseudonym 'Agragrius') in two publications which he edited with Richard Lee: *The Man* and the *People's Hue and Cry*. Petrie, who believed in the abolition of private property, wrote powerfully of women's oppression, but his comments are often overlaid with a highly patronizing, almost bombastic tone.

Petrie (1841); Taylor (1983); Weiner (1969)

Radcliffe, Mary Ann (*c.* 1746–post-1810)

Mary Radcliffe, a Scotswoman, was educated in a convent. She entered into a clandestine marriage whilst still a teenager. Her husband, with whom she had eight children, was an alcoholic, and Radcliffe had to find work to save the family's desperate financial situation. In addition to Gothic novels, Radcliffe published her *Memoirs* (1810) and a tract on the lack of employment opportunities available to women, *The Female Advocate* (1799). Although her feminism was largely driven by personal frustration at women's inability to earn a decent living, rather than deep-seated political principles, her work contains interesting suggestions for greater government interference in the labour market.

Radcliffe (1810)

Reid, Marion (? – after 1872)

Marion Reid (née Kirkland) was born in Glasgow, the daughter of a merchant. In 1839 she married Hugo Reid, a chemist and president of the Hunterian Society, and went to live in Edinburgh. Here she appears to have moved in radical-liberal circles and was spurred to write her *Plea for Woman* when female delegates were denied the opportunity to speak at the World Anti-Slavery Convention in 1840. She travelled considerably during her lifetime and outlived her husband, who died in London in 1872.

Ellsworth (1979)

Richardson, Reginald Jones (1803–61)

Richardson, a master carpenter from Salford, was a founder of the South Lancashire Anti-Poor Law Association, as well as being a member of the Manchester Operative Trades Union. An active Chartist, he composed a number of political pamphlets during his imprisonment in Lancaster Castle for conspiracy in 1840. After his release, Richardson's relationship with the Chartist movement deteriorated and he moved towards more reformist, middle-class initiatives.

His *Rights of Women* (1840) is the fullest elaboration of women's right to vote to emerge from the Chartist movement.

Schwarzkopf (1991); Thompson (1984)

Sharples, Eliza (1803–61)

Eliza Sharples came from a wealthy Wesleyan manufacturing family in Bolton. In 1829 she began to develop an interest in the ideas of Richard Carlile[*]. She turned her back on her family in 1832 and travelled to London to assist Carlile and his associate Robert Taylor, who were imprisoned for blasphemy. A close intimacy soon developed between Carlile and Sharples. Encouraged by Carlile, Sharples delivered public lectures at the radical Rotunda theatre. By the spring she had assumed management of the theatre and Carlile's publishing business. She was now pregnant and persuaded Carlile to announce their union to be a 'moral marriage'. It was also in 1832 that Sharples established her journal, the *Isis*. In 1843 Carlile died, plunging Sharples and their three children into long-term financial problems. Sharples spent a brief period at the abstemious First Concordium community and was later to manage the free-thought Warner Street Temperance Hall in London.

Sharples's confidence in pronouncing herself to be a 'leader of the people' at the Rotunda in 1832, the infusion of her politics with an allegorical Christianity, and her reclamation of Eve as a feminist icon, make her one of the most extraordinary female activists of her day.

Frow and Frow (1989); Rogers (2000); Weiner (1983)

Shelley, Mary Wollstonecraft (1797–1851)

Mary Shelley was the daughter of William Godwin and Mary Wollstonecraft (who died shortly after her birth). She eloped to Europe with the poet Shelley[*], in 1814. Her most famous work, *Frankenstein* (1818) was written whilst she was still a teenager. After Shelley's death, Mary supported herself through her prolific writing. As well as novels and stories, she also produced a highly respected edition of Shelley's poetry. Despite moving in the most radical of circles during her relationship with Shelley, and studying closely the feminism of Godwin, Wollstonecraft and J. H. Lawrence[*], Mary Shelley's own feminism seems somewhat subdued. Certainly in the wake of her husband's tragic death, she seems to have distanced herself from radicalism.

Bennett (1980); Gittings and Manton (1992); St. Clair (1989)

Shelley, Percy Bysshe (1792–1822)

Percy Shelley was the son of Sir Timothy Shelley, and was educated at Eton and Oxford. He was expelled from Oxford for the publication of his *The Necessity of Atheism* (1811). In 1812 he attempted to incite protest against the Act of Union in Ireland. Back in London Shelley became acquainted with William Godwin, who became something of a mentor to him. Shelley also moved into a network of highly progressive families, and adopted their vegetarian diet. In 1814, two years after his marriage to Harriet Westbrook (but in accordance with his principles concerning the impermanence of marriage), he eloped with Godwin's daughter Mary [Shelley][*]. With Mary's stepsister, Claire Clairmont (with whom he may also later have had an affair), they travelled to Europe. His heavily pregnant wife, Harriet, subsequently drowned herself.

Political radicalism infused Shelley's poetry. His *Revolt of Islam* (1818) alluded to the role of a messianic female leader, as well as hinting at the potential of political revolution; whilst the *Masque of Anarchy* (1832) provided a biting indictment of the political authorities. Shelley, with two friends, was drowned off the Italian coast, on his way to a meeting with Leigh Hunt.

Shelley's articulation of women's slave state, and the inadequacy of the marital institution, were to have an abiding hold in radical networks throughout this period.

St. Clair (1989); Tomalin (1982)

Smiles, Samuel (1812–1904)

Samuel Smiles was born to shopkeeping parents in Haddington, Scotland. He originally trained as a surgeon but went on to have a career in railway management and assurance. He is best known for his 1859 work *Self-Help*, but he was earlier involved in radical subcultures. He was a secretary of the Complete Suffrage Union in Leeds in 1842, for example, and was associated with radical unitarians in the metropolis. As editor of the *Leeds Times* (1839–45), and as a contributor to progressive journals such as the *Union, Howitt's Journal* and *Eliza Cook's Journal*, Smiles made an important intervention in radical debates on women. He did not deny the centrality of the domestic sphere as a focus for women's engagement, and was often ambivalent on the question of female employment. Nonetheless he questioned women's political status and their iniquitous education, as well as criticizing conventional habits of dress and upbringing.

Smiles (1905); Tyrell (2000)

Smith, Barbara Leigh, see Bodichon, Barbara Leigh Smith

Smith, James Elishama (1801–57)

James Elishama Smith was born in Glasgow. He was educated at Glasgow University and became a tutor and preacher. In 1830 he joined John Wroe and the Southcottians, in Ashton-under-Lyne. In 1832 he went to London where, moving in Owenite circles, he soon became very popular as a lecturer. Smith, who was closely influenced by both Eliza Sharples* and Anna Wheeler*, became editor of the Owenite *Crisis* newspaper, which published many articles and debates on women's position; he also wrote for the *Pioneer*. In the late 1830s he established his own journal, *The Shepherd*, which provided an organ for his brand of millenarian Owenite views, strongly influenced by both Saint-Simonism and Southcottianism. He also became close to the sacred socialists who were associated with James Pierrepont Greaves*. In the early 1840s he contributed to the Fourierite journal, the *London Phalanx*. Smith achieved a nation-wide reputation for his journal, the *Family Herald*, which he edited from 1842 until his death.

Harrison (1979) and (1969); Smith (1892)

Smith, John Stores (1829–92)

John Stores Smith was born in Manchester. The son of a textile innovator he became a successful business man. An admirer of Thomas Carlyle, Smith moved in radical circles in the 1840s being particularly close to Geraldine Jewsbury*. His *Social Aspects* (1850) was well received in literary and reforming circles, and contained many biting remarks concerning the sexual double standard and the cultural oppression of women.

Howe (1935)

Smith, Julia (1799–1883)

Julia Smith was the daughter of the Unitarian MP, William Smith. She assisted her brother, Benjamin, in raising his five children, following the death of his partner, Anne Longden in 1834. Julia Smith entertained close friends with many of the most advanced intellectual women of the day, including Harriet Martineau* and Elizabeth Jesser Reid (a founder of Bedford College). Smith's political radicalism and pioneering spirit exerted a powerful influence over her niece, Barbara Leigh Smith*. Together they enrolled at Bedford College in 1849 (Smith was herself a member of its council). From her childhood Smith had questioned the social status of women and challenged conventional notions of gender difference.

Burton (1949); Herstein (1985); William Smith MSS,
Cambridge University Library

Smith, Sydney (1771–1845)

Sydney Smith, son of a merchant, was born in Essex. He was educated at Oxford and ordained in 1794. He was a tutor in Edinburgh in 1798, and here he formed friendships with like-minded Whigs such as Henry Brougham* and Francis Jeffrey. Together they established the *Edinburgh Review* in 1802. On returning to London with his wife, Catherine, he became popular in the highest Whig circles. As the vicar of Foston, Yorkshire from 1808, Smith gained a reputation as a benevolent philanthropist. He was rewarded with the canonry of St Paul's Cathedral in 1831, largely due to his support for the Whig plans for electoral reform. Smith does not appear to have advocated any wholesale reform in women's position. Nonetheless, his tremendous faith in women's intellectual abilities, and his dismissal of reactionary fears concerning the implications of female education, made him a respected figure in feminist circles throughout this period.

Holland (1855)

Southcott, Joanna (1750–1814)

Joanna Southcott, a farmer's daughter, came from Devon. A servant and upholsterer, she joined the Wesleyans in 1791, and shortly afterwards began to experience religious visions. Southcott proclaimed herself to be 'the Woman clothed with the Sun' (Revelations, 12: 4): the new Saviour. During her career as a millenarian prophet she was cared for by the wealthy Jane Townley and her companion, Ann Underwood. Southcott died in 1814 following a phantom pregnancy, which she declared would result in the birth of Shiloh, the messiah. Her millenarian prophecies attracted considerable publicity, as did her expansive writings. The widespread Southcottian movement was not inherently radical, but on its fringes it became absorbed into certain chiliastic strands within Owenism and Saint-Simonism. Southcott's recurring emphasis upon women's redemptive role; her liberation of women from the burden of the Fall; and her impassioned imagery, which revolved around marriage and sexuality, articulated a potent vision of women's ills and potential.

Harrison (1979); Hopkins (1983); Taylor (1983)

Southwell, Charles (1814–60)

Charles Southwell, who came from a London working-class family, turned towards radicalism in the 1830s. On returning from Spain in 1837, where he had spent two years fighting with the British Legion, he became an Owenite lecturer, and later founded the *Oracle of Reason* (1841). Jailed for blasphemy in 1844, in the early 1850s he assisted George Jacob Holyoake in promoting secularism. Southwell emigrated in 1855 to Australia, where he continued a career as a lecturer, actor and radical politician. Southwell's own marriage was highly volatile, with both parties committing adultery. His feminist writing tends to be somewhat formulaic; and, as Barbara Taylor points out, he shared with many male Owenites a view of sexuality as a compulsive process.

Taylor (1983)

Stock, Ellen (*c.* 1776–*c.* 1844)

Ellen Stock, née Weeton, came from Lancaster. She took over the management of her mother's school on her death in 1797, before becoming a governess in 1809. Five years later, she married a widowed manufacturer, Aaron Stock. Stock was abusive, violent, and even resorted to forcibly confining his wife. A formal separation was arranged in 1822, but Ellen Stock was left in difficult financial circumstances and only limited contact with their daughter. The editor of her memoirs claims that Stock's spirited response (including, allegedly, window-breaking) to her husband's actions raised the profile of women's desperate legal position. Stock's letters give a bleak portrayal of men as tyrants and oppressors.

Bagley (1969); Vickery (1998)

Taylor, Harriet (1807–58)

Harriet Taylor was born in London to a middle-class medical family. In 1826 she married a druggist, John Taylor, who brought her into the ambit of W. J. Fox's* radical *Monthly Repository* circle (to which she contributed). During this period she met the young philosopher John Stuart Mill*, and the two developed an intense love for one another. They met regularly, with the apparent acquiescence of Taylor's husband. Two years after the death of John Taylor in 1849, Harriet married Mill. Mill and Taylor formed a close intellectual collaboration (although the precise influence of Harriet Taylor is a subject of some scholarly debate). In 1851, Harriet Taylor published an article in the *Westminster Review*, entitled 'The Enfranchisement of Women'. This important essay is a careful consideration of women's lack of civil rights; and forms a detailed rebuttal of conventional arguments against female enfranchisement.

Jacobs and Payne (1998); Hayek (1951); Rossi (1970)

Taylor, Mary (1817–93)

Mary Taylor, a banker's daughter, came from Gomersal, Yorkshire, and was one of Charlotte Brontë's* closest friends. In 1845, frustrated by the lack of opportunities open to British women, she emigrated to New Zealand where she set up a draper's shop. She returned to England seven years later. *The First Duty of Women* (1870) underlined her belief that women could, and should, enjoy a life of paid employment.

Stevens (1972)

Tennyson, Lord Alfred (1809–92)

Alfred Tennyson, a rector's son, was born in North Lincolnshire. He was educated at a grammar school and at Cambridge University. One of the most highly esteemed poets of his day, Tennyson became the Poet Laureate in 1850, and accepted a peerage in 1884. Tennyson indicated a limited sympathy with some aspects of the women's rights agenda, including the importance of educational and legal reform, and the viability of single women having the vote. He did not, however, believe in the concept of women fighting for their rights, adhering rather to a concept of two equal but different partners who would grow together to make an organic whole. Despite his concern with social injustices, Tennyson was more interested in the population's spiritual development than in challenging the established order. In many of his poems, women represent this potential for moral renewal.

Killham (1958); Palmer (1973); Tennyson (1950); Tennyson (1897)

Thompson, William (1775–1833)

William Thompson was from the landowning class in Cork. He earned the nickname the 'Red Republican' locally for his interest in radical political philosophies. He was particularly close to Jeremy Bentham, although he dissented from his economic analyses. Thompson made a major contribution to the development of socialist theory. His *Inquiry into the Principles of the Distribution of Wealth* (1824) argued for workers' rights to the product of their labour. He was a committed campaigner for the co-operative cause, establishing the *Co-operative Magazine* and assisting Lovett in founding the British Association for the Spread of Co-operative Knowledge. His *Practical Directions* (1830) was also eloquent on the benefits of co-operative communities for women. Indeed, Thompson's politics were both more democratic, and more egalitarian than those of his associate, Robert Owen[*]. Thompson's contribution to feminist letters is best known through his *Appeal* (1825). Apparently co-authored with Anna Wheeler[*], it is an extraordinary, wide-ranging consideration of women's cultural, biological, social and political oppression.

Dooley (1996); Pankhurst (1954)

Trelawny, Edward John (1792–1881)

Edward Trelawny, the son of a lieutenant-colonel, was born in London. A self-dramatizing adventurer, Trelawny's own accounts of his life are highly unreliable. However, it seems that prior to his close friendship with Shelley[*] he had travelled widely with the navy. In 1823 he accompanied Byron on his Grecian expedition. In the mid-1830s Trelawny cultivated friendships in radical political circles, (including Anna Jameson[*] and Henry Brougham[*]) and appears to have given some assistance to the campaign for the Infant Custody Act. He was, for four years, an autocratic husband to a young teenage girl, the sister of a Greek chieftain. Claire Clairmont[*] turned down his offer of a common-law marriage, and he later destroyed his long-term relationship with Augusta Goring when he decided to bring a young girl into the household as his mistress. Trelawny's sensual libertinism, his overbearing attitude towards women and insistence on female domesticity make him one of the most unlikely of feminist advocates.

Forman (1910); St. Clair (1977)

Waddington, Samuel Ferrand (fl. 1796–1822)

Samuel Waddington, a Kent hopseller, was closely involved in a whole range of political issues – from colonial trade to the Queen Caroline affair. An acolyte of Carlile's republican circles, he was prosecuted in 1822 for selling Palmer's *Principles of Nature*.

Weiner (1983)

Watkins, John

John Watkins was from Whitby but moved to London, where he established the *London Chartist Monthly Magazine* (1843), a publication critical of his former mentor, Feargus O'Connor. Watkins's feminism is strikingly similar to that of R. J. Richardson*. Noting his image of the 'cottage of content', Jutta Schwarzkopf has argued that Watkins was a persuasive polemicist for Chartist domestic ideology.

Schwarzkopf (1991)

Weeton, Ellen *see* Stock

Wheeler, Anna (1785– *c*. 1850)

Anna Wheeler, née Doyle, came from an Irish upper-class background. At the age of fifteen she married the alcoholic and abusive Frances Massey Wheeler. During their marriage, Wheeler educated herself in radical politics. She left her husband in 1812, taking her daughters to live with relatives in Guernsey. In 1816, she moved to Caen, where she became the centre of a Saint-Simonian circle. From this period onwards, Wheeler became an important mediator between British and French socialism, introducing Flora Tristan and Charles Fourier to Owen, and translating Saint-Simonian articles for the British radical press.

On moving to Britain in 1820, Wheeler developed close relationships with Robert Owen* and Jeremy Bentham, and met William Thompson* at the latter's house. By the mid-1820s Wheeler had become a prominent radical, lecturing on feminism and (often under the pseudonym 'Vlasta') writing articles for Owenite publications. In 1833 she sat on the executive council of the Grand Moral Union of all Productive Classes. Wheeler's most lasting contribution to feminist thought came in 1825 when she collaborated with William Thompson on the writing of the *Appeal*. Wheeler insisted that female emancipation would never be possible unless women could achieve it themselves. Otherwise, she argued, liberation would only ever be won on men's terms.

Dooley (1996)

Wright, Frances later D'Arusmont (1795–1852)

Frances Wright, the daughter of a linen manufacturer, was born in Dundee. Orphaned as a young child she spent much of her childhood with James Mylne, a liberal Scottish philosopher. With her sister, Camilla, Wright travelled to the United States in 1818 (and later to France). On a return journey to America six years later, Wright was deeply affected by a visit to Robert Owen's* New Harmony community in Indiana. She subsequently invested much of her money in a co-operative community near Memphis, peopled by former slaves. The community, which alienated local people because of its progressive approach to marriage, failed in 1830. Shortly afterwards Wright became pregnant. She married her child's father, the Owenite, Phiquepal D'Arusmont, but the relationship ended in divorce. Wright, an advocate of dress reform, was esteemed as a lecturer in radical networks, and her activities and writings widely reported.

Lane (1972)

Notes

1 In compiling these entries, in addition to deriving information from the works of each author, I have drawn heavily upon the following: Banks (1985); Bellamy and Saville (1982); Baylen and Gossman (1984); Blain, Clements and Grundy (1990); Nadel and Fredeman (1983); Shattock (1993); Todd (1989); and the *Dictionary of National Biography*. Any further sources are indicated beneath each entry.
2 Junius Redivivus, 'On the Condition of Women in England', *Monthly Repository* (1833), vol. 7, pp. 228–9.
3 See documents **103** and **47**.
4 See Todd's entry on Hays in Baylen and Gossman (1984).
5 For Hughes's obituary see *Monthly Repository* (1825), vol. 20, pp. 114–16.
6 *Athenaeum* (25 February 1832), no. 226, p. 129.
7 See also document **115**.
8 *British and Foreign Quarterly Review*, vol. 7, no. 13 (1838), p. 394.
9 *Tait's Edinburgh Magazine*, vol. vii, June 1840, p. 397.
10 This is, however, a short piece of work, comprising but 16 pages.
11 See p. 4.

Bibliography

Manuscripts

Birmingham City Library, Hutton Beale Papers
Friends House Library, Anne Knight collection
Girton College, Parkes Papers
Cambridge University Library, William Smith Papers

Newspapers and Periodicals

The years indicated are those studied for this book.

Annual Review (1802–8)
Athenaeum (1831–2)
Black Dwarf (1817–24)
British Co-operator (1830)
British and Foreign Quarterly Review (1838)
British Lady's Magazine and Monthly Miscellany (1815–18)
The Cabinet (1795)
The Charter (1839)
Cooperative Magazine and Monthly Herald (1826–9)
The Crisis (1832–4)
Destructive and Poor Man's Conservative (1833)
Douglas Jerrold's Shilling Magazine (1845–8)
Douglas Jerrold's Weekly Newspaper (1846–8)
Eclectic Review (1848)
Edinburgh Review (1810)
Educational Circular or Communist Apostle (1841–2)
Eliza Cook's Journal (1849–54)
English Chartist Circular (1841)
Hastings and St Leonards News (1847–8)
Howitt's Journal (1847–8)
The Isis (1832)
The Liberator (1840)
The Lion (1828–9)
London Phalanx (1841–3)
London Social Reformer (1840)
The Man. A Rational Advocate (1833)
Metropolitan Magazine (1838–48)
Monthly Repository (1806–38)
Morning Star and Phalansterian Gazette (1840)
The National (1839)
National Association Gazette (1842)

New Monthly Magazine (1832)
New Moral World (1838–45)
Newgate Monthly Magazine (1824–6)
Northern Star (1839–43, 1848–1852)
The People (1848–52)
People's Journal (1846–51)
People's Press (1847–8)
People's Review of Literature and Politics (1850)
The Pioneer (1833–5)
The Promethean; or Communitarian Apostle (1842)
The Prompter (1830–1)
The Reasoner (1846–50)
The Republican (1819–29)
The Shepherd (1834–8)
Social Pioneer (1839)
Star in the East (1836–40)
Tait's Edinburgh Magazine (1832–51)
The Tatler (1830–2)
Truth-Seeker (1846–52)
Truth-Tester, Temperance Advocate and Healthian Journal (1847–8)
Westminster Review (1824–51)
Whittington Club Gazette (1848–51)
The Working Bee and Herald of the Hodsonian Community Society (1839–41)

Printed sources for the extracts cited in the anthology

Aikin, Lucy, *Epistles on Women, Exemplifying Their Character and Condition in Various Ages and Nations* (London: J. Johnson, 1810)

Bailey, Samuel, *The Rationale of Political Representation* (London: R. Hunter, 1835)

Bamford, Samuel, *Passages in the Life of a Radical* (Manchester: Heywood, 1841) 2 vols

Barmby, Catherine, 'The Demand for the Emancipation of Woman, Politically and Socially', *New Tracts for the Times*, vol. 1, no. 3, reprinted in Taylor (1983)

Bagley, J. J. (ed.), *Miss Weeton's Journal of a Governess* (Newton Abbot: David & Charles, 1969) 2 vols

Beddoes, Thomas, *Hygëia: or Essays, Moral and Medical, on the Causes affecting the Personal State of our Middling and Affluent Classes* (London: R. Phillips, 1802) 3 vols

Bell, Thomas, *Kalogynomia, or the Laws of Female Beauty* (London J. J. Stockdale, 1821)

Bennett, Betty T. (ed.), *The Letters of Mary Wollstonecraft Shelley* (Baltimore and London: Johns Hopkins University Press, 1980) 3 vols

Blackburn, Helen, *Women's Suffrage. A Record of the Women's Suffrage Movement in the British Isles* (London and Oxford: Williams and Norgate, 1902)

Bright, John and J. E. Thorold Rogers (eds), *Speeches on Questions of Public Policy by Richard Cobden M.P.* (London: T. Fisher Unwin, 1908; 3rd edn) 2 vols

Brontë, Anne, *The Tenant of Wildfell Hall* (Harmondsworth: Penguin, 1979; first published 1848)

Brontë, Charlotte, *The Professor* (Harmondsworth: Penguin, 1989; first published 1857)

Brontë, Charlotte, *Shirley* (Harmondsworth: Penguin, 1985; first published 1849)

Brontë, Charlotte, *Jane Eyre*, ed. Currer Bell (London: Smith, Elder, 1847)

[Brougham, Henry], Lydia Tomkins, *Thoughts on the Ladies of the Aristocracy* (London: Hodgsons, 1835)

Bush, M. L., *What is Love? Richard Carlile's Philosophy of Sex* (London: Verso, 1998)

Campbell, Alexander, *Letters and Extracts from the MS Writings of James Pierrepont Greaves* (Concordium Press: Ham Common, 1843–5) 2 vols

Cornwallis, C. F., *Selections from the Letters of Caroline Frances Cornwallis*, ed. M.C. Power (London: Trubner, 1864)

Desultory Queries and Remarks proposed to the whole world, in behalf of the Female Sex (Chelmsford: H. Guy, 1828)

Ellis, Lady Mildred, 'The Education of Young Ladies of Small Pecuniary Resources', in *Central Society of Education Papers* (London: Taylor & Watson, 1838), pp. 192–8

Epps, Ellen (ed.), *Diary of the Late J Epps* (London: Kent, 1875)

Erskine, Mrs Steuart (ed.), *Anna Jameson. Letters and Friendships (1812–1860)* (London: T. Fisher Unwin, 1915)

Forman, H. Buxton (ed.), *Letters of Edward John Trelawny* (London: Oxford University Press, 1910)

Fuller, Margaret, *Woman in the Nineteenth Century*, ed. Larry Reynolds (London and New York: W. W. Norton, 1998; first published 1845)

Gamond, Zoë Gatti de, *The Phalanstery; or Attractive Industry and Moral Harmony*, trans. from the French by an 'English Lady' [Sophia Chichester] (London: Whitaker, 1841)

Glasgow Emancipation Society, *Sixth Annual Report* (1840)

'Glorious Deeds of Woman! Forecasting the Failure of the Prosecution of Queen Caroline' (London: William Benbow, 1820)

Grimstone, Mary Leman, *Cleone. A Tale of Married Life* (London: Effingham Wilson, 1834)

Grimstone, Mary Leman, *Woman's Love* (London: Saunders & Otley, 1832)

Haight, Gordon S., *George Eliot and John Chapman. With Chapman's Diaries* (Hamden, Conn., Archon Books, 1969, 2nd edn)

Hansard, *Parliamentary Debates* 3rd Series (1832, 1838)

Hatfield, Miss [S], *Letters on the Importance of the Female Sex. With Observations on Their Manners and on Education* (London: G. and S. Robinson, 1803)

Hays, Mary, *Female Biography; or, Memoirs of Illustrious and Celebrated Women, of All Ages and Countries* (London: Richard Phillips, 1803) 6 vols

Hogg, Thomas Jefferson, *Life of Percy Bysshe Shelley*, with an introduction by Prof. Edward Dowden (London: George Routledge, 1906 first published 1858) 2 vols

Howitt, Mary, *An Autobiography* edited by her daughter, Margaret Howitt (London: Isbister, 1889) 2 vols

Ireland, Annie E. (ed.), *Selections from the Letters of Geraldine Endsor Jewsbury to Jane Welsh Carlyle* (London: Longmans, Green, 1892)

Jacobs, Jo Ellen and Paula Harms Payne (eds), *The Complete Works of Harriet*

Taylor Mill (Bloomington: Indiana University Press, 1998)

Jameson, Anna, *Memoirs and Essays. Illustrative of Art, Literature and Social Morals* (London: Richard Bentley, 1846)

Jameson, Anna, *Winter Studies and Summer Rambles in Canada* (London: Saunders & Otley, 1838) 3 vols

Jewsbury, Geraldine, *The Half Sisters* (Oxford: Oxford University Press, 1998; first published 1848)

A Lady, *Female Rights Vindicated; or, The Equality of the Sexes Proved* (South Shields: James Jollie, 1833; first published 1758)

Lamb, Anne Richelieu, *Can Woman Regenerate Society?* (London: John W. Parker, 1844)

Lamenais, Abbé de, *Modern Slavery*, trans. W. J. Linton (London: J. Watson, 1840)

Lawrence, James Henry, *The Empire of the Nairs; or, the Rights of Women. An Utopian Romance* (New York: Scholars' Facsimile and Reprints, 1975; first published, 1811)

Lawrence, James Henry, *Love: An Allegory* (London: R. Faulder, 1802)

Lawrence, James Henry, *An Essay on the Nair System of Gallantry and Inheritance; shewing its superiority over marriage* (London: J. Ridgway, *c.* 1800)

Le Breton, Philip Hemery (ed.), *Memoirs, Miscellanies and Letters of the Late Lucy Aikin including those addressed to the Rev. Dr. Channing from 1826 to 1842* (London: Longman, Green, Roberts, 1864)

Lynn, Eliza, *Amymone. A Romance of the Days of Pericles* (London: Richard Bentley, 1848) 3 vols

Lytton, Edward Bulwer, *The Life, Letters and Literary Remains of Edward Bulwer, Lord Lytton* (London: Kegan Paul, Trench, 1883) 2 vols

Martineau, Harriet, *Society in America* (London: Saunders & Otley, 1837) 3 vols

Maurice, C. E. (ed.), *Life of Octavia Hill, as told in her Letters* (London: Macmillan, 1913)

Meteyard, Eliza, *Struggles for Fame* (London: T. C. Newby, 1845) 3 vols

Mill, John Stuart, *Principles of Political Economy, with some of their applications to social philosophy* (London: John W. Parker, 1848) 2 vols

Morgan, Lady, *Woman and Her Master* (London, 1840) 2 vols

Morrison, Frances, *The Influence of the Present Marriage System upon the Character and Interests of Females contrasted with that proposed by Robert Owen* (Manchester: A. Heywood, 1838)

New Charter: humbly addressed to the King and both Houses of Parliament, proposed as the basis of a Constitution for the Government of Great Britain and Ireland (London: W. Strange, 1831)

[Norton, Caroline], Pearce Stevenson, *A Plain Letter to the Lord Chancellor on the Infant Custody Bill* (London: James Ridgway, 1839)

Owen, Robert, *Lectures on the Marriages of the Priesthood of the Old Immoral World, delivered in the year 1835* (Leeds: J. Hobson, 1840, 4th edn).

Owen, Robert Dale, *Moral Physiology; or, A Brief and Plain Treatise on the Population Question* (London: E. Truelove, 1831)

Parsons, Benjamin, *The Mental and Moral Dignity of Woman* (London: published for the author, 1842)

Perkins, Jane Gray, *The Life of Mrs Norton* (London: John Murray, 1909)

A Philanthropist, *Domestic Tyranny, or Woman in Chains with an Inquiry as to the*

Best Mode of Breaking Her Bonds Asunder (London: Whittaker, 1841)

Radcliffe, Mary Ann, *The Memoirs of Mrs Mary Ann Radcliffe; in Familiar Letters to her Female Friend* (Edinburgh: 1810)

Reid, Marion, *A Plea for Woman being a vindication of the importance and extent of her natural sphere of action* (Edinburgh: W. Tait, 1843)

Richardson, Reginald J., *The Rights of Woman*, ed. E. and R. Frow (Manchester: Working-Class Movement Library, 1986; first published 1840)

The Rights, Privileges and Laws of Women (London: privately printed, 1815)

Rossi, Alice (ed.) *Essays on Sex Equality* (Chicago: University of Chicago Press, 1970)

Sanders, Valerie (ed.), *Harriet Martineau. Selected Letters* (Oxford: Clarendon Press, 1990)

Shaen, Margaret (ed.) *Memorials of Two Sisters, Susanna and Catherine Winkworth* (London: Longman, 1908)

Shelley, Percy Bysshe, *Queen Mab: A Philosophical Poem: with Notes* (Oxford and New York: Woodstock Books, 1990; first printed 1813)

Smith, John Stores, *Social Aspects* (London: John Chapman, 1850)

Smith, Margaret (ed.), *The Letters of Charlotte Brontë with a selection of letters by family and friends* (Oxford: Clarendon Press, 2000) 2 vols

Southcott, Joanna, *The Second Part of the Continuation of Joanna Southcott's Prophecies of things which are to come* (London: W. Marchant, 1813, 2nd edn)

Southcott, Joanna, *The Kingdom of Christ is at Hand* (London: A. Seale, c. 1805)

Southwell, Charles, *An Essay on Marriage; addressed to the Lord Bishop of Exeter* (London: 1840)

Tennyson, Alfred, *The Princess: A Medley* (London: Edward Moxon, 1847)

Thompson, William, *Appeal of One Half the Human Race, Women, Against the Pretensions of the Other Half, Men, to Retain them in Political, and Thence in Civil and Domestic Slavery* (London: Longman, 1825)

Walker, Alexander, *Woman Physiologically Considered as to Mind, Morals, Marriage, Matrimonial Slavery, Infidelity and Divorce* (London: A. H. Baily, 1839)

[Wright, Frances], *England, the Civilizer: Her History Developed in its Principles* London: Simpkin, Marshall, 1848)

Other Printed Sources

Aaron, Jane, *A Double Singleness. Gender and the Writings of Charles and Mary Lamb* (Oxford: Clarendon Press, 1991)

Ackroyd, Peter, *Blake* (London: Sinclair-Stevenson, 1995)

Anthony, Katharine, *The Lambs. A Study of Pre-Victorian England* (London: Hammond & Hammond, 1948)

Banks, Olive, *Biographical Dictionary of British Feminists, vol. 1 1800–1900* Brighton: Wheatsheaf, 1985)

Bellamy, Joyce M. and John Saville (eds), *Dictionary of Labour Biography* (Basingstoke: Macmillan, now Palgrave Macmillan, 1982), vol. 6

'Barrister of the Middle Temple', *The Lady's Cabinet Lawyer; Being a Familiar Summary of the Exclusive and Peculiar Rights and Liabilities, Legal and Equitable of Women* (London: 1837)

Baylen, Joseph Oscar and Norbert Joseph Gossman (eds), *Biographical Dictionary of Modern British Radicals* (Hassocks: Harvester Press, 1984) vol. 2

Beecher, Jonathan, *Charles Fourier. The Visionary and his World* (Berkeley: University of California Press, 1986)

Belchem, John, *'Orator Hunt'. Henry Hunt and Working-Class Radicalism* (Oxford: Oxford University Press, 1985)

Benger, Elizabeth Ogilvie, *The Female Geniad* (London: T. Hookham & J. Carpenter, 1791)

Berg, Maxine, 'Women's Property in Eighteenth-Century England', *Journal of Interdisciplinary History* (1993), vol. 2, no. 24, pp. 233–50

Betham, Mary Matilda, *Biographical Dictionary of the Celebrated Women of Every Age and Country* (London: B. Crosby, 1804)

Blain, Virginia, Patricia Clements and Isobel Grundy (eds), *Feminist Companion to Literature in English. Women Writers from the Middle Ages to the Present* (London: Batsford, 1990)

Blainey, Ann, *Immortal Boy. A Portrait of Leigh Hunt* (London: Croom Helm, 1985)

Blainey, Ann, *The Farthing Poet. A Biography of Richard Hengist Horne 1802–1884. A Lesser Literary Lion* (London: Longman, 1968)

Bland, Lucy, *Banishing the Beast. English Feminism and Sexual Morality, 1885–1914* (Harmondsworth: Penguin, 1995)

Bridell-Fox, E., *Sarah Flower Adams: A Memoir and her Hymns* (London: Christian Life Publishing, 1894)

Burke, Stephen, 'Letter from a Pioneer Feminist', *Studies in Labour History* (1976), no. 1, pp. 19–23.

Burton, Hester, *Barbara Bodichon, 1827–1891* (London: John Murray, 1949)

Butler, Josephine E., *Memoir of John Grey of Dilston* (Edinburgh: Edmonston & Douglas, 1869)

Caine, Barbara, *Victorian Feminists* (Oxford: Oxford University Press, 1992)

Caine, Barbara, 'John Stuart Mill and the English Women's Movement', *Historical Studies* (1978), vol. 18, pp. 52–67

Campbell, Mary, *Lady Morgan. The Life and Times of Sydney Owenson* (London: Pandora, 1988)

Chapple, J. A. V. and Arthur Pollard, *The Letters of Mrs Gaskell* (Manchester: Manchester University Press, 1966)

Chedzoy, Alan, *A Scandalous Woman. The Story of Caroline Norton* (London: Allison & Bushby, 1992)

Clancy, James, *Essay on the Equitable Rights of Married Women* (Dublin: Charles Hunter, 1819)

Clark, Anna, *The Struggle for the Breeches. Gender and the Making of the British Working Class* (London: Rivers Oram, 1995)

Clark, Anna, 'The Rhetoric of Chartist Domesticity: Gender, Language and Class in the 1830s and 1840s', *Journal of British Studies* (1992), vol. 31, no. 1, pp. 62–88

Clarke, Charles Cowden, *Shakespeare's Characters, chiefly those subordinate* (London: Smith, Elder, 1863)

Clarke, Norma, *Ambitious Heights. Writing, Friendship, Love – the Jewsbury Sisters, Felicia Hemans and Jane Welsh Carlyle* (London: Routledge, 1990)

Colley, Linda, *Britons, Forging the Nation, 1707–1837* (New Haven and London: Yale University Press, 1992)

Combe, George, *The Constitution of Man considered in relation to External Objects* (Edinburgh: John Anderson, 1828)

Coole, Diana, *Women in Political Theory, from Ancient Misogyny to Contemporary Feminism* (Brighton: Harvester Wheatsheaf, 1993)

Cooper, Thomas, *The Life of Thomas Cooper* (London: Hodder & Stoughton, 1872)

Cooter, Roger, *The Cultural Meaning of Popular Science. Phrenology and the Organization of Consent in Nineteenth-Century Britain* (Cambridge: Cambridge University Press, 1984)

Crawford, Elizabeth, *The Women's Suffrage Movement. A Reference Guide 1866–1928* (London and New York: Routledge, 1999)

Cullen, Mary and Maria Luddy (eds), *Women, Power and Consciousness in 19th Century Ireland* (Dublin: Attic Press, 1995)

Davidoff, Leonore, 'The Family in Britain', in F. M. L. Thompson (ed.), *The Cambridge Social History of Britain 1750–1950* (Cambridge: Cambridge University Press 1990), vol. 2, pp. 71–130

Davidoff, Leonore and Catherine Hall, *Family Fortunes. Men and Women of the English Middle Class 1780–1850* (London: Routledge, 1987)

Dickens, Charles, *Dombey and Son* (Harmondsworth: Penguin, 1970; first published 1846–8)

Dooley, Dolores, *Equality in Community. Sexual Equality in the Writings of William Thompson and Anna Doyle Wheeler* (Cork: Cork University Press, 1996)

Dooley, Dolores, 'Anna Doyle Wheeler', in Mary Cullen and Maria Luddy (eds), *Women, Power and Consciousness in 19th Century Ireland* (Dublin: Attic Press, 1995), pp. 19–53

Eccentric Biography or, Memoirs of Remarkable Female Characters, Ancient and Modern (London, T. Hurst, 1803)

Ellsworth, Edward W., *Liberators of the Female Mind, the Shirreff Sisters, Educational Reform and the Women's Movement* (London: Greenwood Press, 1979)

Epstein, James A., *Radical Expression. Political Language, Ritual, and Symbol in England, 1790–1850* (Oxford and New York: Oxford University Press, 1994)

Fox, William Johnson, *Reports of Lectures Delivered at the Chapel in South Place, Finsbury* (London: Charles Fox, 1840)

Fraser, W. Hamish, *Alexander Campbell and the Search for Socialism* (Manchester: Holyoake Books, 1996)

Frow, Ruth and Edmund Frow (eds), *Political Women 1800–1850* (London: Pluto Press, 1989)

Garnett, Richard, *The Life of W. J. Fox, Public Teacher and Social Reformer, 1786–1864* (London: John Lane, 1909)

Gascoigne, John, *Joseph Banks and the English Enlightenment. Useful Knowledge and Polite Culture* (Cambridge: Cambridge University Press, 1994)

Gaskell, Elizabeth, *The Life of Charlotte Brontë* (Harmondsworth: Penguin Books, 1997; first published 1857)

Gittings, Robert and Jo Manton, *Claire Clairmont and the Shelleys 1798–1879* (Oxford: Oxford University Press, 1992)

Gleadle, Kathryn, '"The Age of Physiological Reformers": Rethinking Gender and Domesticity in the Age of Reform', in Arthur Burns and Joanna Innes (eds), *Rethinking the Age of Reform* (Cambridge: Cambridge University Press, forthcoming)

Gleadle, Kathryn, *British Women in the Nineteenth Century* (Basingstoke: Palgrave, now Palgrave Macmillan, 2001)

Gleadle, Kathryn, 'British Women and Radical Politics in the Late Nonconformist Enlightenment, *c.* 1780–1830', in Amanda Vickery (ed.) *Women, Privilege and Power. British Politics 1750 to the Present* (Stanford: Stanford University Press, 2001) pp. 123–51

Gleadle, Kathryn and Sarah Richardson (eds), *Women in British Politics, 1760–1860. The Power of the Petticoat* (Basingstoke: Palgrave, now Palgrave Macmillan, 2000)

Gleadle, Kathryn, *The Early Feminists. Radical Unitarians and the Emergence of the Women's Rights Movement, c. 1831–51* (Basingstoke: Macmillan, now Palgrave Macmillan, 1995)

Gordon, William Clark, *The Social Ideals of Alfred Tennyson. As Related to his Time* (Chicago: University of Chicago Press, 1906)

Haight, Gordon, *The George Eliot Letters* (London: Oxford University Press, 1954) 9 vols

Halévy, Elie, *The Growth of Philosphic Radicalism* (London: Faber & Faber, 1952)

Hall, Catherine, *White, Male and Middle Class. Explorations in Feminism and History* (Cambridge: Polity Press, 1992)

Hamilton, Lady Augusta, *Marriage Rites, Customs and Ceremonies of All Nations of the Universe* (London: Chapple & Sons, 1822)

Hamilton, Elizabeth, *Letters on the Elementary Principles of Education* (London: G. and J. Robinson, 1803) 2 vols

Hammerton, A. James, *Emigrant Gentlewomen. Genteel Poverty and Female Education, 1830–1914* (London: Croom Helm, 1979)

Harrison, J. F. C., *The Second Coming: Popular Millenarianism, 1780–1850* (London: Routledge & Kegan Paul, 1979)

Harrison, J. F. C, *Robert Owen and the Owenites in Britain and America: The Quest for the New Moral World* (London: Routledge & Kegan Paul, 1969)

Harrison, J. F. C., *Learning and Living, 1790–1860: a Study in the History of the Adult Education Movement* (London: Routledge & Kegan Paul, 1961), pp. 118–51

Hayek, F. A., (ed.), *John Stuart Mill and Harriet Taylor: their Correspondence and Subsequent Marriage* (Chicago: University of Chicago Press, 1951)

Mary Hays, *Letters and Essays. Moral and Miscellaneous*, ed. Gina Luria (London: 1974; first published 1793)

Helsinger, Elizabeth K., R. L. Sheets and William Veeder (eds), *The Woman Question. Society and Literature in Britain and America 1837–1883* (Chicago: University of Chicago Press, 1989) 3 vols

Herstein, Sheila R., *A Mid-Victorian Feminist, Barbara Leigh Smith Bodichon* (New Haven: Yale University Press, 1985)

Hill, Christopher, *Milton and the English Revolution* (London: Faber & Faber, 1977)

Hindmarsh, Robert, *A Vindication of the Character and Writings of the Hon. Emanuel Swedenborg* (Manchester: H. and R. Smith, 1822)

Hirsch, Pam, *Barbara Leigh Smith Bodichon, 1827–1891. Feminist, Artist and Rebel* (London: Chatto & Windus, 1998)

Holcombe, Lee, *Wives and Property. Reform of the Married Women's Property Law in Nineteenth-Century England* (Toronto: University of Toronto Press, 1983)

Holland, Lady Saba, *A Memoir of the Reverend Sydney Smith by his Daughter, Lady Holland. With a Selection from his Letters*, ed. by Sarah Austin (London: privately printed, 1855)

Holton, Sandra, 'British Freewomen: National Identity, Constitutionalism and Languages of Race in Early Suffragist Histories', in Eileen Yeo (ed.), *Radical Femininity. Women's Self-Representation in the Public Sphere* (Manchester and New York: Manchester University Press, 1998), pp. 149–71

Hopkins, James K., *A Woman to Deliver her People. Joanna Southcott and English Millenarianism in an Age of Revolution* (Austin: University of Texas Press, 1982)

Houston, Arthur, *Daniel O'Connell: His Early Life and Journal, 1795 to 1802* (London: Sir Isaac Pitman and Sons, 1906)

Howe, Susanne, *Geraldine Jewsbury, Her Life and Errors* (Aberdeen: Aberdeen University Press, 1935)

Hughes, Kathryn, *The Victorian Governess* (London: Hambledon Press, 1993)

Ingpen, Roger (ed.), *The Complete Works of Percy Bysshe Shelley* (London: The Julian Editions, 1926), vol. 9

Isichei, Elizabeth, *Victorian Quakers* (Oxford: Oxford University Press, 1970)

Johnston, Judith, *Anna Jameson: Victorian, Feminist, Woman of Letters* (Aldershot: Scholar Press, 1997)

Jones, David, 'Women and Chartism', *History* (1983), 68, pp. 1–21

Jump, Harriet Devine, *Women's Writing of the Romantic Period, 1789–1836* (Edinburgh: Edinburgh University Press, 1997)

Kelley, Philip and Ronald Hudson, *The Brownings' Correspondence* (Winfield, KS: Wedgestone Press, 1984) vol. 1

Killham, John, *Tennyson and The Princess. Reflections of an Age* (London: Athlone Press, 1958)

Kitchener, Henry Thomas, *Letters on Marriage, on the Causes of Matrimonial Infidelity* (London: C. Chapple, 1812)

Lane, Margaret, *Frances Wright and the 'Great Experiment'* (Manchester: Manchester University Press, 1972)

Latham, J. E. M., *The Search for a New Eden. James Pierrepont Greaves (1777–1842): The Sacred Socialist and His Followers* (London: Associated University Presses, 1999)

Laurence [*sic*], James De, *The Children of God, or the Religion of Jesus Reconciled with Philosophy* (London: John Brooks, 1833)

Lawrence, James Henry, *The Etonian Out of Bounds* (London: Hunt & Clarke, 1828) 3 vols

The Laws Respecting Women (London: Joseph Johnson, 1777)

Leach, Joseph, *Bright Particular Star. The Life and Times of Charlotte Cushman* (New Haven and London: Yale University Press, 1970)

Leneman, Leah, '"The Awakened Instinct": Vegetarianism and the Women's Suffrage Movement in Britain', *Women's History Review* (1997), vol. 6, pp. 271–88

Lewis, Sarah, *Woman's Mission* (London: John W. Parker, 1839, 2nd edn)

Luria, Gina, 'Mary Hays's Letters and Manuscripts', *Signs* (1977), vol. 3, no. 2, pp. 24–30

Lytton, Earl, *Bulwer Lytton* (London: Home & Van Thal, 1948)

Malmgreen, Gail, 'Ann Knight and the Radical Subculture', *Quaker History* (1982), vol. 71, pp. 100–13.

Martin, Emma, *Religion Superseded, or the Moral Code of Nature Sufficient for the Guidance of Man* (London: Watson, 1850)

Mason, Michael, *The Making of Victorian Sexual Attitudes* (Oxford: Oxford University Press, 1994)

Mason, Michael, *The Making of Victorian Sexuality* (Oxford: Oxford University Press, 1994)

McCalman, I., 'Females, Feminism and Free Love in an Early Nineteenth-Century Radical Movement', *Labour History* (1980), vol. 38, pp. 1–25

McLaren, Angus, *Birth Control in Nineteenth-Century England* (London: Croom Helm, 1978)

Mellor, Anne K., *Women's Political Writing in England, 1780–1830* (Bloomington: Indiana University Press, 2000)

Myers, Mitzi, 'Reform or Ruin: A Revolution in Female Manners', *Studies in Eighteenth-Century Culture* (1982), vol. 11, pp. 199–212

Midgley, Clare, 'Anti-Slavery and Feminism in Nineteenth-Century Britain', *Gender and History* (1993), vol. 5, pp. 343–62

Midgley, Clare, *Women Against Slavery. The British Campaigns 1780–1870* (London: Routledge, 1992)

Mineka, Francis E., *The Dissidence of Dissent. The 'Monthly Repository', 1806–1838* (Chapel Hill: University of North Carolina Press, 1944)

Morley, John, *The Life of Richard Cobden* (London: T. Fisher Unwin, 1896)

Nadel, I. B. and W. E. Fredeman (eds), *Dictionary of Literary Biography Vol. 21 Victorian Novelists before 1885* (Detroit, MI: Gale Research Company, 1983)

Orr, Clarissa Campbell (ed.), *Wollstonecraft's Daughters – Womanhood in England and France, 1780–1920* (Manchester: Manchester University Press, 1996)

Palmer, D. J. (ed.), *Tennyson* (London: Bell, 1973)

Pankhurst, R. K. P., *William Thompson 1775–1833. Britain's Pioneer Socialist, Feminist and Co-operator* (London: Watts, 1954)

Parsons, Benjamin, *A Short Memoir of Elizabeth P. Parsons* (Stroud: B. Bucknall, 1845)

Peterson, M. Jeanne, *Family, Love and Work in the Lives of Victorian Gentlewomen* (Bloomington and Indianapolis: Indiana University Press, 1989)

Petrie, George, *The Works of George Petrie: Comprising Equality, and other Poems* (London: John Cleave, 1841)

Philip, Mark, *Godwin's Political Justice* (London: Duckworth, 1986)

Pilkington, Mary, *Memoirs of Celebrated Female Characters who have distinguished themselves by their talents and virtues in every age and nation* (London: Albion Press, 1804)

Place, Francis, *Illustrations and Proofs of the Principle of Population* (London: Longman, Hurst, Rees, Orme and Brown, 1822)

Prochaska, F. K., *Women and Philanthropy in Nineteenth-Century England* (Oxford: Oxford University Press, 1980)

Purvis, June, Hard Lessons. *The Lives and Education of Working-Class Women in Nineteenth Century England* (Cambridge: Polity Press, 1989)

Rees, Joan, *Shelley's Jane Williams* (London: William Kimber, 1985)

Rendall, Jane, '"Friendship and Politics": Barbara Leigh Smith Bodichon (1827–91) and Bessie Rayner Parkes (1829–1925)', in Jane Rendall and Susan

Mendus (eds), *Sexuality and Subordination. Interdisciplinary Studies of Gender in the Nineteenth Century* (Routledge, 1989), pp. 136–70

Rendall, Jane, *The Origins of Modern Feminism: Women in Britain, France and the United States 1780–1860* (Chicago: Lyceum, 1985)

Robinson, Mary, *Letter to the Women of England on the Injustice of Mental Subordination* (Poole: Woodstock Books, 1998; first published 1799)

Roe, Michael, 'Mary Leman Grimstone (1800–1850?) For Women's Rights and Tasmanian Patriotism', *Papers and Proceedings, Tasmanian Historical Research Association* (March 1989), vol. 6, no. 1, pp. 8–32

Rogers, Helen, *Women and the People. Authority, Authorship and the Radical Tradition in Nineteenth-Century England* (Aldershot: Ashgate, 2000)

Rogers, Nicholas, *Crowds, Culture and Politics in Georgian Britain* (Oxford: Clarendon Press, 1998)

Ross, Ishbel, *Child of Destiny. The Life Story of the First Woman Doctor* (London: Victor Gollancz, 1950)

Royle, Edward, *Victorian Infidels. The Origins of the British Secularist Movement, 1791–1866* (Manchester: Manchester University Press, 1974)

Sanborn, F. B., *Bronson Alcott at Alcott House, England and Fruitlands, New England* (Cedar Rapids, IA: Torch Press, 1908)

Schwarzkopf, Jutta, *Women in the Chartist Movement* (Basingstoke: Macmillan, now Palgrave Macmillan, 1991)

Scott, Mary, *The Female Advocate. A Poem occasioned by reading Mr. Duncombe's Feminead* (Los Angeles: 1984; first published 1774)

Shanley, Mary Lyndon, *Feminism, Marriage and the Law in Victorian England 1850–1895* (London: I. Tauris, 1989)

Shattock, Joanne, *The Oxford Guide to British Women Writers* (Oxford: Oxford University Press, 1993)

Shepard, Odell, *Pedlar's Progress. The Life of Bronson Alcott* (Boston: Little, Brown, 1937)

Smiles, Samuel, *The Autobiography of Samuel Smiles* (London: John Murray, 1905)

Smith, F. B., *Radical Artisan. William James Linton, 1812–97* (Manchester: Manchester University Press, 1973)

Smith, Hilda (ed.), *Women Writers and the Early Modern British Political Tradition* (Cambridge University Press, Cambridge, 1998)

Smith, William Anderson, *'Shepherd Smith' the Universalist, the Story of a Mind, Being a Life of the Rev. James E. Smith* (London: Sampson Low, 1892)

Spence, Thomas, *The Rights of Infants; or, the Imprescriptable Rights of Mothers* (London, 1797)

St. Clair, William, *The Godwins and the Shelleys. The Biography of a Family* (London: Faber & Faber, 1989)

St. Clair, William, *Trelawny. The Incurable Romancer* (London: John Murray, 1977)

Staël, Germaine de, *Corinne, or Italy*, trans. by Sylvia Raphael (Oxford: Oxford University Press, 1998; first published 1807)

Stansfield, Dorothy A., *Thomas Beddoes M.D. 1760–1808. Chemist, Physician, Democrat* (Dordrecht, Holland: D. Reidel, 1984)

Stephenson, H. W., *The Author of 'Nearer, My God to Thee'* (London: Lindsey Press, 1922)

Stevens, Joan, *Mary Taylor, Friend of Charlotte Brontë, Letters from New Zealand and Elsewhere* (Oxford: Oxford University Press, 1972)

Stewart, Robert, *Henry Brougham 1778–1868. His Public Career* (London: Bodley Head, 1985)

Stewart, W. A. C., *Progressives and Radicals in English Education, 1750–1970* (London: Macmillan, 1972)

Taylor, Barbara, *Eve and the New Jersualem. Socialism and Feminism in the Nineteenth Century* (London: Virago, 1983)

Taylor, Clare, *British and American Abolitionists. An Episode in Transatlantic Understanding* (Edinburgh: Edinburgh University Press, 1974)

Tennyson, Charles, *Alfred Tennyson* (London: Macmillan, 1950)

Tennyson, Lord Hallam, *Tennyson, a Memoir by his Son* (London: Macmillan, 1897)

Thackeray, William Makepeace, *Vanity Fair* (Harmondsworth: Penguin, 1968; first published 1848)

Thane, Pat, 'Women and the Poor Law in Victorian and Edwardian England', *History Workshop Journal* (1978), vol. 6, pp. 29–51

Thomas, Clara, *Love and Work Enough. The Life of Anna Jameson* (London: Macdonald, 1967)

Thomis, Malcolm and Jennifer Grimmett, *Women in Protest 1800–1850* (London: Croom Helm, 1982)

Thompson, Dorothy, *The Chartists: Popular Politics in the Industrial Revolution* (London: Temple Smith, 1984)

Timpson, Rev. Thomas, *British Female Biography, Being Select Memoirs of Pious Ladies in Various Ranks of Public and Private Life* (London: Aylott & Jones, 1846)

Todd, Janet, *Dictionary of British Women Writers* (London: Routledge, 1989)

Tomalin, Claire, *The Life and Death of Mary Wollstonecraft* (Harmondsworth: Penguin, 1985; first published 1974)

Tomalin, Claire, *Shelley and His World* (Harmondsworth: Penguin, 1982)

Tuchman, Gaye, *Edging Women Out. Victorian Novelists, Publishers and Social Change* (London: Routledge, 1989)

Tyrell, Alex, 'Samuel Smiles and the Woman Question in Early Victorian Britain', *Journal of British Studies* (April 2000), vol. 39, no. 2, pp. 185–216

Tyrell, Alex, 'Women's Mission and Pressure Group Politics in Britain (1825–60)', *Bulletin of the John Rylands University Library* (1980), vol. 63, pp. 194–230

Van Thal, Herbert, *Eliza Lynn Linton, the Girl of the Period* (London: George Allen & Unwin, 1979)

Vicinus, Martha (ed.), *Suffer and Be Still: Women in the Victorian Age* (Bloomington and London: Indiana University Press, 1972)

Vickery, Amanda (ed.), *Women, Privilege and Power. British Politics, 1750 to the Present* (Stanford: Stanford University Press, 2001)

Vickery, Amanda, *The Gentleman's Daughter. Women's Lives in Georgian England* (New Haven and London: Yale University Press, 1998)

Vickery, A. J., 'Golden Age to Separate Spheres: A Review of the Categories and Chronology of English Women's History', *Historical Journal* (1993), vol. 36, no. 2, pp. 383–414

Walkowitz, Judith R., *Prostitution and Victorian Society: Women, Class and the*

State (Cambridge: Cambridge University Press, 1980)

Watts, Ruth, *Gender, Power and the Unitarians in England 1760–1860* (London and New York: Longman, 1998)

Webb, R. K., *Harriet Martineau. A Radical Victorian* (London: Heinemann, 1960)

Weiner, Joel H., *Radicalism and Freethought in Nineteenth-Century Britain. The Life of Richard Carlile* (Westport, CT Greenwood Press, 1983)

Weiner, Joel H., *The War of the Unstamped. The Movement to repeal the British Newspaper Tax 1830–1836* (Ithaca and London: Cornell University Press, 1969)

Williford, Miriam, 'Bentham and the Rights of Women', *Journal of the History of Ideas* (1975), vol. 36, pp. 167–76

Wollstonecraft, Mary, *Vindication of the Rights of Woman* (Harmondsworth: Penguin, 1988; first published 1792)

Woodring, Carl Ray, *Victorian Samplers: William and Mary Howitt* (Lawrence: University of Kansas Press, 1952)

Wright, Mr [H. G.] and Miss Wright, *Retrospective Sketch of an Educative Attempt at Alcott House* (London: V. Torras, 1840)

Wright, H. G., *Marriage and its Sanction* (Cheltenham, 1840)

Yeldham, Charlotte, *Margaret Gillies RWS, Unitarian Painter of Mind and Emotion 1803–1887* (Lampeter: Edwin Mellen Press 1997)

Unpublished works

Plant, Helen, 'Gentlewomen Dissenters: Women of the Rational Dissenting Elite in Yorkshire, 1770–1830', Unpublished paper delivered at 'Feminism and Enlightenment Colloquium', London (27 May 2000)

Rendall, Jane, '"Women That Would Plague Me With Rational Conversation." Aspiring Women and Scottish Whigs, *c.* 1790–1830'. Unpublished paper delivered at 'Feminism and Enlightenment Colloquium', London (27 May 2000)

Index